THE DENT ATLAS OF THE HOLOCAUST

Map 1

This map shows the main deportation railways to the most destructive of all the concentration camps, Auschwitz. From each of the towns shown on this map, and from hundreds of other towns and villages, Jews were deported to Auschwitz between March 1942 and November 1944, and gassed.

As the maps in this Atlas record, Jews were killed in many other concentration camps, as well as at Auschwitz; in death camps and slave labour camps elsewhere, or at the hands of mobile killing squads.

THE DENT ATLAS OF
THE HOLOCAUST

Second edition

Martin Gilbert

Fellow of Merton College, Oxford

JM Dent

First published 1982
Reprinted 1988, 1991
Second edition 1993

Printed and bound in Great Britain by
Butler & Tanner Ltd, Frome and London

J M Dent Ltd
The Orion Publishing Group
Orion House
5 Upper St Martin's Lane
London WC2H 9EA

British Library Cataloguing-in-Publication Data

A catalogue record for this book is available from the British Library.

ISBN 0 460 86171 9 (hardcover)
ISBN 0 460 86172 7 (paperback)

List of Maps

Special symbols used in this Atlas

00,000 numbers of Jews in a particular country, town or village before the Holocaust, according to the last peace-time census

| 11,111 | number of Jews seeking refuge elsewhere, deported, or confined to a ghetto

22,222 numbers killed, or deported to their deaths

➙ the borders of Greater Germany at the time of any particular map

▲▲▲◀ the front lines at the time of any particular map

☀ acts of resistance or revolt by Jewish groups or individuals

Introduction

The map below shows the birthplaces, places of work, and places of execution of 17 Jews who were murdered during the war years. The text which follows on this page tells, briefly, something of their personal stories. If a similarly short reference were made to each Jew murdered between 1939 and 1945, 353,000 such maps would be needed. To draw these maps at the author's and cartographer's fastest rate of a map a day, would take more than 967 years.

Among the 17 people whom I have chosen for this map is the historian, Simon Dubnow, who had taught at Vilna, Kovno and Berlin, and who was murdered in Riga on 8 December 1941, at the age of 81. Among other Jewish historians murdered by the Nazis was Emanuel Ringelblum, born in Buczacz, who survived the Warsaw ghetto revolt, but was later caught by the Gestapo and murdered, at the age of 44, together with his wife and children (page 179).

Many thousands of doctors, medical men and scientists were also killed, among them the pharmacologist Emil Starckenstein, born in the Bohemian town of Pobezovice, who had made major contributions to preventive medicine, first as a Professor at Prague, and after 1938, as a refugee in Amsterdam. In 1941, at the age of 58, he was deported to Mauthausen and killed (page 79).

Charlotte Salomon was a painter. Born in Berlin, she had fled to France in 1939, at the age of 22. Later she was deported to Auschwitz and gassed. One of her paintings bore the caption: 'I cannot bear this life, I cannot bear these times.' Rudolf Levy, also a painter, was born in Stettin in 1875, and worked with Matisse. In the First World War, as a German soldier, he won the Iron Cross. Fleeing from Berlin to Paris in 1933, from Paris to Florence in 1940, he was deported from Italy to Auschwitz in 1943. That same year, the Munich-born painter Hermann Lismann, who had studied in Lausanne and Rome, was deported from France to Majdanek (page 155).

Harry Baur, a Marseilles dock worker who became known throughout France as 'the king of character actors', died in Berlin in 1943, after being tortured by the Gestapo. A fellow French Jew, René Blum, successor to Diaghilev as director of the Monte Carlo ballet, perished at Auschwitz in 1944.

Many poets were also murdered, among them Mordechai Gebirtig, killed in Cracow (page 104), Samuel Jacob Imber, deported to Belzec (page 132), Yitzhak Katznelson, killed at Auschwitz with one of his sons (page 183), and Miklos Radnoti, a 35-year-old Hungarian who, after more than three years in different slave labour camps, died in October 1944 on a death march from Bor in Yugoslavia to Györ in Hungary (page 206).

Among the hundreds of thousands of teenagers killed was the 15-year-old Yitskhok Rudashevski, who recorded in his diary the day-to-day life and moods of the Vilna ghetto (page 156), and Judit Sandor, from Budapest, who survived both the death camps and the war itself, but was too weak to survive the peace, and died at Karlstad, in Sweden, in September 1945, shortly after her seventeenth birthday (page 236).

Janusz Korczak, writer of children's stories, educator and social worker, was murdered at Treblinka with all 200 children from his Warsaw orphanage. He had insisted on acompanying them to the death camp. Alice Salomon, director of the children's home at La Rose, near Marseilles, also voluntarily joined her children, when they were deported to Auschwitz (page 155).

In all, more than a million Jewish children

Map 2

were murdered by the Nazis, among them the three-year-old Pierre Roth, born in Mulhouse *(page 146)*. Thousands of children were shot in the streets, or separated from their parents for the terrible journey to the death camps. Even the tiniest infants were brutally murdered, many wrenched from their mothers' arms, as both were shot, beaten to death, or gassed.

With the death of so many children, future generations were also destroyed, and the natural descent of generation to generation was unnaturally cut off. We shall never know what these million and more children would have made of their lives, had evil men not marked them out to die.

The 314 maps that follow show, in chronological sequence, the destruction of each of the main Jewish communities of Europe, as well as acts of resistance and revolt, avenues of escape and rescue, and the fate of individuals.

The story told in these maps is not complete, nor can the statistics, however carefully researched, be comprehensive. 'With all the resources in the world', as Professor Yehuda Bauer has said, 'it is impossible to show – or even to know – all that was done.'

For each community whose pre-war strength, or war-time destruction, I have been able to plot on one of these maps, two or three other communities existed, particularly smaller ones, for which there is either no room in this Atlas, or for which there is no evidence beyond the knowledge that they were in fact destroyed. The Nazi aim was to blot out these communities and all they represented of life, heritage and culture. Although the Nazis made no specific effort to record every killing, their general efficiency and sense of order was such that much detailed evidence survives of the killings in progress, often as set down at the time by the killers themselves.

The aim of this Atlas is to trace each phase of Hitler's war against the Jewish people: against all those with Jewish blood or of Jewish descent, wherever they could be found. It therefore traces the German conquest of territory in which Jews had lived for centuries, the first random but brutal killings, the enforced expulsions of ancient communities, the setting up of ghettos, the deliberate starvation of tens of thousands – at least 4,000 a month in Warsaw alone – the round-ups and deportations, the creation and

working of the death camps, the slave labour system, the death marches, and the executions up to the very moment of liberation.

The photographs show the places, and some of the people, against whom this enormous organization and effort of murder was directed. Most of them, tragically, are anonymous. Nevertheless, the people in these photographs were real people. Their faces once meant struggle and sorrow, joy and laughter, to those who knew them.

Although this Atlas is one of Jewish suffering, no book or atlas on any aspect of the Second World War can fail to record that in addition to the six million Jewish men, women and children who were murdered at least an equal number of non-Jews was also killed, not in the heat of battle, not by military siege, aerial bombardment or the harsh conditions of modern war, but by deliberate, planned murder. Hence, even in this Atlas, which traces the Jewish story, mention has frequently been made, often as an integral part of the Jewish fate, of the murder of non-Jews. These include Polish civilians killed after Poland's capitulation *(page 38)*, the first, mostly non-Jewish, victims at Auschwitz *(page 46)*, the tens of thousands of victims of the Nazi euthanasia programme *(page 51)*, the non-Jews killed with Jews in the slave labour camps of the Sahara *(page 56)*, the Serbs killed with Jews in April 1941 and January 1942 *(pages 58 and 87)*, the Czech villagers massacred at Lidice *(page 101)*, the Poles expelled and murdered in the Zamosc province *(page 139)*, the Gypsies deported to the death camps *(page 141)*, the non-Jews killed with Jews in the reprisal action in Rome *(page 181)*, Greeks and Italians taken hostage and drowned with Jews in the Aegean *(page 192)*, the French villagers massacred at Oradour-sur-Glane *(page 195)*, and the tens of thousands of Gypsies, Russian prisoners-of-war, Spanish republicans, Jehovah's Witnesses and homosexuals murdered at Mauthausen *(pages 232-3)*.

I have tried in this Atlas to give a chronological presentation of how the Holocaust evolved, and to show how that evolution was bound up with the changing course of the Second World War. The facts set down here will I hope add to our knowledge of what was done to the Jews, with particular reference to where it was done, in what circumstances, and on what massive a scale throughout every territory which came under Nazi domination.

Acknowledgments

The sources for all the facts shown in this Atlas are given in the Bibliography on pages 246-253. In gathering this material, and in preparing the maps themselves, I was particularly inspired by Rabbi Hugo Gryn, a survivor of Auschwitz, whom I first met in the spring of 1974, when work on the Atlas was beginning. His desire to see the story told in as much detail as possible has been a strong influence on my work; as were his personal encouragement and specific suggestions at every stage in drafting the maps and preparing the text.

For Hugo Gryn, as for many of the survivors who have helped me to collect material, or have encouraged me to map particular events, the act of recollection itself is often painful. They feel strongly, however, that unless the full scale and range of the slaughter is set down, many of its episodes will never be recorded, thus blurring the full enormity of the Holocaust, and reducing it to little more than a footnote to the history of the Second World War.

As the work proceeded, I also gained inspiration from the work of the French lawyer and historian, Serge Klarsfeld, whose father was deported from Paris to Auschwitz and perished there, and whose own comprehensive edition of the deportation lists of Jews from France, first published in 1978, is not only a model of scrupulous historical research, but also provided the basic material for thirty-three of the maps in this Atlas.

For the maps themselves, I am indebted to the cartographic work of Terry Bicknell, who transformed my rough and tentative drafts into maps of the highest quality. The Atlas owes much to his skills and patience.

As the maps evolved, I was helped considerably by the kindness and wisdom of Dr Shmuel Krakowski, the Director of Archives at Yad Vashem, Jerusalem, and himself a survivor, who not only provided me with valuable material, but also encouraged me in my researches: his knowledge of the fate of Polish Jewry in the war years, and of events in many other regions, has been an indispensable help, as has been his own pioneering work on Jewish resistance in Poland between 1942 and 1944.

I am also grateful to Professor Yehuda Bauer, of the Institute of Contemporary Jewry at the Hebrew University of Jerusalem, who scrutinized the maps when they were still in draft, and who gave me important guidance as to themes and sources; some of the most important research work on the Holocaust is being done by his pupils, and under his supervision.

When the maps were already at an advanced stage, they were helped by the critical scrutiny of Dr Arthur Cygielman.

Two institutions, Yad Vashem in Jerusalem and the Wiener Library in London, provided me with considerable help from their own substantial holdings, both published and manuscript. I was also helped in my search for materials, and for other reference works, by the late Dr Chaim Pazner, who not only gave me enormous personal encouragement, but also introduced me to the experts at Yad Vashem, whose assistance has been of considerable value.

I am also grateful to Taffy Sassoon, who helped to collate the material once it was assembled, and who translated documents and articles from Hebrew and Yiddish. The typing of the texts was done by Esther Gerber, who came specially from Jerusalem to Oxford for this task, and by Sue Rampton.

In its last phase, the Atlas benefitted from the cartographic corrections of Danuta Trebus, whose work was financed in part by a grant from the Memorial Foundation for Jewish Culture. Work on the original maps was made possible by the generosity of Rex and Deborah Harbour.

My sincere thanks are also due to Frederick A. Praeger, of Westview Press, Boulder, Colorado, for his encouragement of the project in its early stages; to Max J. Holmes, of Holmes and Meier; to Martin Savitt, and the Board of Deputies of British Jews, which published an illustrated 23-map school edition in 1978; to Arthur Wang, of Hill and Wang, who published this school edition in the United States; and to Paul Shaw, then Educational Officer to the Board of Deputies, who gave me good guidance on the presentation and content of many of the maps at this early but important planning stage, and who encouraged me to continue with the present larger work.

I am also grateful to Michael O'Mara, Managing Director of George Rainbird Ltd, whose interest in the project has been a main factor in its fulfilment, as was his appointment of Erica Hunningher as its editor. Her efforts on behalf of the Atlas have been continuous, persistent and substantial.

Many people have written to me with suggestions for specific maps, or have answered my own requests for information. In this regard I should like to thank: Chana Abells; Dr Yitzhak Arad, Chairman of the Directorate, Yad Vashem, Jerusalem; the late Ehud Avriel; Dr Gershon Bacon; Dr Konstantin Bazarov; Professor Shlomo Ben-Ami; Andras Bereznay; Professor Yehuda Blum; John A. Broadwin; Peter Brod; Hyam Corney; Dr Szymon Datner; Professor Dr L. de Jong, Director, Netherlands State Institute for War Documentation; Adina Drechsler; Melvin Durdan; Dr Elizabeth Eppler, Assistant Director, Institute of Jewish Affairs, London; Henning Gehrs, Librarian, Museet For Danmarks Frihedskamp 1940–1945, Copenhagen; Richard Grumberger; Clara Guini, Reference Librarian, Yad Vashen, Jerusalem; Professor Yisrael Gutman; Jerzy Herszberg; Alfred Herzka; Professor Daniel Ivin; Stanislaw Kania, Main Commission for the Investigation of Nazi Crimes in Poland; Hadass Kaufman, Secretary of Archives, Yad Vashem, Jerusalem; Dr Rivka Kauli; Donald Kenrick; Dr J. Kermish, Director of Archives, Yad Vashem; Warren Kimball; Yehudit Kleiman; Erich Kulka; Janet Langmaid; Naomi Laqueur; Curt Leviant; Dr Dov Levin; Karin Levisen, Press and Cultural Department, Royal Danish Embassy, London; Lawrence Litt; Fritz Majer-Leonhard; Hadassa Modlinger; Miriam Novitch; Thomas Orszag-Land; Professor Dr Czeslaw Pilichowski, Director of the Main Commission for the Investigation of Nazi Crimes in Poland; Hayim Pinner; Leon Pommers; Leslie Reggel; Matthew Rinaldi; Dr S. J. Roth, Director, Institute of Jewish Affairs; Dr Livia Rothkirchen, editor of *Yad Vashen Studies,* Jerusalem; Michele Sarfatti, Centro Di Documentazione Ebraica Contemporanea, Milan; Dr. Schulz, Landeshauptarchiv, Koblenz; A. E. Scopelitis, Embassy of Greece, London; Mrs. M. Segall; Tovia Shahar; Dr Shmuel Spector; Jennie Tarabulus; Michael Tregenza; Harold Werner; and K. Zailinger, Director, Service Social Juif, Brussels.

The photographs in this volume come principally from the archives of Yad Vashem, Jerusalem. Others are from Serge Klarsfeld (title page, and 145); The Main Commission for the Investigation of Nazi Crimes in Poland, Warsaw (page 209); The Museum of Denmark's Fight for Freedom 1940–1945, Copenhagen (page 167); I am grateful to those who put these photographic archives at my disposal; and to Tomasz Krasowski, who accompanied me on my own journey through Poland during which I took the photographs on pages 16, 82, 103, 148 and 182. The photograph on page 155 was taken by me in 1976.

As with each of my books, the support and advice of my wife Susie has been of inestimable value, both in terms of the structure of the work, and of her scrutiny of its content at every stage in the long process of evolution; to her are due not only my thanks, but also those of every reader who finds the Atlas of service.

I am most grateful to those who have provided me with extra materials, or have sent in corrections, which I have been able to include in this fourth printing. Special thanks are due to Ben Helfgott, to Professor Gaston L. Schmir, and to Luci Petrovic and A. Mosic (Federation of Jewish Communities in Yugoslavia). Any further material, corrections, or suggestions for new maps, would be much appreciated. My particular thanks are due to the publisher, William Morrow and Company, Inc., and to my editor there, Rose Marie Morse, for giving me the extra pages needed to include an index of the places and of the people mentioned in the atlas. For help in enabling me to compile this index, which will, I hope, add significantly to the usefulness of the atlas, I would like to thank Rachelle Gryn, Kay Thomson, and my son, David.

Martin Gilbert
Merton College
Oxford

22 September 1992

Map 3

ANTI-JEWISH VIOLENCE BEFORE THE FIRST WORLD WAR

Baltic Sea

0 ____ miles ____ 150
0 ____ kilometres ____ 200

TSARIST RUSSIA

Dusyata

Siemiatycze **1**
Bialystok **80**

Minsk

Mogilev

WHITE RUSSIA

Warsaw

POLAND

Lodz
Siedlce **30**
Brest-Litovsk
Pinsk

Gomel **12**
Starodub

Czestochowa
Lublin

THE PALE

Konotop

VOLHYNIA

Nyezhin

Zhitomir
Kiev

Pereyaslav

PODOLIA

Smyela

UKRAINE

Botosani

Elizavetgrad

Ekaterinoslav

Dorohoi
Burdujeni
Sulita

Ananayev

Tirgul Frumos
Jassy

BESSARABIA

Kishinev **49**

Nikolaiev

Melitopol

Bacau

Odessa **300**

Sea of Azov

Akkerman

CRIMEA

RUMANIA

Calarasi **60**

Simferopol

Black Sea

© Martin Gilbert 1982

Jews had lived throughout Europe for more than a thousand years. But no century had passed without their being attacked, expelled and killed.

Before the First World War, several hundred Jews had been killed in a series of violent attacks, or 'pogroms', in all the towns shown above, throughout western Russia and Rumania. As on each of the maps that follow, the numbers of those killed are shown inside a black box.

The murder of 49 Jews in Kishinev in 1903 led to protests throughout the Christian world; but the pogroms had continued.

Immediately after the First World War, tens of thousands of Jews were murdered in the western Ukraine (*opposite*). In a single town, Proskurov, the numbers killed far exceeded the total deaths in 40 years of pogroms throughout Tsarist Russia.

Further killings took place in Hungary in 1919, with the overthrow of the Communist regime, in which some Jews had played a prominent part. In Germany, at Nuremberg, Munich, Rosenheim, Zwickau, Coburg and Salzburg, Adolf Hitler preached hatred of

Map 4

ANTI-JEWISH VIOLENCE IN EUROPE, 1918–1932

the Jew as part of his National Socialist, or 'Nazi', philosophy. 'It is our duty', he declared in 1920, 'to arouse, to whip up, and to incite our people to instinctive repugnance of the Jews.'

In Berlin, in 1922, anti-semites murdered Walter Rathenau, the German Foreign Minister, and in 1923 Jewish houses in Berlin were attacked.

In the Moravian town of Holesov, in 1918, three Jews had been murdered. In eastern Poland, in 1918 and 1919, Jews were attacked and killed in Vilna, Lvov and throughout Galicia, where more than 500 Jews were killed.

In Rumania, in December 1922, restrictions were imposed on the percentage of Jewish students at Cluj University; then at universities in Jassy, Bucharest and Czernowitz, where Jewish students were attacked. Three years later at Piatra, synagogues and schools were looted and the Jewish cemetery desecrated. In 1926 a Jewish student was murdered at Czernowitz, and his murderer acquitted. In 1927, during anti-Jewish riots in Oradea, four synagogues were wrecked, while prayer houses were plundered in Jassy, Targu Ocna and Cluj.

But it was in Germany that anti-semitism

gained its greatest hold. Between 1922 and 1933 there were 200 instances in Nuremberg alone of desecration of Jewish graves. Also in Nuremberg, the first issue of a vicious anti-semitic newspaper, *Der Stürmer,* was published in 1923. The newspaper proclaimed as its banner slogan 'The Jews are our misfortune'.

Following his unsuccessful attempt to seize power in Munich in 1924, Hitler was imprisoned at Landsberg. From there, on 18 July 1925, he published the first part of *Mein Kampf (My Struggle),* in which he wrote with venom of the Jews. The second part was published on 10 December 1926.

Out of prison, Hitler rebuilt his Nazi party, and at 'Party Day' in Weimar in 1926, and again at Nuremberg in 1927, many speakers advocated driving the Jews out of German life. In 1927 Jewish cemeteries were desecrated by Nazi gangs: at Osnabrück and Krefeld the synagogues were wrecked. In Berlin, on 12 September 1931, the eve of the Jewish New Year, Nazi gangs attacked Jews returning from synagogue.

On 30 January 1933, Adolf Hitler became Chancellor of Germany. He was to rule Germany for nearly twelve years, until his suicide in Berlin on 30 April 1945.

15

Map 5

TWO THOUSAND YEARS OF JEWISH LIFE IN EUROPE BY 1933

NORWAY
82 years

ESTONIA
600 years

DENMARK
311 years

LATVIA
400 years

HOLLAND
800 years

MEMEL
269 years

LITHUANIA
600 years

BELGIUM
700 years

WHITE RUSSIA
550 years

DANZIG
400 years

• Wlodawa

GERMANY
1,612 years

POLAND
800 years

UKRAINE
816 years

LUXEMBOURG
647 years

CZECHOSLOVAKIA
1,000 years

CRIMEA
1,900 years

SAAR
312 years

AUSTRIA
1,030 years

HUNGARY
1,900 years

FRANCE
1,930 years

RUMANIA
1,800 years

ITALY
2,100 years

YUGOSLAVIA
1,000 years

BULGARIA
1,900 years

GREECE
2,233 years

0   miles   300

0   kilometres   400

RHODES
2,000 years

© Martin Gilbert 1982

From the moment that Hitler became Chancellor of Germany, he worked to transform one of Europe's most civilised states into a totalitarian dictatorship, and to deny Germany's half million Jews the basic rights of citizenship. Yet Jews had lived on German soil since the time of the Roman Empire. Despite often savage persecution in medieval times, and frequent expulsions from town to town, they had continued, over a period of sixteen centuries, to make their contribution to the development of

Map 6

THE JEWS OF GERMANY AND THE TRIUMPH OF NAZISM, 1933-1938

North Sea

Baltic Sea

MEMEL

DANZIG

EAST PRUSSIA

HOLLAND

Hamburg
19,794

Esterwegen
concentration camp
1933

Sachsenhausen
concentration camp
1933

Berlin
172,672

G E R M A N Y

BELGIUM

Cologne
16,093

Sachsenburg
concentration camp
1933

P O L A N D

Breslau
23,240

UPPER SILESIA

Buchenwald
concentration camp
1937

Leipzig
12,594

Frankfurt
29,385

LUXEMBOURG

SAAR

Nuremberg
8,603

C Z E C H O S L O V A K I A

FRANCE

Dachau
concentration camp
1933

Munich
10,068

45 *Jews murdered*
1933 - 1935

AUSTRIA

SWITZERLAND

HUNGARY

0   miles   100
0   kilometres 160

© Martin Gilbert 1982

modern Germany. Elsewhere in Europe the earliest Jewish communities dated back even further: the map opposite shows the age of those communities in countries which were to come under German rule or influence between 1933 and 1945.

The photograph, taken in 1980, is of a seventeenth-century synagogue in the present-day Polish town of Wlodawa.

From the very first days of Nazi rule in Germany, concentration camps were set up (*above*). Critics of the regime were sent to these camps, as were thousands of individuals against whom Nazi hatred was directed, including homosexuals, for whom the law was particularly severe, socialists, dissident clergymen, and Jews. Brutality by guards led to many deaths in these camps from the first days of Hitler's rule.

In July 1935 the *Manchester Guardian*

published the following description of the interrogation of a prisoner at the hands of the Gestapo: 'His head was wrapped in a wet cloth that was knotted so tightly across his mouth that his teeth cut into his lips and his mouth bled profusely. He was held by three assistants while the official and another assistant took turns in beating him with a flexible leather-covered steel rod (*Stahlrute*). When he fainted from pain and loss of blood he was brought to by means of various other tortures . . . He was told that he might write a letter to his wife, as he would never see her again. The assistants fingered their pistols and discussed which of them should shoot the prisoner. But he remained silent. He was released some time afterwards.' Similar press reports appeared regularly outside Germany: by 1935 at least 45 Jews had been murdered in Dachau alone.

Map 7

THE JEWS OF THE SAAR, 1 MARCH 1935

LUXEMBOURG

GERMANY

Sötern
95

Bosen
25

Bettingen
25

Neunkirchen
213

Tholey
41

Hilbringen
28

Brotdorf
26

Saint
Wendel
130

Merzig
204

S A A R

Diefflen
29

Nalbach
29

Ottweiler
55

Dillingen
135

Pachten
3

Saarwellingen
151

Illingen
107

Saarlouis
274

Fraulautern
37

Merchweiler
26

Waldmohr
21

Bous
5

Wadgassen
6

River Saar

Homburg
128

Differten
8

Saarbrücken
2,650

Saint Ingbert
76

Blieskastel
8

F R A N C E

0 miles 10

0 kilometres 15

©Martin Gilbert 1982

The first territory outside Hitler's control to be incorporated inside Nazi Germany was the Saar (*above*). This small but prosperous province had been separated from Germany in 1919, under the Treaty of Versailles, but was then returned, as a result of a plebiscite, overwhelmingly in Germany's favour. The plebiscite, held under the auspices of the League of Nations, took place on 13 January 1935. Jews had lived in the city of Saarbrücken since the fourteenth century. Under the League of Nations administration between 1920 and 1935, their civil, political and personal rights had been protected by the minority statutes of the League. Outside Saarbrücken itself, there were some 25 rural communities with Jewish inhabitants, ranging in size from the 274 Jews of Saarlouis, to single Jewish families.

On 1 March 1935, six weeks after the plebiscite, the Saar became an integral part

of Germany (*opposite, below*) and was at once subjected to all the rigours of Nazism, including the anti-Jewish legislation, the rule of the Gestapo, and the concentration camps. Almost all the Jews of the Saar chose French or Belgian citizenship. By 1938, when the Saarbrücken synagogue was burned down during the 'night of broken glass' (*page 26*), only 177 Jews were still living in the city.

In Upper Silesia (*opposite*), the first record of a Jewish community dates back to the eleventh century when, in 1060 a synagogue near Ratibor was seized by the town authorities and transformed into a church. There is also a record of Jews being persecuted in Leobschütz a century later, in 1163. Many of the earliest Jewish settlers in this region were poor; fugitives from the crusades or from persecution further east.

Despite more than six centuries of persecution, the Jews of Upper Silesia

THE JEWS OF UPPER SILESIA, 15 JULY 1937

miles 0 — 15
kilometres 0 — 20

P O L A N D

Pitschen
31

Landsberg
20

Kreuzburg
160

Rosenberg
102

Jellowa

Königshuld

Hitler Sea

Guttentag
145

LOWER
SILESIA

Grottkau
40

Falkenburg
51

Oppeln
607

Malapane

UPPER SILESIA
to Germany

Tworog
5

Niesse
220

Gogolin

Gross
Strehlitz
145

Tost

Beuthen
3,500

Patschkau   Ottmachau

Peiskretscham
45

Neustadt
100

Ziegenhals

Oberglogau
50

Cosel
80

Gleiwitz
1,899

Hindenburg
1,200

Leobschütz
111

Stanitz

Bauerwitz
4

Ratibor
640

EAST
UPPER
SILESIA
to Poland

Katscher
42

CZECHOSLOVAKIA

© Martin Gilbert 1982

emerged in the nineteenth century as a small but progressive community. When, after the First World War, the region was returned to Germany, the minority rights of the Jews shown here were protected. This was a result of the German-Polish Convention of 15 May 1922. Even after Hitler came to power in 1933, these minority rights were upheld by the League of Nations, and the imposition of Nazi racial laws was prevented, following a Jewish petition, the 'Bernheim Petition', to the League. But the Convention itself expired on 15 July 1937, bringing the Jews of Upper Silesia, like those of the Saar two years before, within the full rigour of Nazi rule.

THE GERMAN REICH, 1935-1937

North Sea — Baltic Sea

Sachsenhausen

Berlin
GERMANY

Warsaw

UPPER
SILESIA

Prague

Cracow

SAAR

Dachau

Munich

miles 0 — 200
kilometres 0 — 400

© Martin Gilbert 1982

Maps 10 and 11

ANTI-JEWISH RIOTS IN RUMANIA, 1935

ANTI-JEWISH MEASURES, 1935-1939

In the 1930s anti-Jewish violence spread through eastern Europe. It was particularly fierce in Rumania, where attacks on Jews took place in each of the towns shown on the map (left). In universities throughout Rumania, student members of an influential anti-semitic organization, the Iron Guard, prevented Jewish students from attending lectures. From 1934, no new Jewish lawyers were allowed to enter the legal profession. In 1936 the Iron Guard exploded a bomb in a Jewish theatre in Timisoara, killing two Jews, and injuring many more.

In November 1936, at Petrovaradin in Yugoslavia, the editor of an anti-semitic paper modelled on the Nazi Der Stürmer, was tried and acquitted. In August 1937, at Humenne in Czechoslovakia, Jews were accused of sacrilege.

In Lithuania (left, below), severe restrictions were imposed on the number of Jews allowed to enter universities; in the 1936 university entrance, not a single Jewish student was granted admittance to study medicine.

Anti-Jewish laws now began to appear in the statute books of several countries. On 21 January 1938 Rumania formally abrogated the minority right of Jews, and revoked the citizenship of many Jews who had been resident there since the end of the war.

On 29 May 1938 the Hungarian Government passed its first law specifically restricting the number of Jews in the liberal professions, administration, commerce and industry to 20 per cent, while on 3 May 1939 a second 'Jewish Law' forbade any Hungarian Jew to become a judge, a lawyer, a schoolteacher, or a member of Parliament.

Such laws encouraged anti-semitism and led to violence. On 3 February 1939 a bomb thrown into a Budapest synagogue killed one worshipper and injured many more.

But it was in Poland that violence against the Jews was most widespread between 1935 and 1937. In every town and village shown on the map opposite, Jews were attacked in the streets, and Jewish houses and shops were broken up and looted. It was necessary, a Polish Jesuit periodical asserted in 1936, 'to provide separate schools for Jews, so that our children will not be infected with their lower moralty'. On 29 February 1936 Cardinal Hlond declared in a public letter: 'It is true that the Jews are committing frauds, practising usury, and dealing in white slavery. It is true that in schools, the influence of the Jewish youth upon the

Map 12

ANTI-JEWISH VIOLENCE AND JEWISH SELF-DEFENCE IN POLAND, 1935-1937

Jews killed throughout Poland between 1935 and 1937

© Martin Gilbert 1982

Catholic youth is generally evil, from a religious and ethical point of view. But let us be just. Not all Jews are like that. One does well to prefer his own kind in commercial dealings and to avoid Jewish stores and Jewish stalls in the markets, but it is not permissable to demolish Jewish businesses, break windows, torpedo their houses . . .'

On 9 March 1936, in the village of Przytyk *(above),* the murder of three Jews sent further fears through Poland's three million Jews. A few days later, five Jews were murdered in the village of Stawy. Despite Jewish self-defence, as shown here in the Warsaw region and indicated by the star symbol, 79 Jews were killed, and 500 injured.

During 1937 there were further attacks on Jews throughout Poland: 350 attacks in August alone, and in Katowice bombs were thrown into Jewish-owned shops. Tens of thousands of Polish Jews emigrated: to France, Belgium, Holland and Palestine.

THE JEWS OF EASTERN AUSTRIA, 13 MARCH 1938

CZECHOSLOVAKIA

0 miles 20
0 kilometres 30

Gmund 40
Retz 45
Paysdorf 38
Laa 62
Hohenau 70
Horn 55
Mistelbach 95
Hollabrun 78
Angern 63
Stockerau 104
Krems 99
Klosterneuberg 227
Tulln 72
Melk 10
Vienna 176,034
Kittsee 62
Ybbs 130
St. Pölten 310
Modling 302
Bruck 42
Amstetten 28
Baden 1,108
Neusiedlersee
Bad Vöslau 99
Eisenstadt 225
Wiener Neustadt 685
AUSTRIA
Neunkirchen 204
Fruen-kirchen 386
Mattersburg 511
Kobbersdorf 172
Deutschkreuz 433
HUNGARY
Bruck 12
Pinkafeld 34
Liessing 87
Leoben 130
Oberwart 138
Rechnitz 170
Knittelfeld 26
Güssing 74
Judenburg 50
Graz 1,720

© Martin Gilbert 1982

ANTI-JEWISH RIOTS IN POLAND, APRIL-JUNE 1938

Baltic Sea
LITHUANIA
EAST PRUSSIA
Vilna 29 April
GREATER GERMANY
Warsaw 8 to 15 June
SOVIET UNION
POLAND
Dabrowa 15 April
Przemysl 13 June
CZECHOSLOVAKIA
EASTERN GALICIA
Tarnopol 11 and 12 June
Vienna

0 miles 100
0 kilometres 150

© Martin Gilbert 1982

Jews had lived in Austria since Roman times. In 1867, following the abolition of all laws based on religious discrimination, Jews had risen to prominence in Austrian life and culture. They had come to Vienna from all over the Austro-Hungarian Empire, especially from the impoverished province of Eastern Galicia.

In 1919 the Treaty of St Germain guaranteed minority rights to the Jews of Austria. Most lived in Vienna (*left*), but as the map shows, some were to be found in the towns and villages of every region: the Austrian census of 22 March 1934 listed 769 localities with Jewish inhabitants.

Following the violent suppression of the Social Democrat parties in 1934, anti-Jewish discrimination grew, and Austrian Nazism was encouraged by the German Nazis in power across the border.

On 13 March 1938 Germany annexed Austria, and a further 183,000 Jews came under German rule. The activities of all Jewish organizations and congregations were at once forbidden. Many Jewish leaders were imprisoned; several were taken to Dachau and murdered. The Great Synagogue of Vienna was first desecrated by organized hooligans, then 'occupied' by the German army. Many Jews were forced to turn their property over to the Gestapo. Individual Jews were seized in the streets, beaten, and even killed. More then 500 Jews, driven to despair, committed suicide.

In Poland a further spate of anti-Jewish activity broke out within three weeks of the imposition of Nazi rule in Austria (*left, below*). Starting in Dabrowa on April 15, hundreds of Jews had been injured, and much Jewish property destroyed.

From Poland, and from Greater Germany, which now included Austria, tens of thousands of Jews sought safety elsewhere (*opposite, above*). More than 85,000 Austrian Jews found havens in Britain, the United States, and in countries which were later to fall under Nazi rule. From Germany almost half of the country's 500,000 Jews emigrated or fled abroad (*opposite, above*), including more than 33,000 to Palestine, where they joined tens of thousands of recent Jewish immigrants from Poland. But on 5 July 1938, with the opening of the Evian Conference, it became clear that more and more countries wanted to restrict the number of Jewish refugees. The Australian delegate at Evian declared: 'since we have no racial problem, we are not desirous of importing one'.

JEWISH REFUGEES FIND HAVENS IN EUROPE, 1933-1938

NORWAY
2,000

SWEDEN
3,200

DENMARK
2,000

North Sea

Baltic Sea

HOLLAND
30,000

Berlin

POLAND
25,000

UNITED KINGDOM
52,000

GREATER GERMANY

Cologne
Aachen

BELGIUM
12,000

Trier

CZECHOSLOVAKIA
5,000

Vienna

St.Germain

Dachau

AUSTRIA

HUNGARY
3,000

FRANCE
30,000

Bay of Biscay

Evian

SWITZERLAND
7,000

YUGOSLAVIA
7,000

Adriatic Sea

ITALY
5,000

to PORTUGAL
10,000

SPAIN
3,000

© Martin Gilbert 1982

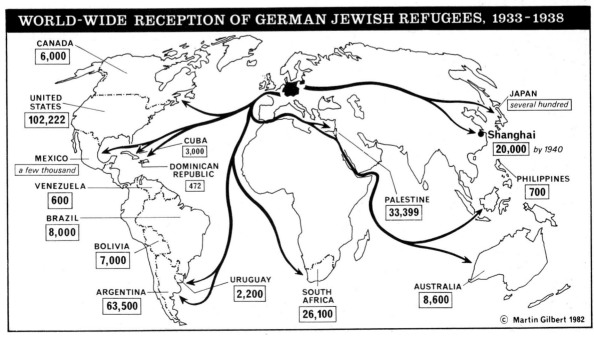

WORLD-WIDE RECEPTION OF GERMAN JEWISH REFUGEES, 1933-1938

CANADA
6,000

UNITED STATES
102,222

JAPAN
several hundred

Shanghai
20,000 *by 1940*

CUBA
3,000

MEXICO
a few thousand

DOMINICAN REPUBLIC
472

PHILIPPINES
700

VENEZUELA
600

PALESTINE
33,399

BRAZIL
8,000

BOLIVIA
7,000

URUGUAY
2,200

SOUTH AFRICA
26,100

AUSTRALIA
8,600

ARGENTINA
63,500

© Martin Gilbert 1982

23

Map 17

JEWS IN THE WESTERN SUDETENLAND

GREATER GERMANY

SAXONY

Abertamy
5

Pernik
5

Nejdek
37

Kraslice
66

Ostrov
30

Chodov
54

Stara Role
19

Olovi
22

Rybare
292

Loket
55

Karlovy Vary
(Karlsbad)
2,120

As
51

Haslov
7

Lazne Frantiskovy
95

Cista
22

Cheb (Eger)
505

Becov
26

Okrouhlov
5

Mnichov
3

Marianske Lazne
(Marienbad)
495

CZECHOSLOVAKIA
SUDETENLAND

Broumov
68

Plana Chodova
13

Tachov
223

Cernosin
16

Tisova
10

Stribro
152

Flossenburg
concentration
camp

Bor
35

Rozvadov
17

Kladruby
21

Primda
3

Straz
45

GREATER

Velky Malahov
2

GERMANY

Bela
8

BAVARIA

Blizejov
7

BOHEMIA

Vseruby
44

0   miles   10

0   kilometres   20

© Martin Gilbert 1982

In October 1938, only six months after the German annexation of Austria, Germany annexed the Sudeten-German region of Czechoslovakia (*opposite*). The area inside the broken line is shown in detail in the map on the left. Here, too, was a long-established Jewish community, whose origins went back, in Cheb for example, to the thirteenth century.

Between the wars the Jews of the Sudetenland were protected by the democratic and egalitarian laws of Czechoslovakia, and were living in towns and villages throughout the region. The map on the left, based on the national census of 1930, shows the Jewish communities in the western areas. The largest of these towns, Karlsbad, known in Czech as Karlovy Vary, had long been a popular resort town and meeting place for Jews. Two Zionist Congresses had been held there in 1921 and 1923. At Marienbad, known in Czech as Marianske Lazne, Jewish doctors had contributed to the development of the spa, whose cures had been popular with Russian Jews during the nineteenth century. In 1937 the Great Assembly of the union of orthodox Jews had been held there.

Beginning in 1933, the Jews of the Sudetenland were increasingly harassed by local, German-speaking, Nazis. During the Sudeten crisis in the autumn of 1938, many synagogues were burned down, including the synagogues at both Cheb and Marienbad on September 23. As the Germans prepared to occupy the region, almost all the 20,000 Sudetenland Jews fled into the still independent Czechoslovak provinces of Bohemia and Moravia. Those who remained were arrested by the Nazis, and sent to concentration camps.

Following the German occupation of the Sudetenland in October 1938, the borders of Greater Germany, as shown opposite, were extended yet again. So too was the concentration camp system, with the opening of a new camp at Flossenbürg, and the enlargement of Dachau. Another new camp, Buchenwald, had been opened on 19 July 1937, for professional criminals. In June 1938 many political prisoners, including Jews, were sent there, followed shortly afterwards by a further 2,200 Austrian Jews.

The photograph shows a rollcall at Dachau in 1938. Often during such rollcalls the prisoners, Jews and non-Jews alike, were forced to stand for many hours, hungry and cold, and were savagely beaten if they fell.

Map 18

THE JEWS OF THE SUDETENLAND, OCTOBER 1938

North Sea

Baltic Sea

MEMEL

DANZIG

EAST PRUSSIA

HOLLAND

Sachsenhausen

Berlin

Warsaw

GREATER

GERMANY

P O L A N D

Buchenwald

SAAR

SUDETENLAND

Prague

TESCHEN

Flossenburg

BOHEMIA

20,000

MORAVIA

Zilina

RUTHENIA

F R A N C E

CZECHOSLOVAKIA

SLOVAKIA

Munkacs

Dachau

Munich

Bratislava

Vienna

A U S T R I A

H U N G A R Y

RUMANIA

0   miles   100

0   kilometres   150

© Martin Gilbert 1982

Map 19

POLISH-BORN JEWS EXPELLED FROM GERMANY, 28 OCTOBER 1938

The next group of Jews to suffer under German policy were 15,000 Polish-born Jews who had been living and working in Germany for 10, 20 and even 30 years. Early in October 1938 the Polish Government announced that all Jews who had lived outside Poland for more than five years would have their passports revoked, and they would thereupon become 'stateless'. The Germans at once announced there would no longer be a place inside Germany for these 15,000 'stateless' Jews.

On October 18 these 15,000 Jews were forced to leave their homes throughout Germany, and to go, with only a single suitcase, to the nearest railway station. The rest of their belongings had to be left behind. Then they were taken through the night to the German-Polish border, and forced over the border at gun point.

At first the Polish Government was reluctant to take them in. Conditions, especially at the border town of Zbaszyn (*above*), were appalling. Learning of this, a member of one of the families which had been expelled, a young man named Herszel Grynszpan, who was living in France, shot and killed a German diplomat in Paris.

Using the diplomat's death as their excuse, the Nazis launched a campaign of terror against all the Jews of Greater Germany. On 9 November 1938, in one night, the so-called 'night of broken glass', hundreds of synagogues were set on fire, Jewish shops looted, and Jews beaten up in the streets. By morning, 91 Jews had been killed. All the towns shown in the map opposite (*above*) were the scene of anti-Jewish violence, as were hundreds of smaller towns, villages and hamlets throughout Greater Germany.

The lower map shows the towns in one small region of Germany, with their Jewish populations of 1932. Each of these little communities was likewise attacked during the 'night of broken glass'.

The photograph shows the fire raging in the principal synagogue in Berlin.

DESTRUCTION OF THE SYNAGOGUES, 9 NOVEMBER 1938

North Sea

Baltic Sea

Danzig

Königsberg

Allenstein

Kiel

Lübeck

Hamburg

Stettin

FREE CITY OF DANZIG

Emden

Bremen

HOLLAND

Hanover

Berlin

Munster

Brunswick

POLAND

Magdeburg

Essen

GREATER GERMANY

Dusseldorf

Glogau

Cologne

Leipzig

Liegnitz

Bonn

Dresden

Breslau

Oppeln

Coblenz

Chemnitz

Hindenburg

Frankfurt

Plauen

SUDETENLAND

Gleiwitz

Darmstadt

91 *Jews killed*

Wurzburg

Karlsbad

Furth

CZECHOSLOVAKIA

Mannheim

LUXEMBOURG

Saarbrücken

Nuremberg

Karlsruhe

FRANCE

Ulm

Augsburg

Linz

Baden

Freiburg

Bad Vöslau

Constance

Salzburg

Munich

Wiener Neustadt

Eisenstadt

Innsbruck

AUSTRIA

HUNGARY

SWITZERLAND

Graz

Klagenfurt

| 0 | miles | 100 |
| 0 | kilometres | 160 |

© Martin Gilbert 1982

JEWS OF THE DARMSTADT REGION

Langen 80

Grafenhausen 44

Egelsbach 52

Babenhausen 52

Gross-Gerau 200

Dieburg 271

Darmstadt 1,646

Gross-Umstadt 60

Pfungstadt

Gross-Bieberau 48

Ober-Ramstadt

Höchst

Wolfskehlen 3

Crumbach

Bad König

Reichelsheim 115

Bensheim 180

Michelstadt

Rimbach 85

Lorsch 70

Heppenheim

Birkenau 37

| 0 | mile | 10 |
| 0 | kilometres | 20 |

© Martin Gilbert 1982

27

Map 22

JEWS SENT TO CONCENTRATION CAMPS, 10 NOVEMBER 1938

Immediately following the 'night of broken glass', more than 35,000 Jews were seized throughout Germany, and sent to concentration camps, bringing to more than 60,000 the total number of Jews in the camps (*above*). Hundreds died of ill-treatment, including 244 at Buchenwald alone in the first month of their imprisonment. Hundreds more committed suicide as a result of the harsh conditions and the brutality of the guards.

In March 1939 Hitler ordered his armies to enter the Bohemian and Moravian provinces of Czechoslovakia (*opposite, below*). Tens of thousands of Jews were trapped, many of them refugees from Germany and Austria who had fled to Bohemia and Moravia a year before. Other Jews fled from Slovakia to Poland, as the Slovak province, where anti-semitic activities had been growing, declared its independence.

Jews had first been mentioned in Prague in AD 970, the first settled community in 1091. They survived repeated expulsions in the seventeenth century, to enjoy religious liberty and their own civil jurisdiction by 1700. Forbidden to follow many of the trades of the time, they had come to excel as shoemakers, tailors, hatters, furriers and goldsmiths. Jewish musicians often played at banquets in the palaces of the nobility. Known as excellent fire-fighters, a group of 400 Jewish firemen were present at all festivities, and at coronations. But no Jew was allowed to call himself a citizen of Prague, and outside the Jewish quarter all Jews were compelled to wear yellow badges and peaked yellow hats.

Slowly, the situation improved: in 1677 a royal edict had been issued against throwing stones at Jews. By 1800 Prague had become a centre of Hebrew printing, learning and scholarship, and in the century before 1938 the Jews of Prague knew emancipation, cultural vitality, prosperity, and hope.

When German troops entered Prague on 15 March 1939, the city's 31,571 Jews, ten per cent of the total population, had been joined by a further 25,000 refugees from the towns and villages of Bohemia shown here (above, left), whose Jewish populations are given according to the census of 1930.

Thousands of Czech Jews sought to escape, both by legal and illegal means. By the end of 1939 more than 19,000 had succeeded in leaving Europe altogether. But the rest were trapped.

Six days after the German occupation of Prague, Hitler sent his forces into Memel (above, right). Here, the local Jewish community could trace its origins back to the sixteenth century. In 1924 Memel had become an autonomous region under Lithuanian sovereignty. Its minorities were protected by the League of Nations. By 1939, the 2,470 Jews of Memel had been joined by 7,000 Lithuanian Jews.

With the German occupation of Memel, most Jews fled into Lithuania.

Map 26

THE GERMAN INVASION OF POLAND, 1 SEPTEMBER - 5 OCTOBER 1939

Baltic Sea

strong Polish resistance

LITHUANIA

Hel

Danzig

Königsberg

EAST PRUSSIA

GREATER

Bialystok

River Vistula

POZNAN

P

O

Warsaw

strong Polish resistance

Kalisz

Lodz

L

Brest-Litovsk

3,000 *Jews*

and

7,000 *non-Jews*

killed by German bombing of Warsaw September 1939

Breslau

A

strong Polish resistance

N

GERMANY

LOWER SILESIA

D

strong Polish resistance

River Vistula

River San

strong Polish resistance

Moravska Ostrava

Cracow

WESTERN

GALICIA

Lvov

strong Polish resistance

Przemysl

Sanok

Dobromil

MORAVIA

EASTERN GALICIA

Zilina

S L O V A K I A

RUTHENIA

HUNGARY

0 *miles* 40

0 *kilometres* 60

© Martin Gilbert 1982

Map 27

THE JEWS OF RURAL POLAND ON THE EVE OF WAR: A SAMPLE

Blazowa 930

Dubiecko 977

Pawlokoma 8

Nienadowa 75

Polanki 14

Bachorz 12

Babice 39

Krzywcza 203

Ostrow 65

River San

Dynow 1,273

Nozdrzec 10

Dabrowka 12

Tarnawka 92

Korytniki 33

Krasiczyn 46

Kruhel 10

Przemysl 17,326

Hludno 41

Wara 15

Piatkowa 44

Bachow 82

Pikulice 68

Hermanowice 17

Zalesie 10

Zohatyn 35

Kotow 10

Brzuska 61

Rokszyce 13

Grochowce 12

Obarzym 6

Lipa 33

Korzeniec 30

Fredropol 10

Brzozow 1,127

Jablonka 3

Ulucz 210

Bircza 1,038

Huwniki 22

Sierakosce 21

Krzemienna 27

Temeszow 3

Leszczawa 31

Rybotycze 314

Kalwaria Paclawska 3

Mrzyglod 60

Dobra 25

Kuzmina 15

Leszczyny 6

Dobromil 2,119

Debna 11

Jurowce 12

Kostarowce 19

Tyrawa Woloska 299

Zaluz 31

Trzcianiec 7

Stankowa 48

Wojtkowa 113

River San

Sanok 4,067

Ropienka 54

Wojtkowka 58

Chyrow 919

Niebieszczany 8

Zagorz 392

Lukawica 33

Rudenka 22

Jankowa 29

Dzwiniac Dolny 45

Bukowsko 129

Tarnawa Dolna 13

Uherce 51

Olszanica 73

Kroscienko 241

Tarnawa Gorna 14

Lesko 2,388

Myczkow 49

Ustianowa 96

Jasien 69

Ustrzyki Dolne 1,768

Plonna 36

Wysoczany 4

Hoczew 59

Wies 38

Solina 33

Rownia 29

Hoszow 32

Nowosiolki 35

Kulaszne 29

Srednie 38

Berezka 26

Bandrow Narodowy 38

Rzepedz 28

Szczawne 38

Myczkow 6

Polanczyk 11

Rabe 53

Czarna 132

Turzansk 32

Mchawa 31

Gorzanca 15

Komancza 74

Baligrod 515

Steznica 34

Polana 19

Lutowiska 1,264

Rabe 5

Terka 12

River San

Kolonice 4

Chmiel 8

Smolnik 79

Jablonki 5

Zatwarnica 82

Cisna 118

Dolzyca 22

Kalnica 23

Liszna 7

Smerek 43

Przyslup 6

Ustrzyki Gorne 56

Wetlina 8

Tarnawa Nizna 42

0   miles   10
0   kilometres   16

© Martin Gilbert 1982

On 1 September 1939 the German army invaded Poland, advancing across a land where Jews had lived for over 800 years. The map above shows the number of Jews living in a small area of Poland, which in September 1939, was on one of the lines of advance of the German army as it drove through Poland.

The map on the left shows the main line of advance of the German army: the thicker arrows show the advance in the first five days of September, the thinner arrows, the advance in the next two weeks.

Rapid though the German advance was, the Polish forces fought with skill and bravery at many points, checking the German forces in a series of fierce battles. During the fighting, more than sixty thousand Polish soldiers were killed, of whom some 6,000 were Jews. In addition 3,000 Jewish civilians were among those killed during the bombing of Warsaw.

Map 28

POLAND'S LARGEST JEWISH COMMUNITIES ON THE EVE OF WAR

Baltic Sea

Vilna
55,006 *28%*
14th century

Bialystok
39,165 *45%*
18th century

Grodno
21,159 *42%*
14th century

Pinsk
20,220 *75%*
16th century

Lodz
202,497 *33%*
18th century

Warsaw
352,659 *29%*
15th century

Siedlce
14,685 *48%*
16th century

Brest-Litovsk
21,440 *52%*
14th century

Kalisz
16,220 *35%*
12th century

Miedzyrzec
12,000 *75%*
17th century

Kowel
12,785 *61%*
16th century

Radom
25,159 *23%*
17th century

Lublin
38,937 *35%*
14th century

Czestochowa
28,486 *30%*
18th century

Chelm
13,537 *47%*
15th century

Rowne
22,737 *71%*
16th century

Kielce
18,083 *40%*
16th century

Luck
17,366 *48%*
10th century

Bedzin
21,625 *45%*
17th century

Przemysl
17,326 *34%*
14th century

Lvov
99,595 *33%*
14th century

Sosnowiec
20,805 *22%*
19th century

Tarnopol
14,000 *44%*
16th century

Tarnow
19,330 *44%*
15th century

Cracow
56,515 *26%*
14th century

Drohobycz
17,000 *44%*
15th century

Kolomyja
15,000 *33%*
16th century

Rzeszow
14,000 *36%*
15th century

Stanislawow
24,823 *41%*
17th century

0 *miles* 100
0 *kilometres* 100

© Martin Gilbert 1982

The map above shows those Polish cities with 12,000 or more Jewish inhabitants at the time of the census of 1931. Also given is the percentage of Jews among the total population of the town.

On the map opposite are some of the towns in which, from the first days of the German occupation, Jews were singled out for abuse, violence, and death. The figures show only some of those killed, mostly in savage attacks on Jews at prayer, or in random shootings. Thousands of Jews, and thousands of non-Jews, were killed during these early days of German rule. Jews, who formed a tenth of the Polish population, accounted for nearly a third of those killed. The photograph, taken by a German soldier, shows a typical incident, 'mocking a Jew'.

Map 29

GERMAN ATROCITIES AGAINST JEWS, 2 SEPTEMBER-13 NOVEMBER 1939

Bydgoszcz

Aleksandrow
60
September 7

16
September 16

Nowe-Miasto
7
September 14

Pultusk
14
September 14

Ostrow **30**
September 8

560
September 11

River Bug

Wyszkow
65
September 11

Wegrow

Siedlce

Wloclawek

River Vistula

Of **16,336** Polish civilians executed
in 714 localities, in the first six weeks
of the war, at least **5,000** were Jews

Ozorkow
24
September 5

Zgierz
7
September 7

Warsaw
53
November 13

Rawa
Mazowiecka
23 *September 10*

Minsk
Mazowiecki

20
September 20

Lukow
100
September 19

Laskarzew
20
September 17

Turek
15

Zloczew **80** *September 4*

Sieradz
33 *September 20*

Zdunska Wola
3 *September 3*

Wieruszow
17
September 3

P O L A N D

Kruszyna
12 *September 4*

Lelow
4 *September 3*

Czermno **3** *September 12*

Konskie
20 *September 4*
20 *September 12*

**GREATER
GERMANY**

SILESIA

Czestochowa **180**
September 3

Zarki **90** *September 4*

Bedzin

Wolbrom

Trzebinia
37
September 8

River Vistula

Tarnobrzeg
5

River San

Sosnowiec
13
September 4

Karwodrza
12 *September 11*

Mielec
35
September 13

Strzyzow
4 *September 15*

14 *September 15*

0 — miles — 40
0 — kilometres — 60

© **Martin Gilbert 1982**

Map 30

THE JEWS OF DANZIG, 1 - 17 SEPTEMBER 1939

Baltic   Sea

GREATER

GERMANY

Hel Peninsula

Hel ●

Gulf of Danzig

Gdynia

Zoppot
1,500

THE POLISH CORRIDOR

Danzig
4,000

Stutthof
*concentration
camp*

Langenau ●

D A N Z I G

Hohenstein
33 ●

Neuteich
● 40

Elbing

POLAND

River Vistula

EAST

PRUSSIA

| 0 | miles | 20 |
| 0 | kilometres | 30 |

© Martin Gilbert 1982

Following the German invasion of Poland, and even while that invasion was in progress, German troops entered the Free City of Danzig, which was immediately annexed to the German Reich. With the dominance of the local Nazi Party in Danzig in 1937, many of Danzig's 9,000 Jews had managed to emigrate to western Europe, Britain, the United States and Palestine. But more than 5,000 Jews, many of them old people, were trapped in the city as the German army entered on 1 September 1939 *(above)*.

On September 2, as German control was imposed throughout the Danzig territory, a concentration camp was opened at Stutthof, and two weeks later several hundred leading Danzig Jews, including the writer and journalist, Jacob Lange, and the cantor of the Danzig synagogue, Leopold Shufflan, were deported there. Within a week most of them had died as a result of deliberate brutality.

On September 9, while German troops still battled with Polish forces, all Jewish men in the small Ruhr town of Gelsenkirchen *(opposite, above)* were deported to the concentration camp of Sachsenhausen,

near Berlin. Of the original Jewish community of 1,400 in 1933, nearly 700 had managed to emigrate by 1939. Now, scarcely a week after the outbreak of war, the men were sent eastwards, and the women and children left to fend for themselves.

By the end of the German-Polish campaign, 6,000 Jewish soldiers had been killed and as many as 400,000 Polish soldiers had been captured, of whom some 61,000 were Jews. The Jews were at once separated from the Poles: thousands were sent to prisoner-of-war camps inside Germany, where they were denied the basic rights of prisoners-of-war and treated instead as if they were concentration camp inmates, with less rations than other prisoners, forced to do especially heavy work. At Lamsdorf 5,000 Jewish prisoners were housed in barns, 700 or 800 to each barn, without any floor covering, and one loaf of bread had to be shared by six or eight men. At Rathorn the two days' ration for five men was one loaf of bread and half a jar of soup. At Stablack, as a result of savage beatings by the German overseers at the various construction works

THE GELSENKIRCHEN DEPORTATION, 9 SEPTEMBER 1939

JEWISH PRISONERS-OF-WAR IN GERMANY, 1939-1940

to which they were sent, 10 to 15 Jews died each day. At Neubrandenburg the German commander issued instructions in October 1939 to the effect that all 'Aryan' prisoners-of-war were entitled to the uniforms and personal effects of their fellow Jewish prisoners. As a result, the Jews were sent to work half-naked and barefoot, and many of them froze to death.

These Jewish prisoners-of-war were among the first victims of a Nazi policy that, while severe at all times against conquered peoples, singled out Jews for particularly savage treatment. For the fate of some surviving Jewish prisoners-of-war in 1944 and 1945, see pages 204, 211 and 217.

Map 33

THE GERMAN-SOVIET PARTITION OF POLAND, 28 SEPTEMBER 1939

SWEDEN

Baltic Sea

Memel

LATVIA

LITHUANIA
*annexed by
Lithuania*

Swieciany

Vilna

Königsberg

Danzig

EAST
PRUSSIA

2,400

S

Lida

Grodno

Bydgoszcz

Lomza

Wolkowysk

Poznan

Pultusk

Bialystok

Baranowicze

*annexed by
Germany*
678,000

Warsaw

Brest-
Litovsk

Pinsk

SOVIET
UNION

Kalisz

Lodz

Siedlce

Wielun

Radom

250,000

*escape
eastward*

Lublin

*annexed by
the Soviet Union*
1,309,000

GREATER
GERMANY

VOLHYNIA

GENERAL
GOVERNMENT
1,139,000

Chelm

Luck

Rowne

UPPER
SILESIA

Zamosc

20,000

*escape
southward*

Brody

PROTECTORATE OF
BOHEMIA & MORAVIA

Bielsko

Cracow

Tarnow

Lvov

Dynow

Przemysl

Tarnopol

S = Suwalki region
of Poland.
2,400 Jews
expelled to
Lithuania

AUSTRIA

EASTERN
GALICIA

Stanislawow

SLOVAKIA

RUTHENIA

Kolomyja

RUMANIA

HUNGARY

- - - The frontiers of Poland
between 1918 and 1939

── The eastern frontier of Greater
Germany from October 1939

0   miles   50

0   kilometres   75

© Martin Gilbert 1982

On 28 September 1939 Poland was partitioned between Nazi Germany and the Soviet Union, while Lithuania annexed the Vilna region. In the following two months, before the border was sealed, more than a quarter of a million Jews escaped from the German to the Soviet side. These Jews were to constitute the majority of the survivors of Polish Jewry by the end of the war *(page 242)*.

The map above shows the number of Jews living in the three principal divisions of Poland at the time of the German invasion. With the eastward extension of the frontiers of Greater Germany, nearly two million more Jews were brought under German rule: four times the number of Jews who had been living in Germany when Hitler came to

power in January 1933.

The first German acts of terror in Poland had been the September murders *(page 33)*. Now a new policy was put briefly and brutally into operation: expulsion. The figures shown on the map opposite give some of the main expulsions eastward, where figures are available. By the end of 1939, tens of thousands of Jews had been driven to the border rivers and forced to swim them. Hundreds had been drowned as they tried to cross. Others had been shot and killed as they swam.

Of the 1,800 Jews driven from Chelm, only 400 survived the perils of expulsion. Hundreds of others were denied refuge at the last moment when Soviet soldiers refused to allow them to cross into Soviet territory.

Map 34

JEWS MURDERED, OR DRIVEN EASTWARD DURING OCTOBER 1939

Ostrolenka

Przasnysz

Bialystok

River Narew

7,000

Ostrow

Pultusk
8,300

Wyszkow

Kaluszyn

Warsaw

Brest-Litovsk

River Vistula

*annexed by
Germany*

*annexed by
the Soviet Union*

River Bug

Kowel

Chelm
1,800

of whom 1,400
*were murdered
on the march*

Hrubieszow

Luck

Tarnobrzeg
3,800

Rozwadow

Sokal

River Vistula

Lezajsk
2,000

Lancut

10,000   Jaroslaw

Lvov

River San

Przemysl

over 500 *murdered*

Rymanow
1,000

*between 14 and 28 September
before the Germans handed the
city to the Russians.
Among the dead*

Sanok

Dr. Asscher Gitter

and other leading citizens

0   *miles*   40

0   *kilometres*   60

SLOVAKIA

HUNGARY

© Martin Gilbert 1982

Map 35

JEWISH PRISONERS-OF-WAR AND NON-JEWISH CIVILIANS MURDERED, 1939-1940

In the opening months of the Second World War the Germans particularly ill-treated Jewish soldiers who had been taken prisoner while fighting with the Polish army. Some were sent to Germany (*page 35*). Others, kept in Poland, were also treated savagely from the first days of their capture. Those at the assembly points of Lomza and Zambrow (*above*) were to be transferred under German escort to the German side of the partition line. But of the 1,200 assembled at Zambrow, 250 were murdered on the spot.

At the transit camp at Zyrardow, the Jewish prisoners-of-war were kept in the local stadium for 10 days without food, surviving only because local Poles managed to throw food in to them. On the Day of Atonement, 24 September 1939, these Jewish prisoners-of-war were forced to clean the latrines with their bare hands, and treated with particular brutality.

Another group that suffered terribly were the Jewish soldiers whom the Germans took prisoner during the Polish campaign, whose birthplaces were in those parts of eastern Poland which had just been annexed by the Soviet Union. One train load was brought to Wlodawa, to be sent eastward across the border; 200 had died of hunger or had frozen to death during the journey from central Poland. Near Wlodawa, the survivors were made to take the corpses out of the train. The SS guards then opened fire, killing 120 more of the prisoners.

A further group of Polish Jewish prisoners-of-war was brought to Lublin. They were told that they were to be sent to Soviet Russia. On the march northwards, ostensibly towards the border, almost all of them were killed. The survivors were held in the prisoner-of-war camp at Biala Podlaska, where another 200, denied medical attention, died of typhus. Extreme brutality against Jewish prisoners-

38

Map 36

of-war was also recorded at transit camps set up at Krosniewice, Zyrardow and Radom.

Thousands of non-Jews, as well as Jews, suffered cruelty during these early days of the German occupation of western Poland. Between September 1939 and June 1940, in each of the towns and villages shown in small type *(left)*, Polish civilians were shot, some at random, some because they were the political, religious, or intellectual leaders of their community: as many as 360 at Skloby. As with the killing of Jews, the method was barbaric. At Szalas, for example, all 300 males over the age of 15 were seized, many machine-gunned, and the rest locked in a school which was then set on fire. The list, even for the region shown here, is incomplete. Elsewhere in the occupied regions, the scale of killing of non-Jews was similar; more than 16,000 in the first month and a half of the occupation *(page 33)*, and continually increasing during 1940. At Torun *(right)*, twelve young boys aged 11 to 16 were shot as a reprisal for the breaking of a window in the local police station.

On 12 December 1939 two years' forced labour was made compulsory for all Jewish males between the ages of 14 and 60. Labour camps were set up throughout the General Government and in the Warthegau *(right)*. At first Jews were seized in the streets in order to fill the camps. Later, organized conscription took place. Many died in the camps of brutality, and exhaustion. The photograph shows part of the barracks of one such labour camp, near Dabrowa.

EASTERN LABOUR CAMPS BY JANUARY 1940

Map 37

'LUBLINLAND' DEPORTATIONS, OCTOBER 1939 - APRIL 1940

North Sea

Baltic Sea

Hamburg
21 October 1939

Stralsund
15 February 1940

Stettin
15 February 1940

1,000

Schneidemühl 160
12 March 1940

Ciechocinek

Inowroclaw   Nieszawa

Poznan   Gniezno

Lipno   Warsaw

Konin

Kalisz

Lodz

GREATER
GERMANY

Moravska
Ostrava
17 October 1939

Prague
26 October 1939

Brno
26 October
1939

Vienna
20 October 1939

Nisko

95,000
in Lublinland
in April 1940

Lublin
Piaski
Belzyce   Glusk
Zarzecze

THE
SOVIET
UNION

SLOVAKIA

0   miles   80
0   kilometres   140

© Martin Gilbert 1982

Even before the new German-Soviet border had been fixed, the Germans were planning to drive the Jews from hundreds of towns and villages in the nearly annexed territories. As Hitler himself declared: 'Out with them from all the professions and into the ghetto with them: fence them in somewhere, where they can perish as they deserve.'

On 21 September 1939 it was decreed that all communities with less than 500 Jews were to be dissolved, and that the Jews were hereafter to live in certain restricted areas in the larger cities, or in a special area set aside for them in the poor village region between Lublin and Nisko, the so-called 'Lublinland reservation' (above).

Even Jews waiting at Hamburg for the next ship to the United States, then neutral, were deported eastwards, as shown here. Also deported were Jews from Vienna, from three former Czechoslovak towns, Prague, Brno and Moravska Ostrava, as well as from the Baltic ports of Stralsund and Stettin.

By the end of the winter, lacking proper housing, food or medical help, hundreds, if not thousands of these deportees to Lubinland had died. Others worked in harsh conditions, savagely beaten by guards, in a forced labour camp set up near Zarzecze, and many died. Some, who managed to escape eastwards into the Soviet Union, were immediately deported to labour camps in Siberia, where many of them also died.

Meanwhile, on 30 October 1939, the head

of the SS, Heinrich Himmler, had fixed the following three months as the period during which all Jews had to be cleared out of the rural areas of western Poland. In the Poznan region, 50 communities were at once uprooted: seven of them are named opposite.

From Lodz, hundreds of women, children and old people were deported eastward by train in sealed freight-cars, mostly to the Lublin region. At the same time, Jews living in the rural areas of western Poland were forced to leave their homes, taking with them only what they could carry in sacks or bundles, and to go to the towns and cities shown on the right-hand map. An idea of the numbers of those uprooted can be seen in the boxes: 4,700 Jews, for example, were forced into the city of Ozorkow, bringing the total population to more than 9,000. Hundreds of communities were involved: those from the region west of Ozorkow are shown above. In some of the smaller villages, such as Drzewce, there was only a single Jewish family. They too were driven out. In one of these villages, Chelmno, lived a total of 33 Jews, all of whom were forced to leave. Just over a year later, their village became the site of the first death camp (page 82).

In the cities to which Jews were driven, overcrowding was severe. Poverty followed swiftly for tens of thousands of families, already stripped of their possessions, and now without a livelihood. The photograph (left) is of one such deportee, a Jewish boy in Lublin.

POLISH JEWS EXPELLED FROM WESTERN POLAND, SEPTEMBER - NOVEMBER 1939

Baltic *Sea*

Strzelno 1
Puck 31
Wejherowo 62
Chylonia 5
Gulf of Danzig

Danzig

POMERANIA

THE POLISH CORRIDOR

Kartuzy 35

Skarszewy 40
Tczew 93

EAST PRUSSIA

Koscierzyna

Zblewo 12
Starogard 125

Brusy 24
Karsin 3
Czersk 5
Gniew 20

Chojnice 110
POLAND
Skorcz 19
Nowe 31

Osie 26
Lubawa 26

Kamien 12
Tuchola 118
Grudziadz 297
Lasin 23
Nowe Miasto 61

Sepolno 183
Bukowiec 12
Swiecie 171
Radzyn 12

Sypniewo 3
Wiebork 64
Chelmno 74
Lisewo 9
Wabrzezno 92
Brodnica 56
Lidzbark 60
Dziadlowo 35

Chelmza 72
Golub 104
Gorzno 1

Torun 354
Mlyniec 3

Borders of 1919 to 1939

miles 0 — 5
kilometres 0 — 40

© Martin Gilbert 1982

JEWS EXPELLED INTO WARSAW, NOVEMBER - DECEMBER 1939

DANZIG WEST PRUSSIA
GREATER EAST PRUSSIA
SOVIET UNION

Bydgoszcz
River Vistula
Zuromin
Sierpc
Biezun
Lipno
Raciaz

40,000
expelled

Poznan
WARTHEGAU
Kaluszyn
Warsaw
Konstancin

Konin
GENERAL GOVERNMENT

Aleksandrow
Kalisz
Lodz
Brzeziny

Sieradz
Kozienice

miles 0 — 40
kilometres 0 — 60

© Martin Gilbert 1982

As the eastward expulsion of Jews continued, incredible distress was caused, both in the uprooting of settled communities, and in the disruption of life in the towns to which they were sent. The German plan was carefully prepared and ruthlessly pursued. As Hitler had made clear to the Reichstag on 6 October 1939, strict measures were needed for what he descibed as 'adapting and regulating the Jewish problem'. By the end of January 1940 some 78,000 Polish Jews had been driven out of their homes.

The map on the right shows the new German administrative division, and the first three provinces — Greater Danzig and West Prussia, Greater East Prussia, and the Warthegau — from which Jews were expelled during the first few months of the German conquest of Poland. The map below, with figures for the number of inhabitants at the time of the 1931 census, shows how Jews from the city of Poznan, and from several of the villages around it, were first driven westwards to a central collecting point, then eastwards into the General Government, and then dispersed. Also dispersed were the Polish Jews of the new Greater Danzig region (opposite, above). This region had been part of the German Empire before 1914.

But the largest single destination for those who had been uprooted was Warsaw (opposite, below), a city that was already the home of more than 350,000 Jews.

THE FIRST KALISZ EXPULSIONS, 12 DECEMBER 1939

GREATER
EAST
PRUSSIA

SOVIET
UNION

WARTHEGAU

Kozminek
labour camp
1,300

Kalisz

Warsaw

Kaluszyn

Biardy

Lukow

Glogau

Rembertow

15,000
expelled

Lublin

GENERAL
GOVERNMENT

S I L E S I A

Sandomierz

Lezajsk

Cracow

Rzeszow

Lancut

Tyczyn

0   miles   40

0   kilometres   60

© Martin Gilbert 1982

GERMANY MOVES NORTH, APRIL 1940

0   miles   200

0   kilometres   400

North
Atlantic
Ocean

NORWAY

FINLAND

S
W
E
D
E
N

Oslo

EST.

LAT.

North
Sea

Baltic Sea

LIT.

DENMARK

SOVIET UNION

EIRE

BRITAIN

HOLLAND

Berlin

BELGIUM

GREATER GERMANY

FRANCE

SLOV.

HUNGARY

SWITZ.

© Martin Gilbert 1982

As the Polish expulsions continued, ancient communities were dispersed. The map above shows the first expulsions from Kalisz, where Jews had first come from the Rhineland more than seven centuries before. In 1919, at the beginning of Polish rule, two Kalisz Jews had been killed by local anti-semites (*page 15*). At the outbreak of the Second World War, 20,000 Jews in the town made up almost half the population. Of those expelled, some 7,000 Kalisz Jews reached Warsaw by the end of the year. But more than 1,000 able-bodied men were sent to a nearby labour camp at Kozminek.

In April 1940 the German army moved again, northwards into Denmark and Norway (*left*). In Denmark, 6,000 Jews were left unmolested at the insistence of the Danish authorities, as were the 1,400 Jewish refugees who had reached Denmark from Germany, Austria and Czechoslovakia, in 1938 and 1939. In Norway (*right*), some 1,400 Norwegian Jews, and about 300 refugees, were likewise unmolested, but only for six months. In October 1940 they were forbidden to continue in all academic or other professions. There were, however, none of the killings, beatings, forced labour and expulsion which had become daily events in German-occupied Poland.

Map 46

THE JEWS OF NORWAY AT THE TIME OF THE GERMAN INVASION

Arctic Ocean

FINNMARK
7

TROMS
22

NORDLAND
13

North Atlantic Ocean

NORWAY

SWEDEN
neutral

NORD-
TRÖNDELAG
1

miles 0 — 80
kilometres 0 — 100

SOR
TRÖNDELAG
227

MORE
34

HEDMARK

OPLAND
3

14

BUSKERUD
25

Bergen
27

Oslo
749

AKERSHUS
134

TELEMARK
5

OSTFOLD
38

Gulf of Bothnia

ROGALAND
10

AUST-
AGDER
1

VESTFOLD
50

Baltic Sea

VEST-
AGDER
4

© Martin Gilbert 1982

Map 47

THE FIRST DEPORTATION TO AUSCHWITZ, 14 JUNE 1940

SWEDEN
neutral

North Sea

Baltic Sea

EAST PRUSSIA

Danzig

Stutthof

SOVIET UNION

Sachsenhausen

Berlin

Warsaw

London

Dover

GREATER GERMANY

Breslau

Tarnow

Buchenwald

Auschwitz

Cracow

Flossenbürg

LUXEMBOURG

SLOVAKIA

Paris

FRANCE

Dachau

Munich

HUNGARY

SWITZERLAND
neutral

0 miles 100
0 kilometres 200

↓ Lines of German advance 4-14 June 1940

Areas conquered by Germany by 14 June 1940

© Martin Gilbert 1982

On 10 May 1940 the German army invaded Holland, Belgium, Luxembourg and France (*above*). Within five weeks, on June 14, as German forces approached Paris, yet another concentration camp was being set up in German-occupied Poland. Situated just outside the town of Auschwitz, it was intended as a punishment camp for Polish political prisoners, not as a concentration camp for Jews. But in order to prepare the old barracks, 300 Jewish forced labourers had been brought from Auschwitz town.

The first inmates were mostly non-Jewish Poles, 728 in all, from a prison in Tarnow. Many of them had been caught at the eastern border trying to get to France through Hungary. Other Poles taken in that first train to Auschwitz were schoolteachers and priests. Three Jews were also among these first inmates: Emil Wieder and Isaac Holzer, both lawyers, and Maximilian Rosenbusch,

the Director of the Hebrew school in Tarnow. As the deportees' train was passing through Cracow, they heard the station announcer report the fall of Paris.

Like all concentration camp inmates, these first Auschwitz prisoners were put to forced labour, often doing heavy work that was not needed, such as digging ditches. At times they were tormented by having to queue on their knees for their daily bowl of soup. After the first successful escape, on July 6, there was a punitive 20-hour rollcall. After a second escape on October 28, a rollcall was held in bitter weather from 12 noon to 9 p.m., during which 200 prisoners died.

Elsewhere in Poland, thousands of Jews were being sent to forced labour camps, mostly to build fortifications along the new Soviet frontier (*opposite*). Thousands of other Jews were brought from Slovakia to these labour camp regions.

Map 48

SLAVE LABOUR ON THE GERMAN BORDER, MAY–DECEMBER 1940

Baltic Sea

Danzig

EAST PRUSSIA

SOVIET-OCCUPIED POLAND

Mlawa

Rypin

POLESIA

River Vistula

Pultusk

Nasielsk

Serock

Warsaw
May 1940

Miedzyrzec

border fortifications

GERMAN-OCCUPIED POLAND

Radom
May 1940
2,000
almost none survived

Lublin
May 1940

River Bug

VOLHYNIA

Czestochowa
August 1940
1,000
almost none survived

Zamosc

Belzec

SILESIA

Cieszanow

River Vistula

Mielec

the 'Otto line'

Cracow

Tarnow

Auschwitz

EASTERN GALICIA

PROTECTORATE OF BOHEMIA & MORAVIA

Zilina

Presov

Ruzomberok

Humenne

S L O V A K I A

Banska Bystrica

Kosice

HUNGARIAN-OCCUPIED RUTHENIA

HUNGARY

© Martin Gilbert 1982

JEWS DEPORTED FROM GERMANY TO THE PYRENEES, 22 OCTOBER 1940

North Sea

Baltic Sea

Hamburg

Danzig

Stettin

Torun
POLAND

Berlin

Poznan

Warsaw

River Vistula

Aachen

Cologne
RHINELAND
Erfurt

Coblenz

Leipzig

GREATER

Chemnitz

Breslau

Cracow

Auschwitz

River Seine

GERMAN-
OCCUPIED
FRANCE

15,000
deported

River Rhine

GERMANY

Nuremberg

BAVARIA

*Lieba Lust
born Auschwitz 26 December 1875
died Gurs 3 December 1940*

Augsburg

Munich
Salzburg

Vienna

AUSTRIA

Budapest

HUNGARY

SWITZ.

Graz

'VICHY'
FRANCE

ITALY

YUGOSLAVIA

River Danube

Zagreb

Récébédou
Noé 302
Gurs
1,260 200

Pyrenees

Rivesaltes
102

SPAIN
neutral

0   miles   100

0 kilometres   200

© **Martin Gilbert 1982**

On 22 October 1940 the German Government deported more than 15,000 German Jews from the Rhineland to internment camps in France, at the foothills of the Pyrenees. As a result of the conditions in the camps, nearly 2,000 of the deportees died. The towns shown on the map above are the birthplaces of some of the deportees, including Danzig, Warsaw, and even Auschwitz.

The small map *(right)* shows the numbers deported to Gurs from part of the upper Rhine. These Jews had been German patriots. From Mannheim alone, 126 Jews had died fighting for Germany in the First World War: among them five soldiers with the common Jewish surname Mayer.

The map on the far right gives the birthplaces, names and ages of deportees with the surname Mayer who died while in Gurs internment camp.

JEWS DEPORTED TO GURS, 22 OCTOBER 1940

PALATINATE

Weinheim
40

Speyer
55

Mannheim
2,000

SAAR

Landau
89

Bruchsal
79

Mosbach
51

Saarbrücken
177

River Rhine

Pforzheim
183

Ettlingen
9

BADEN

Offenburg
91

ALSACE

Alt Breisach
34

0   miles   40

0   kilometres   60

© **Martin Gilbert 1982**

Map 51

TWENTY JEWS WITH THE SURNAME MAYER WHO DIED IN GURS

Rimbach
Mina Mayer, aged 75

Frankfurt-am-Main
Julius Mayer, aged 54

Mühlheim
Marie Mayer, aged 78

Osthofen
Emanuel Mayer, aged 68

Grossbockenheim
Max Mayer, aged 63

Grünstadt
Johanna Mayer, aged 84

Mannheim
Julius Mayer, aged 56

Mergentheim
Meta Mayer, aged 53

Ulmet
Salo Mayer, died before his first birthday

Neidenstein
Lehmann Mayer, aged 86

Niederhochstadt
Laura Mayer, aged 63

Germersheim
Selma Mayer, aged 71

Bruchsal
Rosalie Mayer, aged 80

Iggelheim
Michel Mayer, aged 82

Malsch
Frieda Mayer, aged 77

Rastatt
Cecile Mayer, aged 75

Julius Mayer, aged 27

Nonnenweier
Maier Mayer, aged 74

Ichenhausen
Eva Mayer, aged 79

Freiburg
Joseph Mayer, aged 59

River Rhine

River Main

River Rhine

River Danube

0   miles   20

0 kilometres 20

© Martin Gilbert 1982

Map 52

JEWS FORCED INTO GHETTOS, OCTOBER 1939 TO DECEMBER 1940

Plonsk
August 1940

Wloclawek
November 1940

Wolomin
15 November 1940

River Bug

River Vistula

W A R T H E G A U

Zychlin
19 July 1940

Warsaw
15 November 1940

Kutno
16 June 1940

Siedlce
6 May 1940

Tuliszkow
January 1940

Kolo
December 1940

Bolimow
11 June 1940

Chocz
March 1940

Glowno
29 December 1940

Lodz
I May 1940

Kozminek
January 1940

Deblin
April 1940

Lutomiersk
July 1940

Tomaszow
1 June 1940

Zdunska Wola
September 1940

Piotrkow
28 October 1939

T H E

G E N E R A L

Radomsko
20 December 1939

G O V E R N M E N T

Czestochowa
March 1940

Chmielnik
March 1940

Jedrzejow
January 1940

Pinczow
February 1940

River Vistula

| 0 | miles | 40 |
| 0 | kilometres | 60 |

© Martin Gilbert 1982

Starting with the town of Piotrkow on 28 October 1939, the Germans began to confine the Jews in Poland to a particular area of each town in which they lived. Sometimes this area was the already predominantly Jewish quarter. But often it was a poor or neglected part of the town, away from the centre. Jews from the rest of the town were then forced to leave their homes, and to move into this other, often much smaller area, in which even the basic amenities were not available.

Not only the Jews of each of the towns shown in the map on the left, but also deportees from the Warthegau, and from the surrounding rural communities, were forced to move into these new ghetto confines; at Piotrkow 8,000 local Jews were joined by a further 8,000 deportees.

In each ghetto food supplies and medical provisions were restricted. Intense overcrowding, hunger and disease led to widespread suffering, and death. The photograph was taken in the Lodz ghetto, where 5,000 were to die from starvation in the first six months of 1941 (page 54).

Meanwhile, in Germany itself, experiments had been tried on non-Jewish, and also on some Jewish patients from mental homes and old people's homes. The aim of the experiments was to kill all whom the Nazis judged unfit to live. The victims, including the children, were killed by gas in the euthanasia centres shown here.

After the German conquest of Poland more than 1,000 Poles were taken from nearby psychiatric clinics to a wood outside the Polish village of Piasnica Wielki, where they were shot. In October 1940, 290 Jews, old people, cripples, and the mentally ill from the Old Age Home in Kalisz, were put in a lorry to be taken to the town of 'Padernice' (below). No such town existed. Just outside Kalisz, in the woods at Winiary, all 290 were gassed inside the lorry by exhaust fumes, and buried in the woods.

Map 55

WARSAW JEWS EXPELLED INTO THE WARSAW GHETTO, NOVEMBER 1940

Just over a year after the establishment of the first ghetto, at Piotrkow (*page 50*), orders were given to confine all the Jews of Warsaw, as well as all the Jews who had already been deported to Warsaw, inside one section of the city. The Warsaw ghetto was to become the largest of all the ghettos established by the Germans in Poland. The section of the city chosen for it was one in which more than 280,000 Jews were already living.

In October 1940 a wall was built around the area designated for the ghetto. Jews were made both to build the wall and to pay for it. As soon as it was built, the thousands of Jews who lived elsewhere in Warsaw were forced to leave their homes, to abandon most of their possessions, and to move into the new ghetto area (*above*). One Warsaw Jew, Chaim Kaplan, wrote in his diary of the expulsion from the Praga suburbs: 'By the thirty-first of October, Praga must be empty of its Jewish inhabitants, who were rooted to its soil for hundreds of years. Most of them are poor. They have no money to move their belongings. And where would they move them to?' Many Poles, Kaplan added, 'drove the Praga Jews from their apartments in advance, before the fixed date'.

Early in 1941, 72,000 Jews were expelled from towns throughout the Warsaw region

Map 56

JEWS DEPORTED INTO THE WARSAW GHETTO, FEBRUARY - MARCH 1941

72,000 deported into Warsaw

© Martin Gilbert 1982

(above), and driven into the ghetto, bringing the total number of refugees to 150,000. Conditions inside the ghetto were appalling: terrible overcrowding, minimum rations, and almost no contact with the outside world for 400,000 people.

Under the ration scales imposed by the Germans, all Germans in Warsaw were entitled to 2,310 calories a day, foreigners to 1,790 calories, Poles to 934 calories, and Jews to a mere 183 calories. Yet Jews had to pay twice as much as Poles, and nearly 20 times as much as Germans, for each calory. Inside the ghetto, food distribution was organized by the Jews themselves. The photograph, one of more than 300 photographs taken by a member of the Warsaw photographic studio, Studio Forbert, was entitled simply 'meal time'. More than 13,000 Jews died of starvation in Warsaw between January and June 1941 (page 54).

Attempts to make conditions as bearable as possible were made by a special Jewish Council, set up by the Germans. The Council provided what relief it could, and arranged cultural activities, concerts, and education. There were many orphanages in the ghetto, their difficult work inspired by the leadership of their directors, including Janusz Korczak. On 12 August 1942 he was to insist on accompanying his children in one of the Warsaw deportations (page 112).

Map 57

THE SPREAD OF TERROR AND DEATH, JANUARY TO JUNE 1941

North Sea

Amsterdam
`400`
22 February 1941

Baltic Sea

Warsaw
`13,000`
died of starvation and disease January - June 1941

Bremen
hundreds
early 1941

Kalisz
`439`
gassed 1 January 1941

Lublin

Lodz
`5,000`
died of starvation and disease January - June 1941

Biala Podlaska
`12`
prisoners of war 15 May 1941

BELGIUM

Suresnes
Paris
`3,600`
interned 14 May 1941

GERMAN-OCCUPIED FRANCE

GREATER GERMANY

Mauthausen

Kielce
Opole
Lagow
Modliborzyce
Cracow

Vienna
`5,004`
15 February - 12 March 1941

RUMANIA
Bucharest
`120`
murdered in the streets 22-23 January 1941

VICHY FRANCE

Zagreb
`6`
April 1941

Adriatic Sea

Black Sea

Noé
Le Vernet
Gurs
Rivesaltes
Les Milles
Argelés
internment camps

SPAIN
neutral

Mediterranean Sea

TURKEY
neutral

`791`
on board the "Darien" reached Palestine by sea 9 March 1941

```
0    miles    200
0  kilometres  300
```

several thousand deported to the Sahara, for slave labour see page 56

Map 58

BIRTHPLACES OF JEWS EXECUTED IN FRANCE FOR RESISTANCE, 1941

© Martin Gilbert 1982

During the first six months of 1941, the rigour of Germany's policy towards the Jews was constant and severe. On 1 January 1941 a further 439 old and sick Jews were taken from the Old People's Home at Kalisz, and gassed by exhaust fumes in a nearby wood (*see also page 51*). At Biala Podlaska, 12 more defenceless Jewish prisoners-of-war were savagely murdered. In each of the ghettos shown on page 50, death from starvation and disease was a daily occurrence, with more than 18,000 dead in Warsaw and Lodz. From 22 February 1941 any Pole selling food to a Jew outside the Warsaw ghetto was automatically sentenced to three months' hard labour, and the ghetto ration was reduced to three ounces of bread a day. 'Although the ghetto of Lodz was intended as a mere trial,' the Cologne *Zeitung* reported on 5 April 1941, 'a mere prelude to the solution of the Jewish question, it has turned out to be the best and most perfect temporary solution of the Jewish problem.' Nine days later, any Jew leaving the Lodz ghetto was ordered to be shot on sight.

More than 40,000 German and Belgian Jews were deported into the Warsaw ghetto. New ghettos were also set up in Cracow, Lublin and Kielce. From Vienna, more than 5,000 Jews were deported to these eastern ghettos and labour camps, while from Amsterdam, more than 400 Jews were seized as hostages and deported to the stone quarries of Mauthausen concentration camp; the events leading to this deportation are described on pages 78-9.

In Paris, several thousand foreign-born Jews were seized and interned in May 1941. At the same time, thousands of Polish- and German-born Jews, who had fought in the French Foreign Legion against Germany in 1940, were deported to slave labour camps in the Sahara. Outside Paris, at Suresnes, 133 Jews were shot for resistance during 1941, the first executions taking place on 16 April 1941. The map above shows the birthplaces of some of those shot, as recorded by the Gestapo: 10 had been born in Warsaw, and almost all had been born within the borders (shown here dotted) of the former Russian Empire. Many, like Charles Weinberg from Kishinev, were in their fifties. One of those shot, Antoine Hajje, had been born in Cyprus; another, Elias Salomon, in Beirut.

Outside Greater Germany, anti-semitic violence in Bucharest left 120 Jews dead in the streets (*left*): men, women and children who had been hunted down by armed gangs. A few survivors managed to reach Palestine by sea.

The photograph shows work on the Sahara railroad (*see also page 56*).

Map 59

SLAVE LABOUR CAMPS OF THE SAHARA, 1941-1942

SPAIN
neutral

● Granada

Algiers ●

Mediterranean Sea

Gibraltar
British

*Atlantic
Ocean*

Oran ●

Boghari ●
labour camp

Tangier ●

SPANISH MOROCCO

Djelfa ●
labour camp

Berguent ●
punishment camp

M O R O C C O

Missour ●
labour camp

Tendrara ●
labour camp

Bouârfa ●
*labour
camp*

Hadjerat-M'Guil ●
*punishment camp and
isolation camp*

Kenadsa
labour camp

Ain el Ourak ●
labour camp

Meridja ●
labour camp

Béchar ●
labour camp

Abadla ●
labour camp

A L G E R I A

Beni Abbès ●
labour camp

+ + + The Trans-Sahara railway,
being built by slave labour
in 1941 and 1942.

Adrar
● *labour camp*

0   miles   100

0 kilometres 100

© **Martin Gilbert 1982**

In April 1940 more than 1,500 Jews were serving in the French Foreign Legion, hoping to fight against Nazi Germany. But with the German conquest of France in June 1940 they were first 'demobilized', then interned, and finally sent to labour camps in French North Africa (*above*). Many of these Jews were refugees from Germany and Austria who had been in France at the outbreak of war.

A law of 4 October 1940 gave Vichy France the power to intern Jews even inside the Unoccupied Zone, and on 22 March 1941 a law signed by Marshal Pétain authorized the construction of a Trans-Sahara railway. The work was done, in harsh conditions, by all who had been interned: former Spanish Republican soldiers, Poles, Czechs, Greeks and Jews.

The camp at Hadjerat-M'Guil was opened on 1 November 1941, as a punishment and isolation camp. It contained 170 prisoners, nine of whom were tortured and murdered in conditions of the worst brutality. Two of those murdered were Jews, one of whom had earlier been in a concentration camp in Germany but had been released in 1939 and

SLAVE LABOUR CAMPS ON THE RIVER BUG, FEBRUARY 1941

GREATER GERMANY

Warsaw

Lodz

Kielce

Lublin

Lukow

Bialystok

Brest-Litovsk

Kowel

Belzec

'Otto Line'

Lvov

SOVIET UNION

UPPER SILESIA

see map 61

River Vistula

River San

River Bug

border

fortifications

SLOVAKIA

RUTHENIA

BUKOVINA

RUMANIA

Vienna
5,004

AUSTRIA

HUNGARY

TRANSYLVANIA

© Martin Gilbert 1982

had fled to France. This young man's parents had become refugees in London. On learning of their son's murder in the Sahara, they committed suicide.

Shown above is the deportation of more than 5,000 Jews from Vienna to the Kielce and Lublin ghettos, and to the labour camps along the River Bug (above). There, together with Jews deported from Warsaw and Lodz, they were forced to drain marshes and build fortifications on the Soviet border, the 'Otto Line', intended to act as a barrier against Soviet tanks. One of the main labour camps, at Belzec, was later to become one of the four eastern death camps (page 90).

Another group of Jews who were sent to forced labour were skilled workers living in the region of the Upper Silesian coalfields. There were 93,628 Jews living in this region, in 32 communities, the six largest of which, among them the town of Auschwitz, are shown here (right). Thousands of able-bodied Jews were rounded up in these towns and sent to work in German mining, metallurgy and textile plants and factories in the region, as many as 5,000 men from Bedzin.

SLAVE LABOUR GANGS, MARCH 1941

Zawierce
5,472

Bedzin
25,171

Dabrowa Gornicza
5,564

Sosnowiec
24,149

UPPER SILESIA

coal fields

Chrzanow
8,229

EAST UPPER SILESIA

River Vistula

Auschwitz
6,454

© Martin Gilbert 1982

Map 62

THE GERMAN CONQUEST OF YUGOSLAVIA AND GREECE, APRIL 1941

GREATER Graz
GERMANY

HUNGARY

TRANS *YLVANIA*

ITALY

Subotica
250

Timisoara

BACSKA

Zagreb

RUMANIA

Fiume

Novi
Sad
250

BANAT

Belgrade

Bucharest

YUGOSLAVIA

Zara
(Italian)

Sarajevo

Adriatic Sea

Dubrovnik

Nis

BULGARIA

70,000 *Jews in 1940*

Skopje

Sofia

ITALY

Bari

ALBANIA *occupied by Italy from April 1939*

Valona

CORFU

Salonica

GREECE

Aegean Sea

Ionian Sea

ZANTE

Athens

TURKEY *neutral*

75,000 *Jews*

| 0 | miles | 100 |

| 0 | kilometres | 150 |

Mediterranean Sea

CRETE

© Martin Gilbert 1982

On 6 April 1941 the German armies invaded
Yugoslavia and Greece, and by the end of
the month a further 145,000 Jews had been
brought under Nazi tyranny *(above)*. Those
of the Banat, shown opposite according to
the Yugoslav census of 31 March 1931, lived
in small and scattered communities north of
Belgrade, between the River Tisa and the
Rumanian border. Numbering over 3,000

people, they were all driven from their
homes by the Germans in August 1941,
within four months of the German conquest
of Yugosalvia. Taken to Tasmajdan camp,
near Belgrade, they were shot in the camp
itself, and on the banks of the Danube, in
daily executions: on 20 August 1941 the
whole Banat region was declared *Judenrein,*
'purged of Jews'.

Map 63

THE JEWS OF THE BANAT

HUNGARY

Krstr
11

Arandelovo
39

Nova
Kanjiza
46

Coka
49

Mokrin
38

Kikinda
100

Sajan
9

Padej
28

R U M A N I A

Novi Becej
167

Torda
10

Jasa Tomic
56

River Tisa

Kumani
14

Melenci
32

Veliki
Beckerek
1,352

Boka
3

BACSKA

Aradac
4

Ecka
33

Jarkovac
5

B A N A T

Vrsac
404

Perlez
18

Seleus
5

River Danube

Kovacica
37

Padina
33

Alibunar
31

Bela Crkva
67

Y U G O S L A V I A

Novo Selo
1

SREM

Pancevo
507

Delibiato
10

Gaj
6

Kovin
75

River Danube

Tasmajdan
concentration camp
3,000

Belgrade
*Sajmiste
concentration camp*

SERBIA

© Martin Gilbert 1982

By the end of October 1941 almost no Banat Jews were left alive in Tasmajdan: the life, the culture and the achievements of more than 30 communities had been destroyed for all time.

West of the Banat, the towns of Sobotica and Novi Sad were occupied by Hungarian forces on 11 April 1941. In Subotica the Germans executed 250 members of a Jewish youth movement who had carried out the first acts of sabotage against the occupation forces. In Novi Sad, Hungarian troops and local Germans murdered at random 250 Jews and 250 Serbs.

From the outset of the war, Jews were active in the Yugoslav resistance. The first secret radio in Zagreb was operated by two Jewish brothers. More than 2,000 Yugoslav Jews later fought with Tito's partisans, and a specifically Jewish unit of 250 men, formed in 1943, lost more than 200 fighting against the Germans. One leading resistance fighter, Moša Pijade, a Jew, later became a Vice-President of Yugoslavia.

Map 64 and 65

THE JEWS OF WESTERN CROATIA ON THE EVE OF WAR

Cakovec 533
Varazdin 486
Ludbrijeg 74
Koprivnica 339
Virje 15
Djurdjevac 29
HUNGARY
Donji Miholjac 119
Krapina
Zlata 13
Zabok 6
Klanjec
Krizevci 126
Loka 1
Sevnica 4
Zagreb 8,702
River Drava
Bjelovar 360
Virovitica 233
Slatina 174
Osijek
see map 66
Dugo Selo 23
Klostar Ivanic 5
Ivanic 16
Samobor 8
CROATIA
Daruvar 136
Nasice 161
Jastrebarsko
Lekenik 11
Sisak 230
Pakrac 209
Pozega 248
Pisarovina 15
Petrinja 14
Jasenovac 2
Vinica 23
Karlovac 347
Sunja 9
Slavonski Brod 462
Leskovac 93
Kostajnica
River Sava
Nova Gradiska see page 75 207
Ogulin 21
Dvor 1
BOSNIA
Cazin 1
Bihac 149

© Martin Gilbert 1982

0 miles 30
0 kilometres 40

RABBIS AND CANTORS MURDERED BY CROAT 'USTACHI'

0 miles 30
0 kilometres 50

Murska Sobota
M. Roth, aged 70

Cakovec
Elia Gruenwald chief rabbi aged about 55

Ludbrijeg
(Ludberg)
Dr. Deutsham aged about 70

Varazdin
Dr. Rudolf Guech aged about 70 Jakob Kohn

Koprivnica
Leo Wolfenzon, aged about 55 Dr. N. Kohn, aged about 58

N. Schwartz aged about 45

Paul Froehlich, aged 28 Isidor Guren, aged about 60 Dr. Simon Ungar, aged about 60

Krizevci
Lavoslav Buchsbaum aged 72

Virovitica
Adolf Springer, chief cantor aged 45

Donji Miholjac

Bjelovar
Izidor Dolf aged about 45

Zagreb

Slatina
Hinko Gruenwald, aged about 95

Osijek

Vijoslav Mandel, aged about 32

Vucovar

Daruvar
Josip Gilman aged about 65 Leopold Katz, aged 65

Nasice
Jakov Schmelzer aged 35

Karlovac
David Meissl, cantor aged about 45 killed with his son, his three daughters were saved

Sisak
Dr. M. Heisz, chief rabbi aged about 60 Jakov Klinkovstein chief cantor, aged about 65

Pakrac
Izak Freides, aged about 55

Pozega
Mordeschil Rikow aged about 70

Dakovo
Alexander Roth, cantor

Vincovci
Izidor Hersmovic aged about 60 Mijo Propper, aged about 60

Nova Gradiska
Andrija Trilnik aged about 30

Brcko
Leon Katan, aged 66

Zagreb
*David Atijas, cantor
Arnold Basch, cantor
Miroslav Freiberger, chief rabbi
Lavoslav Kahn, cantor, 45
M. Loewy, Dean of the Rabbanical School, 70
Eugen Mandel, cantor, 35
Samuel Singer, cantor 65
Dragutin Vogel, cantor, 27
Josip Weissmann, retired chief cantor, 73*

Banja Luka
N. Kohn, rabbi and cantor

Travnik
Izak Baruch

© Martin Gilbert 1982

THE JEWS OF EASTERN CROATIA AND THE SREM ON THE EVE OF WAR

0 miles 20
0 kilometres 30

HUNGARY

Popovac 11

Knezevi Vinograd 25

Belisce 96
Darda 23
Valpovo 30
Osijek 2,600
Koska 15

EASTERN CROATIA
Cepin 9
Dalj 16
Podgorac 9
Ernestinova 3
Bobuta 7
Vukovar 306
Semeljci 10
Vinkovci 647
River Danube
Cerevic 7
Beocin 37
Sremski Karlovci 2
Dakovo 254
Ivankovo 15
Slakovci 8
Sarengrad 4
S R E M
Maradik 3
Indija 39
Andrijevci 10
Erdevik 27
Sid 59
Ruma 215
Stara Pazova 68
Babina Greda 5
Zupanja 75
Zemun 523
Vrbanja 10
Drenovci 5
Sremska Mitrovica 115
Nikinci 4
Belgrade
Rajevo Selo 6
River Sava
Brcko 112
Racinovci 2

© Martin Gilbert 1982   for Bosnia, see page 75

Following the German conquest of Yugosalvia on 17 April 1941, Croatia became an independent State, ruled by the pro-Nazi 'Ustachi'. The top maps show the Jewish communities of Croatia and the Srem according to the Yugoslavia census of 1931. The areas plotted are shown on the small map *(right)*.

Persecution of the Jews began at once. In Ruma, the synagogue was demolished. In Vukovar, the community leaders were arrested, and then 'ransomed' back to the community. In Osijek, German soldiers, local Germans and Croat 'Ustachi' burned the main synagogue, destroyed the Jewish cemetery, looted Jewish property, and imposed a crippling 'fine' on the Jewish community.

The map opposite *(below)* gives the names of some rabbis and cantors who were murdered during the late spring and early summer: some were venerable rabbis, scholars and teachers; others were young men embarking upon their careers. Doctors, nurses, midwives, chemists, dentists and vets, whose work had been for the whole Croatian community, were also killed. Many young Croat Jews were to fight with Tito's partisans.

GERMANY AND CROATIA

Baltic Sea

0 miles 200
0 kilometres 300

Berlin

GREATER GERMANY
Warsaw

Prague
Lvov

Vienna
SLOVAKIA

Budapest
HUNGARY
RUMANIA

CROATIA
YUGOSLAVIA
DALMATIA
Banja Luka
Travnik
BOSNIA
Belgrade
SERBIA

Adriatic Sea

ITALY

© Martin Gilbert 1982

Map 68

THE JEWISH COMMUNITIES OF SERBIA

CROATIA

BANAT

River Danube

Veliko Gradiste
9

Zemun
concentration camp established April 1941

Belgrade
7,906
122 shot
29 July 1941

Pozarevac
62

Zabrezje
1

River Sava

Umka
3

Smederovo
78

Sabac
89

Obrenovac
10

Ripanj
3

Mladenovac
2

Loznica
3

Palanka
8

Arandelovac
3

Lapovo
4

Kamenica
2

Valjevo
25

Jagodina
24

Cuprija
1

River Drina

Kragujevac
95

Paracin
6

Rogacica
47

Cacak
7

Uzice
21

Kraljevo
9

Aleksinac
6

Pozega
248

Krusevac
12

SERBIA

Priboj
1

Raska
2

Sjenica
19

Duja Poljana
9

Novi Pazar
249

| 0 | miles | 25 |
| 0 | kilometres | 40 |

Tutin
6

© Martin Gilbert 1982

After 500 years of struggle, persecution and expulsion, the Jews of Belgrade achieved full civil rights in 1878 in the newly independent Serbia. Between the wars they were active in Serbian professional and business life. Smaller Jewish communities settled throughout Serbia, as in the region south of Belgrade (*above*).

On 14 April 1941, within a few hours of the German occupation of Belgrade, Jewish shops were looted, and within a few weeks all Jewish communal activity was forbidden.

On 29 July 1941 the Germans executed 122 'Communists and Jews' for resistance.

Undeterred, Jews from the youth movement joined the resistance, sabotaging German military installations.

By November 1941 more than 15,000 Jews had been deported from throughout Serbia to the concentration camp at Zemun, where by June 1942 they had been killed in mobile gas units, disguised as Red Cross vans.

On 29 August 1942 Berlin was informed officially that the Jewish problem was 'totally solved' in Serbia, 'the only community', the report boasted, 'in which this has been achieved'. Of Serbia's 23,000 Jews, 20,000 had been murdered.

Map 69

EASTERN ESCAPE ROUTES OF POLISH JEWS, MAY 1940 - MAY 1941

© Martin Gilbert 1982

In the year before the German invasion of the Soviet Union, hundreds of Jews living in the Soviet-annexed regions of Poland and the Baltic States, as well as refugees from German-occupied Poland, tried to escape to potentially safer regions. In the Lithuanian city of Kovno, the British Consul, Thomas Preston, helped provide 400 'illegal' Palestine certificates for Jews who were then able to make their way through Istanbul to Jerusalem, while a further 800 received legal certificates. A few hundred Jews were able to cross the Baltic Sea to Sweden. The leaders of several Jewish youth movements,

however, decided to return to Warsaw, to help organize resistance there.

Several hundred Polish and Lithuanian Jews managed to get permission to enter Japan. A few others received transit visas, issued between 20 and 31 August 1940 by Sugehara, the Japanese Consul in Kovno, enabling them to cross the Trans-Siberian railway to Japan, ostensibly for the Dutch East Indies. They were then able to move on to Australia, the United States and Canada.

But those who managed to escape were only a fragment of those trapped in eastern Poland, the Baltic States and western Russia.

Map 70

RUSSIAN JEWRY, A SAMPLE

```
0    miles    40
0  kilometres  60
```

Orel
3,597

Kromy
56

Starodub
3,317

Novozybkov
4,825

Dimitrovsk
21

Maloarchangelsk
28

Dimitriev
186

Gluchov
2,551

Kursk
4,154

Berezna
697

Sosnitsa
1,141

Lgov
183

Korop
787

Myena
1,321

Borzna
697

Oboyan
118

Konotop
5,763

Sudzha
53

Nezhin
6,131

Sumy
2,627

Priluki
11,163

Romny
8,593

River Donetz

Lubny
6,039

Mirgorod
1,994

Kharkov
81,138

Cherkassy
10,886

Poltava
18,474

Chigirin
408

Kobelyaki
1,400

Izium
268

River Dnieper

Kremenchug
28,969

Novomoskovsk
1,421

Aleksandrija
4,395

Pavlograd
3,921

Elizavetgrad
18,358

Ekaterinoslav
62,073

Chaplino
59

Bobrinets
2,265

Krivoi Rog
6,430

Zaporozhe
11,319

UKRAINE

Nikopol
2,699

Tokmak
1,898

Mariupol
7,332

Nikolaiev
21,787

Berislav
395

Melitopol
11,438

Nogaisk
186

Berdiansk
2,138

Cherson
14,837

Genichesk
1,776

Sea of Azov

Dzhankoi
3,294

CRIMEA

Kerch
3,067

Eupatoria
2,409

Saki
53

Karasubazar
190

Feodosia
3,248

Bakchisarai
275

Black Sea

Sevastopol
5,204

Simferopol
21,500

Balaklava
70

Yalta
2,353

© Martin Gilbert 1982

On 22 June 1941 German forces invaded the Soviet Union. As they advanced they moved through areas of dense Jewish settlement, in which lived more than 2,700,000 Jews as well as several hundred thousand Jewish refugees from western Poland.

The figures shown here (*left*) of the number of Jews in some of the cities, towns and villages of western Russia are taken from the Soviet census of 1926. In cities such as Kharkov Jews constituted more than 20 per cent of the total population, and between 1926 and the outbreak of war, the Jewish population of most of the towns shown here had increased. Some had almost doubled: there were as many as 150,000 Jews in Kharkov on the eve of the German invasion. In the Crimea, ancient Jewish communities dating back to Greek and Roman times, and Jewish collective farms set up in the 1920s, existed side by side.

The Jews of several towns shown on the left-hand map had lived through the pogroms in Tsarist times (*page 14*). Many more had been the victims of the massacres of 1918 and 1919, which had claimed 85,000 lives (*page 15*). Some of the towns, such as Starodub, had taken a lead in organizing Jewish self-defence during that period. Others, a few years later, had been at the centre of the famine region, when millions of Soviet citizens had perished.

During the early 1920s tens of thousands of Russian Jews had emigrated, some to avoid Communist persecution, others to escape the all-pervading poverty. But the majority had no choice but to remain in their homes and with their families, working in shops and offices, tilling the fields, and simply trying to exist in the harsh world of Stalinism.

Hitler had other plans for these millions of Jews. He wanted them neither as subjects, nor as slaves. He had made his plans before the German invasion: in May 1941, at Pretzsch, in Saxony, special mobile killing squads, the 'Einsatzgruppen', were set up. Each squad had been allocated a particular area of the Soviet Union for its future activities. Thus Einsatzgruppe A was to be responsible for the murder of Jews in the Baltic States, while Einsatzgruppe D was to work in the Ukraine and the Crimea.

Just as the German army was confident that it could defeat the Soviet Union, and conquer all of western Russia, so the SS was convinced that it could, by mass executions on the spot, 'solve' the Jewish question in

Map 71

THE GERMAN INVASION OF RUSSIA, AND MASS MURDER PLANS, 22 JUNE 1941

Russia, by murdering all the Jews it could
catch. No family was to be spared. Nor were
any resources to be wasted in setting up
ghettos, nor in the deportation of Jews to
distant camps or murder sites. The killing
was to be done in the towns and villages, at
the moment of military victory.

When the German army invaded Russia in
June 1941, its advance was so rapid that less
than 300,000 Jews were able to escape
eastward, to safety beyond the Volga.

The photograph, taken from the personal
album of one of the officers in the picture,
shows the arrival of a detachment of
Einsatzgruppe D in the town of Drohobycz,
in the Polish province of Eastern Galicia,
which Russia had annexed in October
1939. Part of the task of these killing squads
was to recruit local anti-semites, whether
Ukrainians, Lithuanians, or Latvians, who
could help them to round up, terrorize and
destroy each Jewish community, however
small. For the work of this particular
detachment in Drohobycz itself,
see page 67.

The map above shows the regions
allocated to the different killing squads, and
the initial points of attack of the German
army and its Rumanian ally on 22 June 1941.

Map 72

SOME JEWISH COMMUNITIES IN THE VOLHYNIA ON THE EVE OF WAR

0   miles   16

0   kilometres   24

Pohost
894

Serniki
1,073

Lubieszow
17

Wysock
1,060

Kamen Kashirski
750

P O L E S I A

Dabrowica
3,225

Wlodzimierzec
1,500

Bereznica
1,372

Tomaszgrod
193

Maniewicze
549

Rafalowka
651

Klesow
90

Trojanowka
212

Antonowka
578

Sarny
4,950

Rokitno
788

Poworsk
37

Mielnica
1,040

Stepan
1,588

Holoby
209

Sokul
167

Kolki
860

Osowa
832

Berezne
2,818

Rozyszcze
4,070

V O L H Y N I A

Derazno
741

Kostopol
3,920

Ludwipol
1,088

Torczyn
1,758

Zofjowka
1,825

Siedliszcze
788

Luck
15,879

Klewan
1,814

Aleksandrja
1,536

Miedzyrzecz
2,330

Olyka
2,479

Nieswicz
30

Ostrozec
751

Tuczyn
2,622

Rowne
25,000

Korzec
4,895

Targowica
784

Mlynow
731

Zdolbunow
1,500

Hoszcza
963

Boreml
1,018

Warkowicze
1,053

Ozieriany
946

1921 - 1939

Demidowka
707

Dubno
7,000

Mizocz
1,048

Beresteczko
2,625

Kozin
653

Ostrog
9,240

WESTERN
UKRAINE

EASTERN
GALICIA

Rachmanow
62

Polish - Soviet border

Radzwillow
3,120

Krzemieniec
6,240

Szumsk
2,040

© Martin Gilbert 1982

In the first three weeks of their invasion of the Soviet Union, the German forces made rapid advances. In their wake, the specially trained mobile killing squads began the systematic murder of Jews, in every city, town and village of western Russia. The map above shows the number of Jews living in the larger towns and villages of part of the Volhynia, an area inside the Russian Empire until 1914, and within the independent Polish

Map 73

JEWS MASSACRED BETWEEN 22 JUNE AND 16 JULY 1941

state between the wars. The Volhynia was annexed by Russia at the time of the Nazi-Soviet partition of Poland in October 1939. In the area shown here, there were also more than 100 smaller Jewish communities.

In all, more than a quarter of a million Jews were living in the Volhynia in 1939. The figures above show some of the German killing squad massacres during the first three weeks following the invasion.

Map 74

JEWS MASSACRED BETWEEN 17 JULY AND 31 AUGUST 1941

Gulf of Riga

ESTONIA

Sea

LATVIA

Liepaja 3,000

Baltic

LITHUANIA

Dvinsk ○

Moscow ○

EAST PRUSSIA

Volkavyskis 900

see map 75

○ Kovno

Augustow 1,500

Wolozyn 1,000

GREATER

Stawiski 2,000

Iwje 225

Oszmiana 700

Korelicze 105

Stolpce 80

Tykocin 2,100

Zdzieciol 120

Lubotyn 228

Zambrow 1,100

Slonim 1,200

○ Warsaw

GERMANY

Czyzew 3,500

THE   SOVIET   UNION

German forces advancing

POLAND

Pripet marshes

Pinsk 11,000

Kamen Kashirsky 88

Pohost 150

Sarniki 150

Korzec 312

Bereczteczko

Dubno 80

Zborow 850

Zborow 300

○ Lvov

see map 76

Kiev ○

German forces advancing

Stanislawow ○

Zhitomir 2,530

UKRAINE

RUTHENIA

Hotin 3,000

Kamenets Podolsk 14,000

mostly deportees from Hungarian-occupied Ruthenia (see page 184)

Kirovo 6,000

HUNGARY

Czernowitz 4,000

Kalinindorf 1,875

Orgeev 200

Jassy 4,000

Nikolaiev 5,000

RUMANIA

Kishinev 12,287

0   miles   100
0   kilometres   150

Kilia 2,000

Black Sea

Sea of Azov

CRIMEA

© Martin Gilbert 1982

During the second six weeks of the German advance into Russia, the work of the killing squads continued without respite. This map, like the previous map and the maps on the right, shows only a small percentage of the total killings. For many places, particularly the smaller villages and hamlets, no record survives. Nor was the killing confined to SS units. In Lithuania local non-Jews were among the most savage killers, while in the south, Rumanian troops and militia murdered thousands of Jews in the area of

MORE JEWS MASSACRED, 17 JULY - 31 AUGUST 1941

Joniskis
355

Pasvalys
1,349

L A T V I A

Dagda
216

Rokishkis
4,188

Dvinsk
21

Aglona Mental Home
544

Seduva
664

Panevezhys
8,837

Zarasai
2,569

Raseiniai
3,043

L I T H U A N I A

Kedainai
2,201

Utena
1,038

Agriogala
38

Wilkia
402

Ukmerge (Vilkomir)
1,647

River Niemen

Jonava
552

P O L A N D

Kovno
2,581

Kaisiadorys
1,911

Vilna
1,000

Wilejka
250

Prienai
1,078

Ponary

20 July - 8 August
444

12 - 31 August

0 miles 40
0 kilometres 60

Marijampole
156

Alytus
952

© Martin Gilbert 1982

EASTERN GALICIAN KILLINGS. SUMMER 1941

Mosty
Wielkie
119

River Bug

Krzemieniec
800

Brody
250

VOLHYNIA

U K R A I N E

Busk
30

Lvov
2,000

Zloczow
300

Tarnopol
3,000

Bobrka
63

Jezierno
180

Mikulince
30

Podwoloczyska
70

Trembowla
40

E A S T E R N
G A L I C I A

Stryj
10

Husiatyn
200

Buczacz
350

Czortkow
400

Stanislawow
1,000

Zaleszczyki
800

0 miles 30
0 kilometres 40

© Martin Gilbert 1982

Rumanian military advance. Throughout Eastern Galicia (*right*) Ukrainian peasants frequently set upon the Jews, murdering hundreds before the German killing squads arrived. But it was the German squads whose work was on the larger scale, including the first 'five figure' massacre of Jews by Einsatzgruppe D in Kishinev between 17 and 31 July 1941 (*page 71*). A second 'five figure' massacre took place on August 27 and 28, of Jews who had earlier been deported to Kamenets Podolsk from Hungary. These were not Hungarian citizens but Jewish refugees who had fled to Hungary and Ruthenia in 1938 and 1939 from Germany, Austria, Slovakia and Poland. Some had lived in Hungary as 'Aryans', on false identity papers. Others had obtained the right to live in Hungary as 'transients' on their way to Palestine. Rounded up and deported eastward during July, over 18,000 had been sent to camps in and around Kamenets Podolsk. On 27 August 1941 heavily armed SS units, with Ukrainian militia support, marched 14,000 of these refugees some 10 miles to a series of bomb craters, ordered them to undress, and opened fire with machine-guns. Many of those who died had been buried alive.

Map 77

THE JEWS OF BESSARABIA ON THE EVE OF WAR

Hotin 5,786

Romancauti 180

Secureni 4,216

Noua Sulita 4,154

Briceni 5,354

Otaci 2,785

Zgurita 2,541

Soroca 5,452

Lipcani 4,698

Edineti 5,349

Chetrosu 140

Liublin 274

Vartujeni 1,834

Rascani 2,060

Dumbraveni 1,198

Vascaut 34

Vadu Rascu 1,970

Marculesti 2,237

Alexandreni 1,018

Floresti 529

Cotiugeni 367

Glodeni 214

Capresti 1,815

Raspopeni 158

Rezina 2,889

Balti 14,259

Limbeni 39

Sangerei 167

Chiperceni 208

Falesti 3,258

Telenesti 2,811

Bravicea 413

Susleni 110

Valea lui-Vlad 1,281

Sculeni 1,207

Cornesti 338

Orhei 6,408

Parlita 1,064

Calarasi 3,662

Peresecina 241

Criuleni 240

Ungheni 1,390

Varzaresti 205

Vadu lui-Voda 9

Nisiporeni 380

Ciuciuleni 291

Kishinev 41,405

Tighina (Bendery) 8,294

Lapusna 165

Hancesti 1,523

Carpineni 271

Gura Galbena 111

Taraclia 151

Causani 1,870

Olanesti 110

Palanca 24

Leova 2,326

Cimislia 925

BESSARABIA

Romanesti 1,995

Volintiri 420

Cazaci 136

Comrat 392

Borodino 50

Cetatea Alba (Akkerman) 4,239

Baimaclia 509

Berezina 125

Saba 159

Tarutino 1,546

Gotesti 35

Sarata 316

Arciz 842

Cahul 803

Taraclia 46

Tatar Bunar 1,202

Tuzla 118

Colibasi 2

Bolgrad 1,222

Kilia 1,969

Reni 1,201

Ismail 1,680

Black Sea

River Dniester

River Pruth

0 miles 30

0 kilometres 50

© Martin Gilbert 1982

Until 1941 Bessarabia was part of the Tsarist Empire. The murder of 49 Jews during the Kishinev pogrom in 1903 (*page 14*) had led to protest demonstrations in London, Paris and New York, and a letter of rebuke from Theodore Roosevelt to the Tsar. In 1918 the region became part of Rumania but remained strongly anti-semitic. The city of Kishinev was a focal point of Jewish culture and political life, while Jewish agricultural communities thrived throughout the province.

With the return of Soviet rule to Bessarabia in June 1940, all Jewish

Map 78

MASSACRES, DEPORTATIONS AND DEATH MARCHES FROM BESSARABIA, from July 1941

PODOLIA

Bar
camp under
German control

Zhmerinka
3,274
in ghetto

Copai Gorod
2,200
in ghetto

Murafa 4,500 in ghetto

Lucenets
2,897
in ghetto

Shargorod 5,300 in ghetto

Djurin
3,500
in ghetto

REICHSKOMMISSARIAT
UKRAINE

River Bug

Manicovca

Secureni

Otaci

Mogilev-Podolsk
15,000
in ghetto

Crijopol

Obadowka

Balanowka

Tibulovca

camp
under
German
control
from
1942

Bershad
9,200 in ghetto

see
page
87

Briceni

Lipcani
800 8 July
1.200
on death
march
20 July ·
6 Aug

Edineti
1,000
5-7 July

Jampol

T R A N S N I S T R I A
under Rumanian administration

Soroca

Zgurita

River Dniester

Olgopol

Balta
2,723
in ghetto

BESSARABIA
under Rumanian
control
from July 1941

Vascaut

Vartujeni

Cotiugeni

Cusminca

Rezina

Birzula

Ramnita

Marculesti

148,000
Jews from Bessarabia
perished in Transnistria

River Pruth

Limbeni

Parlita

Falesti

Rautel forest
many thousands

Balti
50 8 July
44 9 July

Orhei
200
6 August

several hundred
escape to
Soviet central Asia
June - July

Dubossary

Criuleni

RUMANIA

MOLDAVIA

Jassy

0   miles   50
0   kilometres   80

© Martin Gilbert 1982

10,000 17-31 July
1,411 1 August
551 7 August
325 8 August
41,000 after deportation

Kishinev

Tiraspol

Tighina

institutions were closed and on 13 June 1941 many of the Jewish leaders, as well as wealthy Jews, were exiled to Siberia, where many died. But with the arrival of the Nazi killing squads in July 1941, the scale of murder, as indicated above, exceeded anything previously known.

Following the initial killings, internment camps were set up throughout the province. At the camp in Edineti, after the initial slaughter, 70 to 100 people died every day in July and August 1941, mostly of starvation.

Then in September the Jews of Bessarabia were forced out of the province in hundreds of death marches, some of which are shown above. In all, more than 148,000 Bessarabian Jews perished in the ghettos and camps of Transnistria. During these marches more than half of the victims died: of exposure, disease, hunger, thirst and the savage brutality of the Rumanian and German guards, who would often pick a group of marchers at random, order them aside, and shoot them.

Map 79

THE JEWS OF THE BUKOVINA ON THE EVE OF WAR

0 miles 10

0 kilometres 20

Kolomyja

GREATER GERMANY (EASTERN GALICIA)

Sniatyn

Cincau 57

Dorosauti 58

Ocna **115**

Zastavna **635**

Davidesti 48

Cozmeni **640**

Lujeni **381**

Sadagura **1,488**

River Pruth

RUMANIA (BESSARABIA)

Banila pe Ceremus **517**

Milie **197**

Ispas **143**

Kuty

Vijnita 2,666

Berhomet **979**

Rastoace 71

Mareniceni 25

Gura Putilei **115**

Dintinet 56

Toraceni 58

Putila **382**

Sarghieni **204**

Plosca 99

Seletin **737**

Stanestii **622**

Broscauti **115**

Costesti **274**

Cabesti **120**

Jadova 50

Panca 25

Czernowitz (Cernauti) **42,932**

Nova Jadova **325**

Mihova **243**

Banila **688**

Cires 100

Storojinet **2,482**

Iordanesti 99

Budinet 8

Ciudeiu **570**

Petrauti **138**

Crasna Putnei **169**

Crasna Iliesti 97

Igesti 100

Fradautii Noui **104**

Siret 2,121

River Siret

RUMANIA (MOLDAVIA)

Zamostea **129**

Zvorastea 28

Straja **134**

Vicovul de Sus **334**

Bainet 23

Brodina **234**

Putna **214**

BUKOVINA

Argel 11

Sucevita 10

Marginea 23

Radauti **5,647**

Dornesti 84

Serbauti 14

Granicesti 9

Clit 4

Darmanesti 92

River Ceremos

Moldovita **452**

Poiana 11

Moldova Sulita 55

Vatra **136**

Frumosul 88

Vama **392**

Ilisesti **131**

Suceava **3,533**

Liteni 11

River Moldova

Breaza 94

Carlibaba **154**

HUNGARY (TRANSYLVANIA)

Campulung-Moldovenesc **1,488**

Frasin **156**

Gura Humoruliu **1,951**

Paltinoasa 14

Ciocanesti 7

Stulpicani **151**

Iacobeni **228**

Ostra 10

RUMANIA

Vatra Dornei 1,750

© Martin Gilbert 1982

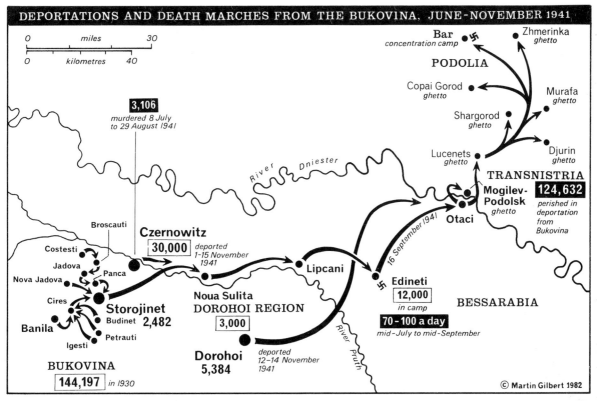

DEPORTATIONS AND DEATH MARCHES FROM THE BUKOVINA, JUNE-NOVEMBER 1941

Bar
concentration camp

Zhmerinka
ghetto

PODOLIA

Copai Gorod
ghetto

Murafa
ghetto

3,106
murdered 8 July
to 29 August 1941

Shargorod
ghetto

Djurin
ghetto

Lucenets
ghetto

TRANSNISTRIA
124,632
perished in
deportation
from
Bukovina

Mogilev-
Podolsk
ghetto

Broscauti

Czernowitz
30,000
deported
1-15 November
1941

River Dniester

Otaci

16 September 1941

Costesti

Jadova
Panca

Nova Jadova

Cires

Banila

Storojinet
Budinet 2,482

Igesti
Petrauti

Lipcani

Noua Sulita
DOROHOI REGION
3,000

Edineti
12,000
in camp

BESSARABIA

70-100 a day
mid-July to mid-September

River Pruth

Dorohoi
5,384

deported
12-14 November
1941

BUKOVINA
144,197 in 1930

© Martin Gilbert 1982

THE BUKOVINA

Oslo
Stockholm
Leningrad

North
Sea

Moscow

Warsaw
Berlin
Kiev

Paris

GREATER
GERMANY

Lvov
BUKOVINA

Vienna
HUNGARY

RUMANIA

Black
Sea

Rome
Belgrade

Istanbul

Athens

© Martin Gilbert 1982   CRETE

The Jews of the Bukovina, like those of
Bessarabia, were driven eastwards to ghettos
in Transnistria. Uprooted from more than
100 communities, they too were marched
away, interned, and then marched off again.
Within a year more than 120,000 had died
(page 87). The photograph was taken at the
start of a Bukovina death march.

THE JEWS OF ESTONIA ON THE EVE OF WAR

FINLAND

Helsinki

Gulf of Finland

Leningrad

German front line 1 September 1941

Baltic Sea

Tallin 4,213

Paldiski 1

Nomme 109

Keila 1

Rakvere 100

Johvi 8

Narva 370

ESTONIA

Tapa 16

Mustvee 6

DAGO 10

Haapsalu 11

Türi 2

Paide 31

Jogeva 5

Lake Peipus

SOVIET UNION

OSEL

Karuse 37

Poltsamaa 2

Pärnu 500

Viljandi 226

Tartu 1,766

Lake Pskov

Kuressaare 37

Kilingi-Nomme 1

Moisaküla 1

Torva 1

Voru 199

Pskov

Valga 521

Anstla 3

Petseri 5

Gulf of Riga

LATVIA

© Martin Gilbert 1982

0   miles   40
0   kilometres   60

ESTONIA CONQUERED, 3 SEPTEMBER 1941

Oslo

Stockholm

Helsinki

Leningrad

North Sea

Baltic Sea

Pskov

ESTONIA

Moscow

Vilna

German front line

Berlin

Warsaw

GREATER GERMANY

1 September 1941

Vienna

Czernowitz

Budapest

Loborgrad

BOSNIA

Bucharest

Belgrade

Black Sea

Adriatic Sea

Sarajevo

Sofia

Rome

Ankara

0   miles   200
0   kilometres   400

© Martin Gilbert 1982

The Jewish community of Estonia owed its origins to the Cantonists: Jewish boy soldiers conscripted for the army of Tsar Nicholas I at the age of 12, and sometimes even at eight or nine. These boys served a compulsory 25 years, a system which had started in 1827 and which continued for more than 20 years. On demobilization, many Cantonists settled in Tallin, known in Russian as Reval. A further 2,000 Russian Jews came in Tsarist times to live in the university town of Tartu, known to the Jews by its German name, Dorpat.

In the inter-war years Estonia was the only country in eastern Europe to adhere to the minority treaties of the League of Nations. Jewish autonomous institutions, set up in 1926, were controlled by a Jewish Cultural Council. For ten years Jewish life flourished. But from 1934, a local fascist movement encouraged anti-semitism.

In 1940 Estonia was annexed by the Soviet Union. Five hundred Jewish communal leaders, as well as many 'capitalist' Jews, were then deported to Siberia, where many died. But following the German invasion of Russia in June 1941, some 3,000 Estonian

JEWISH COMMUNITIES IN BOSNIA ON THE EVE OF WAR

CROATIA

River Sava

Jasenovac

Bosanska Dubica 7
Stara Gradiska concentration camp set up in April 1941
Bosanska Gradiska 28
Bosanski Brod 79
Odzak 3
Bosanski Samac 29
Derventa 143
Modrica 13
Gradacac 45
Brcko 112
Bijeljina 321
Prijedor 45
Ljubija 6
Doboj 54
Gracanica 22
Janja 4
Dubrava 20
Banja Luka 368
Tesanj 18
Teslic 16
Tuzla 314
Zvornik 75
Zivinice 7
Kljuc 4
Zepce 71
Vlasenica 60
Ljubovija
Kladanj 12
Srebrenica 4
Jajce 31
Travnik 364
Zenica 234
Olovo 30
Donji Vakuf 3
Kruscica concentration camp set up in April 1941
Visoko 113
Visegrad 107
Fojnica 3
Kiseljak 17
Sarajevo 8,196

BOSNIA

miles 25 / kilometres 40

© Martin Gilbert 1982

Jews found refuge in the Soviet Union. After the German occupation of Tallin in September, the remaining 1,000 Jews were murdered by the SS killing squads.

After the German invasion of Bosnia, a few Jews managed to flee over the mountains into Italian-occupied territory, but the majority were deported to concentration camps controlled by the Croat fascist 'Ustachi'. The majority died in the camps.

The Jewish community of Sarajevo had been built up during the sixteenth century by Jewish refugees from Spain. These 'Sephardi' Jews spoke their own language, Ladino, and helped, as merchants and traders, to link Bosnia with the outside world. After the Austrian annexation of Bosnia in 1878, hundreds of Ashkenazi Jews, from Vienna, Prague and Budapest, joined the local communities. Between the wars, during the 'Yugoslav era', the Jews of Bosnia enjoyed full civil liberties. But disaster struck from the first days of the German occupation, with the burning down of the synagogue by German troops and local Muslims.

By November 1941 a total of 14,000 Bosnian Jews had been deported to the camps shown here (right). Less than 1,000 survived the war.

THE JEWS OF BOSNIA MURDERED

0 miles 40 / 0 kilometres 60

Loborgrad 4,000 women

CROATIA

Jasenovac 4,000 men

Stara Gradiska 6,000 children

children
men
women

Tuzla

BOSNIA

Travnik

Kruscica

Sarajevo

Italian zone

DALMATIA

Mostar 1,600

Adriatic Sea

© Martin Gilbert 1982

Map 86

MASSACRE AND REVOLT IN SEPTEMBER AND OCTOBER 1941

Zagare
2,236 *murdered*
150 *shot*

Nevel
710

Moscow

Yanovichi
1,180

Krasnopole
1,940

Vitebsk
3,000

Krupki
1,500

Rudnya
6,200

see map 87

Vilna

Shklov
3,000

Lida

Borisov
8,000

Tatarsk
*resistance
25 October 1941*

Lomza
3,500

Mogilev
2,760

Zambrow
1,000

see map 88

Bobruisk
380

Starodub 270
*resistance
25 October 1941*

Pripet marshes

Parichi
1,700

Lelchitsy
1,400

Ostrog

Ovruch
30

Chernigov
280

Radomyshl
13,020

Toporow 120

Komarno
300

Przemyslany
500

Kozowa 300

Korosten
340

Zhitomir
7,500

Kiev
33,771
29-30 September

Buczacz
400

Bolechow
1,000

Stanislawow
10,000

Litin
2,000

Babi
Yar

Skvira
1,000

Voronezh

HUNGARY

Sniatyn
400

Vinnitsa
28,000

Uman
24,000

Kremenchug
7,000

Kosow
2,200

Zbaraz
70

Berdichev
14,803

Ananayev
300

Kirovograd
5,000

Dnepropetrovsk
15,000

Delatyn
1,950

Dubossary
6,000

Nikolaiev
5,000

Melitopol
2,000

Mariupol
8,500

Taganrog
3,000

RUMANIA

Kherson
410

Odessa
48,000

Sea of Azov

SERBIA

Belgrade
449
II October

Kakhovka
740

Black Sea

0   miles   100
0   kilometres   150

© Martin Gilbert 1982

German front line, October 1941

As the German armies approached Moscow, the killing squads continued their work behind the lines. The map above shows some of the main killings. The map opposite (*above*) shows the details in the Vilna region of Lithuania, where a German lieutenant carefully recorded for his superiors the precise number of those killed on each day of his squad's activities, dividing his statistics into men, women and children.

The killing squads were heavily armed and had strong local support. The Jews were unarmed, and surrounded by an extremely hostile peasantry, who sometimes attacked them even before the killing squads had arrived. In some cases this random butchery of so many Jews led the SS to order the locals to stop the killing, in order to put it on a 'systematic' basis, according to the killing squad schedules. Despite the overwhelming odds against them the Jews rose in revolt wherever they could. The first revolts, as shown above, were at Tatarsk and Starodub. To crush this resistance, German regular

KILLINGS IN THE KOVNO AND VILNA REGIONS, SEPTEMBER-OCTOBER 1941

Ukmerge (Vilkomir)
4,000

Swieciany
8,000 *killed*

hundreds *escape*
26 September 1941

Jonava
1,556

Polygon
3,726

Lintup

Glebokie

Danilowicze

LITHUANIA

Sakiai
890

Kovno
1,500
4 October
9,000
28 October

Niemenczyn
403

Kobylnik
48

Lake Narocz

Naumiestis
650

Semiliski
962

Vilna
19,311

Nowo Wilejka
1,159

Trakai
1,446

Ponary

Alytus
1,279

Jahiunai
575

Marijampole
7,000

GREATER
GERMANY

Butrimonys
976

Eisishkes
3,446

0   miles   40

0   kilometres   60

© Martin Gilbert 1982

army units were brought in. Where necessary, as resistance spread, the Germans used artillery fire, and even air support.

At Kiev the Jews were driven into Babi Yar, a ravine in the suburbs, and then machine-gunned by an SS killing squad, helped by Ukrainian militiamen.

At Vilna the Jews were confined to a ghetto inside the city, where hundreds were murdered. Others were taken away in batches of a thousand and more to pits eight miles away, at the village of Ponary. Here too, they were shot.

Any Jews who managed to escape from their executioners at the pits were killed by a special unit of Germans and Lithuanians. Hundreds of other Jews were murdered inside Vilna itself, and in the notorious Lukiszki prison. In two months, throughout the former eastern provinces of Poland (*right, below*), more than 20,000 Jews were murdered.

On 26 September 1941 the Jews of Swieciany were rounded up and taken to a former army camp in the nearby Polygon woods, where they were massacred. On the evening before, several hundred young men and women had managed to break through the Lithuanian police cordon and escape eastwards, to towns not yet reached by the killing squads. These Jewish communities were liable at any moment to be subjected to the activities of the killing squads, for, as the map opposite shows, the front line, with its chaos and confusion had long since moved much further east.

FURTHER KILLINGS, SEPTEMBER-OCTOBER 1941

LITHUANIA

Olkieniki
1,000
25 September

WHITE
RUSSIA

Szczuczyn
50

Lida
2,000
28 October

Koidanov
1,500

Nieswiez
5,000
30 October

Kleck
4,000
31 October

Slutsk
300

Lachowicze
2,000
28 October

POLESIA

Hancewicze
3,000
13-15 September

Antopol
150
October

Pripet marshes

GREATER
GERMANY

1921 to 1939

VOLHYNIA

Kostopol
1,400
women and children
October

Miedzyrzec
1,500
October

Poland's eastern border with Russia

Ostrog
2,500
September

EASTERN
GALICIA

River Bug

0   miles   50

0   kilometres   80

© Martin Gilbert 1982

Map 89

THE DESTRUCTION OF THE JEWS OF CROATIA, 1941-1944

GREATER
GERMANY
Klagenfurt

annexed by Germany, April 1941

AUSTRIA

S L O V E N I A

annexed by Italy April 1941

Trieste

ISTRIA

Danica
2,000

Zagreb

CROATIA

Karlovac

Loborgrad
hundreds

Jasenovac
20,000

Gradiska
2,000

Jadovno
2,000

under Croat control April-September 1941

3,000
escape

Zara
Italian

DALMATIA

Adriatic Sea

ITALY

Split

under Italian control, 1941-1943

BOSNIA

H U N G A R Y

Osijek

BACSKA
annexed by Hungary

Dakovo
2,000

BANAT

R U M A N I A

Belgrade

S E R B I A
under German occupation from April 1941

© Martin Gilbert 1982

Following the German army's conquest of Yugoslavia, a pro-German regime was established in Croatia, with its capital at Zagreb (*above*). On 30 April 1941 this new Croat State introduced its first racial laws, removing Jews from public office and ordering all Jews to wear a yellow badge. Within a few weeks, several wealthy Jews had been seized in Zagreb and held as hostages until local Jews could provide 100 kilogrammes of gold for their release, thus impoverishing the community. By the end of May all Jewish cultural institutions had been closed, synagogues ransacked, and cemeteries destroyed.

In May 1941 the first Croat concentration camp was set up, at Danica. It was quickly followed by four more camps, at Jadovno, Gradiska, Loborgrad, and Dakovo. More than 6,000 Croat Jews were deported to these camps, and during July and August almost all of them were murdered. On 1 October 1941 a further camp was established at Jasenovac.

By the end of 1942 the remaining 20,000 Croat Jews had been rounded up and sent to Jasenovac, where most of them were starved to death, beaten to death or shot. By the spring of 1945, as the Soviet army and Yugoslav partisan forces approached the camp, only a few hundred were still alive (*page 220*).

Between April 1941 and April 1942 more than 3,000 Croatian Jews escaped over the mountains to Italy and the Italian-controlled coastal zone. But by a law of 30 April 1941, people with only one Jewish parent were 'protected' from deportation.

Because of the successful intervention by the Catholic Church and the Papal Nuncio to save the Jewish partners in mixed marriages, 1,000 Croat Jews survived the war.

In Holland the Jews had been confined to special parts of the towns, denied the right to teach or to remain in the civil service, and ordered to wear a yellow star. Nazi agitators repeatedly raided the Jewish quarter of

DUTCH JEWS DEPORTED TO MAUTHAUSEN

MAUTHAUSEN AND ITS SUB-CAMPS

Amsterdam, beating up Jews in the streets. At the beginning of February 1941 a Dutch Nazi had been killed when the Jews resisted one such attack. At the same time the Germans accused a Jewish tavern owner, Ernst Cahn, of daring to resist a German patrol. Cahn was shot, the first Dutch citizen to die in front of a German firing-squad. A few days later, on 22 February 1941, the SS raided the Jewish quarter of Amsterdam as a reprisal for the earlier resistance: 425 Jews were arrested, beaten, and deported to Buchenwald (above, right). Some died there. The rest, among them the distinguished Czech pharmacologist, Emil Starckenstein, were transferred shortly afterwards to Mauthausen. Within three days of their arrival, they were killed in the stone quarry, the centre of Mauthausen's forced labour network (right).

The photograph is of the gallows at Mauthausen, photographed at liberation (pages 234-5).

Map 92

TWELVE EASTWARD DEPORTATIONS, 16 OCTOBER - 29 NOVEMBER 1941

North Sea

Baltic Sea

Riga
LATVIA

REICHSKOMMISSARIAT
OSTLAND

Minsk

WHITE
RUSSIA

Hamburg
1,034

Emden

RUHR
Düsseldorf
984
Cologne
2,007

Berlin
4,187

GREATER GERMANY

Lodz

Warsaw

Lublin
GENERAL
GOVERNMENT

BOHEMIA

EASTERN
GALICIA

Würzburg
202

Frankfurt
1,113

Prague
5,000

Brno
3,000

Luxembourg
512

Nuremberg
618

Vienna
5,000

Munich
1,000

AUSTRIA

0   *miles*   150
0 *kilometres*   200

© Martin Gilbert 1982

In the autumn of 1941 the SS decided to deport more than 22,000 Jews to the ghettos of Lodz, Warsaw and Lublin, and to the former Soviet cities of Riga and Minsk (*above*). The first of these deportation trains left on 16 October 1941. On reaching the ghettos, the Jews were faced with starvation. On reaching Riga and Minsk, many were taken to nearby woods and shot.

Meanwhile, beginning on 10 October 1941, thousands of Slovak Jews were sent to labour camps at Sered, Vyhne and Novaky, while the remaining Jews living in what had once been Czechoslovakia were ordered out of their homes and sent to specially designated 'ghetto areas' in 14 selected towns (*opposite, above*). Already, on 1 September 1941, these Jews had been

ordered to wear the yellow star, and to cease all business activity. In Slovakia alone more than 10,000 Jewish shops and businesses had been closed down.

The largest of the new ghettos was established on 24 November 1941 in the small fortress town of Theresienstadt, known in Czech as Terezin. By the end of the war, 73,614 Jews had been deported to Theresienstadt from Bohemia and Moravia, and thousands more from elsewhere in Greater Germany.

In November the eastward deportations continued, as did the work of the mobile killing squads (*right*). At the same time, as an experiment, 1,200 prisoners at Buchenwald were taken to the euthanasia institute at Bernberg, and gassed.

BOHEMIAN, MORAVIAN AND SLOVAK JEWS FORCED INTO GHETTOS, 10 OCTOBER 1941

SUDETENLAND

GERMANY

Usti
Teplice
Theresienstadt
Cheb
Karlovy Vary
Marianske Lazne
Plana
Plzen
Mlada Boleslav
Brandys
Prague
Hradec Kralove
Pardubice
Kolin
BOHEMIA
Klatovy
MORAVIA
Unicov
Moravska Ostrava
Olomouc
Boskovice
Lipnik
Holesov
Kromeriz
Zilina
Bardejov
Trebic
Brno
Ruzomberok
Poprad
Presov
Uhersky Brod
Ivancice
Mikulov
Breclav
Trencin
Novaky
SLOVAKIA
Kosice
GREATER
Trnava
Sered
Nitra
Vyhne
Bratislava
Galanta
Dunajska Streda
Levice
Komarno
FELVIDEK
annexed by Hungary

0   miles   60
0   kilometres   80

© Martin Gilbert 1982

MASSACRE AND DEPORTATION, NOVEMBER 1941

North Sea

Baltic Sea

Borisov 7,000
Monastyrshchina 1,010
Riga 10,000
Rumbuli forest
GERMAN-OCCUPIED-RUSSIA
Vitebsk 4,090
Kovno 5,000
Berezino 1,000
Lyubavichi 700
Vilna 1,341
Ponary
Minsk 12,000
Mogilev 3,730
Nowogrodek 400
Wolozyn 300
Rogachev 3,500
Swierzen 500
Bobruisk 20,000
RUHR
Essen 252
Berlin
Bernberg
Lodz
Mir 1,500
Gomel 4,000
Düsseldorf 489
Buchenwald 1,200
Bayreuth 50
Theresienstadt
Slonim 9,000
Rowne 15,000
Kremenchug 8,000
RHINELAND
Kamionka Strumilowa 500
Berdichev 2,000
UKRAINE
BAVARIA
TRANSNISTRIA
Boryslaw 1,500
Lvov 3,000
Stryj 1,200
Czernowitz 30,000
Nadworna 2,500
Odessa 25,000
Przemyslany 400
Kolomyja 1,000
Belgrade
Black Sea

0   miles   100
0   kilometres   200

© Martin Gilbert 1982

Map 95

CHELMNO DEATH CAMP, THE FIRST VICTIMS, 8-14 DECEMBER 1941

River Warta

Kolo **2,300** *8 December*

Kolo station

Powierce station

Zawadki mill

Chelmno wood

Chelmno

River Ner

Wladyslawow
115

Brudzew
20

Tuliszkow
232

River Warta

Dabie
975
14 December

Turek
1,757

Uniejow
492

Kowale Panskie
4,000 *interned*
1,100 *deported*
10 December

Dobra
350

| 0 | *miles* | 2 |
| 0 | *kilometres* | 4 |

© Martin Gilbert 1982

Map 96

DEPORTATION, MASSACRE AND THE FIRST DEATH CAMP , DECEMBER 1941

North Sea

Baltic Sea

Riga **15,000**
Liepaja **3,500**
Nevel **43**
Rzhev **840**
Moscow
German military advance by December 1941

Jody **700**
Polotsk **7,000**
Mekhov **200**

Vilna **385**
Mogilev **315**

Nowogrodek **400**
Parichi **1,500**
Bobruisk **5,280**
Koryukovka **90**

Munster **403**
Chelmno
Warsaw **29,538**
died of starvation July–December 1941

Warendorf **6**
Brzezany **1,000**
Slaviansk **1,000**
Artemovsk **90**

GREATER GERMANY

Fulda **131**
Horodenka **500**
Feodosia **2,000**

Karasubazar **2,500**

Zabie **500**
Zablotow **1,000**

CRIMEA

Zemun **15,000** Belgrade
December 1941–January 1942

0 miles 200
0 kilometres 300

Black Sea

© Martin Gilbert 1982

The successful gassing of 1,200 Jews from Buchenwald in November 1941 was followed two weeks later by a second gassing experiment. The place chosen was a wood near the Polish village of Chelmno; the victims were Jewish villagers from several nearby communities (*opposite*). The method chosen was to bring the Jews by narrow guage railway from Kolo to Powierce, drive them with whips to the river, lock them overnight, without food or water, in the mill at the hamlet of Zawadki (seen here in a photograph taken in 1980), and then, in the morning, drive them in lorries to the woods near Chelmno, gassing them by exhaust fumes during the journey. The bodies were then thrown into deep pits, while the lorries returned to the mill for more victims. In all, five lorries were used, three of which held up to 150 people, and two up to 100. By noon, the whole trainload had usually been destroyed.

The first gassing at Chelmno took place on 8 December 1941. It was judged a success, and was continued on an ever widening scale. The next 1,000 victims had already been

taken by truck from six villages to Kowale Panskie, and were held there until the journey to Chelmno on 10 December 1941.

Even as the gassings at Chelmno began, the deportations from Germany to Riga continued, as did the mass murder of deportees almost immediately after their arrival (*above*). Thus on 13 December 1941 the last six Jews living in Warendorf were deported to Riga and killed: their small community dated back to 1387, and had been 41 strong in 1933. Most had managed to emigrate by 1939. In the south-east, German forces had conquered the Crimea. Here too, community after community was being wiped out by the killing squads.

It was not only at Chelmno that mobile gas vans were being used. At the concentration camp at Zemun, just outside Belgrade, some 15,000 Jews from all over Serbia were gradually but systematically being gassed in vans disguised as Red Cross vehicles. By June 1942 all had been killed: an average of 120 every day. No sooner had the vans completed their task at Zemun than they were transferred to Riga (*page 104*).

GLOBAL WAR: THE U.S.A., THE AXIS POWERS, AND JAPAN

Arctic Ocean

CANADA

BRITAIN

THE
SOVIET UNION

Leningrad
Moscow
Stalingrad

USA

Atlantic
Ocean

CHINA

INDIA

JAPAN

Pearl
Harbor

Cairo

Pacific
Ocean

Indian
Ocean

AUSTRALIA

© Martin Gilbert 1982

THE KILLING OF JEWS CONTINUES: THE BALTIC STATES

FINLAND

Lake
Ladoga

0   miles   100
0   kilometres   150

Gulf of Finland

Leningrad

Baltic Sea

Tallin

ESTONIA
1,000

Lake
Peipus

Lake
Ilmen

Tartu

Riga
26,900

S O V I E T

LATVIA

229,052

Dvinsk

German front line, December 1941

LITHUANIA

Moscow

Kovno

U N I O N

Vilna

GREATER
GERMANY

Smolensk

© Martin Gilbert 1982

Map 99

JEWS MARKED OUT FOR DEATH, 20 JANUARY 1942

ESTONIA
"Free of Jews"

USSR
5 million

NORWAY
1,300

LATVIA
3,500

DENMARK
5,600

LITHUANIA
34,000

HOLLAND
160,800

BALTIC STATES

BIALYSTOK
DISTRICT
400,000

WHITE
RUSSIA
446,484

BELGIUM
43,000

EASTERN TERRITORIES

Berlin
Wannsee

GENERAL
GOVERNMNT
2,284,000

420,000

GERMANY
131,800

UKRAINE
2,994,684

FRANCE
OCCUPIED ZONE
165,000

BOHEMIA
& MORAVIA
74,200

88,000

SLOVAKIA

FRANCE
UNOCCUPIED ZONE
700,000
*including
French North Africa*

AUSTRIA

HUNGARY
742,800

43,700

10,000

CROATIA
40,000

SERBIA

RUMANIA
342,000

ITALY
58,000

BULGARIA
48,000

ALBANIA
200

GREECE
69,600

KOS

RHODES

MOROCCO

ALGERIA
French North Africa

TUNISIA

0   miles   200

0 kilometres 300

CRETE

© Martin Gilbert 1982

By December 1941 the German armies were masters of Europe, and on 7 December 1941 the Japanese entered the war against the United States and Britain (*opposite, above*).

From Estonia the killing squads reported to Berlin with their usual precision the murder over the previous six months of 229,052 Jews in Latvia and Lithuania (*opposite, below*). All 1,000 Jews caught in Estonia had also been killed.

At the Wannsee suburb of Berlin, German officials gathered on 20 January 1942 to discuss the final destruction of European Jewry. They also noted, as seen on the map above, what they believed to be the precise number of Jews still to be killed. The 'low' figures for the Baltic States indicate their knowledge that so many thousands had been killed already. At the Wannsee Conference plans were made for what was called the 'Final Solution', to be carried out by means of slave labour for all able-bodied Jews, the separation of men from women, and mass deportation.

85

Map 100

JEWS MARKED OUT FOR DEATH, JANUARY 1942, BUT BEYOND NAZI RULE

Arctic Ocean

North Atlantic Ocean

SWEDEN
8,000

FINLAND
2,300

GREAT BRITAIN
330,000

North Sea

Baltic Sea

German front line, January 1942

Moscow

Riga

Minsk

Berlin
Wannsee

Chelmno

REPUBLIC OF IRELAND
4,000

PORTUGAL
3,000

SWITZERLAND
18,000

Bogdanovka · Atmicetka

Jasenovac

Gurs

SPAIN
6,000

TURKEY-IN -EUROPE
55,000

Black Sea

Yalta

Mediterranean Sea

0 miles 300
0 kilometres 400

© Martin Gilbert 1982

Among the statistics presented by the SS to the Wannsee Conference were the number of Jews in Britain and Finland, as well as in all the neutral countries of Europe, whom the Gestapo hoped eventually to bring within the scope of the 'Final Solution'.

In 1942 the Finns agreed to deport 11 Jewish refugees. But when these 11 were murdered by the Gestapo, the Finnish Government refused to allow any further deportations (page 244).

Meanwhile, the gassings at Chelmno, and the killing squad slaughter in Russia, continued, as did the deaths from starvation in the Warsaw ghetto, and the death marches from the Bukovina (opposite, above).

Those Jews in Odessa who had not been murdered earlier were deported to concentration camps, where thousands died of brutality, starvation and disease. At Novi Sad, on 23 January 1942, Hungarian fascists drove 550 Jews and 292 Serbs to the river and on to the ice, and, after firing on the ice to break it up, shot all those who managed to stay afloat. In Titel 35 of the 36 Jews of the town were shot.

In the Crimea (opposite, below) ancient communities and modern collective farms were being wiped out so thoroughly that on 16 April 1942 Berlin was officially informed by the local SS: 'the Crimea is purged of Jews' (page 97).

DEPORTATION AND MASSACRE, JANUARY 1942

WHITE RUSSIA

German front line, January 1942

0 ___ miles ___ 150
0 ___ kilometres ___ 200

Bugaj `600`
12 January

Izbica Kujawska `1,000`
14 January

Brdow `600`
12 January

River Pripet

Mozyr `1,500`

Kiev `8,000`

Kharkov `14,000`

Drobitzky Yar

Artemovsk `3,000`

Warsaw

Pripet marshes

Northern Bug

Chelmno

Klodawa `1,140`
9 January

Lodz `3,000`
16 January

Brzezany `400`

River Vistula

Khmelnik `6,800`

Vinnitsa `5,000`

Southern Bug

Novomoskovsk `140`

River Dnieper

Pavlovgrad `3,670`

`5,123`
deaths from starvation

TRANSNISTRIA

River Dniester

🕇 **Dumanovka** `18,000`
🕇 **Bogdanovka** `48,000`
🕇 **Atmicetka** `5,000`
🕇 **Vertugen** `23,000`

1942 to 1943

Mielec `500`

Dolina `2,000`

BUKOVINA
deportations continue

BESSARABIA
deportations continue

HUNGARY

Sea of Azov

Odessa `19,852`
12 January to 23 February

CRIMEA

Black Sea

in all `2,550` *Serbs*
and `700` *Jews*

killed by Hungarian fascists in occupied Yugoslavia

● **Titel**
● **Novi Sad**

© Martin Gilbert 1982

THE MASSACRE OF THE JEWS OF THE CRIMEA, JANUARY-APRIL 1942

Putrid

Sea of Azov

Gulf of Perekop

eighty six Jewish agricultural settlements and collective farms

Sea

Tongue of Arabat

Dzhankoi `455`
30 December 1941

Kerch `4,500`
29 November 1941

Evpatoria
`1,300` *1-15 January 1942*
`22` *17 January 1942*

CRIMEA
`91,678`
total killed

Karasubazar `76`
14 December 1941

Feodosia `1,000` *November - December 1941*
`36` *28 February 1942*
`22` *1 May 1942*
`64` *2 April 1942*

Simferopol `14,300`
13-15 December 1941

Sebastopol

Yalta `1,500`
18 December 1941

Bakhchisarai `90` *13 December 1941*

Black Sea

0 ___ miles ___ 20
0 ___ kilometres ___ 40

© Martin Gilbert 1982

Map 103

EASTERN KILLINGS, AND THE 'STRUMA'

WHITE RUSSIA

Lepel `1,000` *28 February*

SOVIET UNION

Pyshno `26`

Cherven `1,800` *1 February*

Kursk `100` *1 February*

VOLHYNIA

under German occupation

German front line, January 1942

Shamovo `500` *2 February*

UKRAINE

Brailov `3,000` *12 February*

Hulievca `650` *13 March*

Czernowitz

Cihrin `722` *9 March*

Taganrog

Jassy

Sea of Azov

RUMANIA

CRIMEA

Caucasus

Bucharest

Simferopol `300`

Constanta *12 December 1941*

Black Sea

BULGARIA

sunk 24 February 1942

Istanbul *arrived 15 December 1941*

Sile

`709` *drowned*

`1` *saved*

Sea of Marmara

TURKEY *neutral*

KOS *under German occupation*

RHODES *under German occupation*

SYRIA

CYPRUS

CRETE *under German occupation*

intended route

Mediterranean Sea

Haifa

Tel Aviv

PALESTINE

British Mandate

Alexandria

EGYPT

TRANS-JORDAN

SAUDI ARABIA

miles 150

kilometres 300

© Martin Gilbert 1982

The eastern killings continued during February 1942, with shootings such as those at Radom, and the deportation by lorry from Sierpc to Mlawa, when hundreds were murdered on the journey itself.

Hundreds of Jews were also deported to slave labour camps, such as the one at Cieszanow *(right),* where conditions were so harsh that almost no one survived.

Jewish resistance also grew. A group of Jews from Tomaszow Lubelski *(right)* organized a partisan unit which fought the Germans for some months, until it was betrayed by local Poles. Elsewhere, small groups of Jews still managed to escape, and to maintain themselves in the woods. Thus the four Jewish families living in the village of Hola *(opposite, below),* who were about to be deported to the ghetto in Wlodawa, escaped to the woods east of Zamolodycze, where they found several families already in hiding. Within a short time, armed Ukrainian peasants forced the families out of the forest, locked them into a barn, and then betrayed them to the Germans. Only four Jews managed to escape, to the Skorodnica forest. There they found 100 other Jews in hiding, but when German troops attacked them 75 were shot. The survivors fled to the woods near Maryanka, and managed to acquire a rifle from Lubien village. Later they helped smuggle 75 Jews from the Wlodawa ghetto, and a further 46 men, women and girls from the village of Adampol. The group then set up its base deep in the Skorodnica forest, built up an armoury of 15 rifles and, in an ambush on a German truck, killed 10 Germans. Later the group joined other Jewish partisans in the Parczew forest *(pages 122 to 123).*

The SS killing squads were also still at work *(left),* in White Russia and the Ukraine in February, and in the Transnistrian deportee camps in March. Meanwhile, the Jews of neighbouring Rumania, as well as thousands of Jewish refugees who had managed to reach Rumania from Poland and Czechoslovakia, sought boats in which to escape across the Black Sea, and on to Palestine. Boats were scarce, German submarines patrolled the Black Sea, and British officials pressed the Turkish Government not to allow the boats through the Sea of Marmara, hoping thereby not to offend Arab opinion in Palestine.

One such ship was the 'Struma', which had left Rumania on 12 December 1941. The ship was flying the neutral Panamanian flag,

DEPORTATION, MASSACRE AND REVOLT, FEBRUARY 1942

Sompolno 1,000

Mlawa
death march

Sierpc 500 6 February

River Vistula

River Bug

Warsaw 4,618 deaths from starvation in February

Chelmno 5

G R E A T E R

WARTHELAND

see below
Wlodawa

Pripet marshes

resistance led by
Mendel Heler and
Meir Lalimacher

POLAND

Radom 40
'Bloody Thursday' 19 February

U K R A I N E

G E R M A N Y

Tomaszow Lubelski 1,500
25 February

Belz 1,000

Cieszanow
slave labour camp

Brailov

E A S T E R N

G A L I C I A

SLOVAKIA

© Martin Gilbert 1982

ESCAPE, BETRAYAL, MASSACRE AND SURVIVAL WEST OF WLODAWA

Krywowierba

woods

Lubien

Wola

Adampol 46 escape

Adampol estate

River Bug

Zamolodycze

woods

Hola

21 killed
4 survived

25 in hiding

100 in hiding
75 shot

Wlodawa

Maryanka

25 in hiding

Skorodinica

75 escape

Suchawa

© Martin Gilbert 1982

but while it was still in the Black Sea, Germany and Italy declared war on Panama, following the United States' entry into the war a week earlier. As a result, the ship was flying, in German eyes, an 'enemy' flag. After four days in the Black Sea, it reached Istanbul. But under British pressure, the Turks ordered the ship back into the Black Sea, where it was sunk, probably by the Germans, on 24 February 1942. All but one refugee was drowned. 'Palestine', commented the British High Commissioner in Jerusalem, 'was under no obligation to them', and he went on to explain, that he was acting in accordance with the 'basic principle that enemy nationals from enemy or enemy-controlled territory should not be admitted to this country during the war', a principle, he insisted, that applied even to refugees from enemy territory.

Map 106

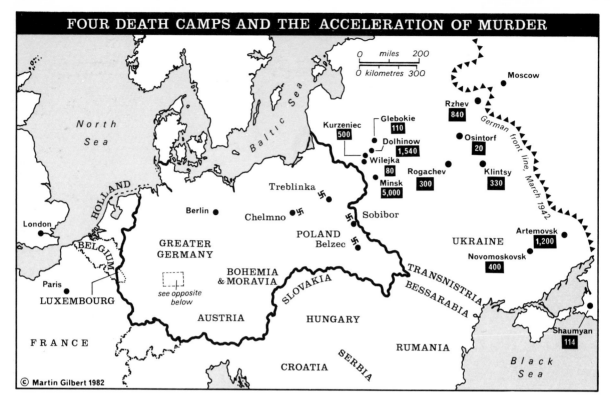

FOUR DEATH CAMPS AND THE ACCELERATION OF MURDER

© Martin Gilbert 1982

The death camp at Chelmno had been in operation for more than six weeks by the time of the Wannsee Conference of 20 January 1942 (*page 85*). In March 1942 the town-by-town killings in the east continued (*above*), while at the same time (*also above*), three new death camps were being prepared, at Belzec, Treblinka and Sobibor, where, as at Chelmno, no-one was kept alive for slave labour. These four camps had a single purpose: to kill every Jew within a few hours of arrival.

As soon as these four 'death' camps were in operation, thousands of Jewish communities were marked out for deportation, first from German-occupied Poland, then from elsewhere in Greater Germany, and finally, from western and southern Europe. The deportees were told they were going to Poland to be 'resettled' in farms and labour camps. In fact, their only destination was a death camp and immediate death.

Between 8 December 1941 and 28 February 1942, more than 13,000 Jews had been deported to Chelmno and gassed. Adolf Eichmann himself had witnessed this process. Then, on 17 March 1942 the first deportations took place to the second of the death camps, just south of the village of Belzec. The deportees came from as far west

as Mielec (*opposite above*), as well as from Lublin, and from the village of Belzec itself. In all, 6,786 Jews were murdered in this first set of deportations. A group of a dozen or so Jews from the nearby village of Lubycza Krolewska, who had been at work for more than a month finishing construction in the camp, were also killed.

The gas chambers at Belzec operated for more than nine months, the killing process being supervised by SS men, assisted by Ukrainian and Estonian guards. A special rail spur from the main line to the unloading ramp could take 20 goods wagons at a time: these wagons were shunted on, leaving the rest of each train to wait its turn.

Hardly had the first Jews been gassed at Belzec, than the German authorities began a search throughout the western provinces of Germany for those Jews, often only a single family, living in isolated communities in remote country regions. From one such region, in the hills above Bad Kissingen (*opposite, below*), 83 Jews were seized, as well as 23 in Bad Kissingen itself. Deported eastward across Germany, Bohemia and Poland to Belzec, they were first held in two nearby internment camps, Izbica Lubelska and Piaski, and then sent on to Belzec, where they were gassed (*pages 92 and 93*). Not a single one of these deportees survived.

FIRST DEPORTATIONS TO BELZEC, 17 MARCH 1942

0 miles 25
0 kilometres 40

Lublin `1,600`

Trawniki

Piaski

Dubienka `843`

River

VOLHYNIA

Krasnystaw

Izbica
Lubelska

LUBLIN
REGION

Hrubieszow `1,343`

Bug

GENERAL

GOVERNMENT

Szczebrzeszyn

Zamosc

Zwierzyniec

Tomaszow
Lubelski

Belzec village `500`

Belzec
camp

Lubycza
Krolewska

Mielec `4,500`

WESTERN GALICIA

Lubaczow

EASTERN
GALICIA

Debica

Rzeszow

Jaroslaw

© Martin Gilbert 1982

GERMAN JEWS SEARCHED OUT FOR DEPORTATION TO BELZEC, 24 MARCH 1942

Höchheim `9`

Bad Neustadt `3`

Brückenau `4`

River Saale

Kleineibstadt `6`

Geroda `6`

Steinach `4`

Platz `2`

Kleinbardorf `3`

Schondra `6`

Poppenlauer `14`

0 miles 5
0 kilometres 10

Völkersleier `4`

Bad Kissingen `23`

Massbach `3`

Lendershausen `2`

Pfaffenhausen `13`

Kleinsteinach `4`

© Martin Gilbert 1982

THE JEWS OF THE WURZBURG REGION ROUNDED UP FOR DEPORTATION

Laudenbach **11**

Thungen **3**

Schwanfeld **8**

River Main

Theilheim **31**

Zeilitzheim **7**

Gerolzhofen **19**

Lülsfeld **3**

Rimpar **6**

Estenfeld **4**

Nordheim **4**

Altenschönbach **5**

Prichsenstadt **7**

Veitshochheim **4**

Höchberg **4**

Würzburg

320 deported 24 March

Grosslangenheim **2**

Wiesenbronn **3**

Kitzingen **76**

Oberalterheim **4**

Reichenberg **12**

Mainbernheim **2**

Geroldshausen **2**

Gossmannsdorf **3**

Acholshausen **2**

Marktbreit **23**

Huttenheim **3**

Giebelstadt **5**

Obernbreit **5**

Allersheim **2**

Gaukönigshofen **25**

0 miles 5
0 kilometres 10

© Martin Gilbert 1982

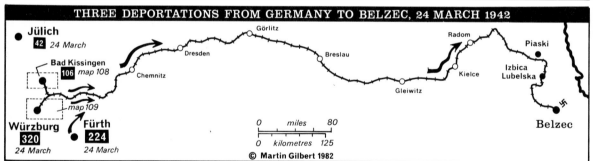

THREE DEPORTATIONS FROM GERMANY TO BELZEC, 24 MARCH 1942

Jülich **42** 24 March

Görlitz

Radom

Piaski

Bad Kissingen **106** map 108

Dresden

Breslau

Izbica Lubelska

Chemnitz

Kielce

map 109

Gleiwitz

Würzburg **320** 24 March

Fürth **224** 24 March

0 miles 80
0 kilometres 125

© Martin Gilbert 1982

Belzec

The search for the remaining Jews of Germany continued during the last week of March 1942 and the first three weeks of April. Throughout the Würzburg region (*top*) single families and small communities were seized and taken to Würzburg, from where, on 24 March 1942 the first of three deportations took place, with 320 deportees. Together with the Jews collected at Bad Kissingen, Jülich and Fürth, all were deported eastwards (*above*), held for a few days in the village of Piaski, and then taken to Belzec (*opposite*); not one survived.

Throughout March Jews were also deported to Belzec from Eastern Galicia and the Lublin region. From Lublin itself almost all the city's large Jewish community was deported within two weeks.

The deportation of Jews to Chelmno also continued (*opposite*). In the deportations from Opole were many Austrian-born Jews who had been deported from Vienna to Poland two years before (*page 40*).

In Warsaw thousands of Jews continued to die of starvation. In other towns, such as Rohatyn and Tarnopol, the Jews were driven to nearby woods, and murdered. Near Ilja, on March 14, Jews who had been sent to

Map 111

MASS MURDER, DEPORTATION AND REVOLT, MARCH 1942

Baltic Sea

REICHSKOMMISSARIAT
OSTLAND

resistance led by
Josef Rodblat
and David Rubin

Ilja
900
17 March

resistance led by
R.M.Bromberg
M.P.Malkevich
and Hersh Smolar

Minsk
5,000
2 March

Baranowicze
3,000
4 March

GREATER GERMANY

WARTHEGAU

Krosniewice
900
2 March

Kutno
7,000

Chelmno

Zychlin
3,200
3 March

Warsaw
at least **4,000** deaths
from starvation in March

REICHSKOMMISSARIAT
UKRAINE

Radoszkowicze
850
11 March

Ozorkow
500

Poddebice
2,000

Kozminek
1,000

Kazimierz
Dolny
2,000

Lublin
10,000
18-25 March

Wawolnica
1,500

Piaski
3,400

Izbica
Lubelska
2,200
24 March

Siennica Rozana
272

Opole Lubelskie
3,000
31 March

Rawa Ruska
1,500
20 March

Zamosc
hundreds

GENERAL
GOVERNMENT

Bilgoraj
2,500

Belzec

Tomaszow
Lubelski
hundreds

Zolkiew
700
15 March

Lvov
15,000

Drohobycz
1,500

Rohatyn
2,000
20 March

Tarnopol
1,000
25 March

EASTERN GALICIA

Stanislawow
6,000
31 March

0 miles 40
0 kilometres 80

© Martin Gilbert 1982

work on a farm joined a group of Soviet partisans, and went into hiding in the forest. Three days later two Jewish leaders at Ilja, who had refused to hand over partisan sympathizers to the SS, themselves escaped to the forest to join the partisans. As a reprisal, the Germans shot all old and sick Jews in the street, then forced 900 more into a building, locked it, and set it on fire. All 900 perished.

In Minsk 5,000 Jews were taken from the ghetto to a newly dug pit on the outskirts of the town and machine-gunned. No ammunition was wasted on the hundreds of Jewish children seized that day: they were thrown into the pit alive to die of suffocation. The Jews of Minsk tried to organize a resistance group. But on 31 March 1942 the Gestapo raided the ghetto, capturing several of the resistance leaders.

FIRST DEPORTATIONS TO AUSCHWITZ, 26-27 MARCH 1942

North Sea

GREATER GERMANY

0   miles   100
0   kilometres   200

Majdanek

Belzec

Auschwitz

Compiègne

Drancy

Zilina

Nitra

SLOVAKIA

Trnava

Paris
1,112
27 March to Auschwitz

Komarno

FRANCE

Bratislava
2,000
26-27 March to Auschwitz

© Martin Gilbert 1982

BIRTHPLACES OF SOME OF THE FIRST PARIS DEPORTEES

North Sea

Copenhagen

Dvinsk

Kovno

Smolensk

London

Grodno

Minsk

Atlantic Ocean

Berlin

Saar

Leipzig

Warsaw

Tatarsk

Zhitomir

Line of German advance

Kiev

Rouen

Drancy

Paris

Nancy

Nuremberg

Prague

Auschwitz

Lvov

Zloczow

Zablotow

Nikolaiev

Skole

Kishinev

Odessa

Budapest

Ismail

Simferopol

Perpignan

Black Sea

Constantinople

Salonica

Bursa

Salomon Benatore aged 39

Bergama

Bizerta

Smyrna

Moreno Cohen aged 41

Oran
Robert Cohen aged 21

Algiers

Bône
Jacob Aziz aged 32

Tunis

Marrakech
Aron Cohen aged 46

0   miles   200
0   kilometres   400

Mardoche Douani aged 40

Mediterranean Sea

Haifa
Ignatz Baum aged 41

Alexandria

German forces

© Martin Gilbert 1982

Map 114

BIRTHPLACES OF POLISH JEWS IN THE FIRST PARIS DEPORTATION

© Martin Gilbert 1982

The first deportations from western Europe to Belzec had taken place on 24 March 1942 (*page 91*). Two days later, the first deportations of Jews to Auschwitz began, first from Slovakia, and on the following day from France (*opposite*). At Auschwitz, all were sent to the barracks. No gassings took place there until 4 May 1942 (*page 100*).

The first Jews deported to Auschwitz from France on 27 March 1942 were all foreign-born Jews who had been rounded up in Paris seven months earlier, and interned. Their birthplaces ranged from Marrakech to Haifa, and from London to Simferopol (*opposite, below*). Many had left their birthplaces between the wars, to seek a new livelihood in France. Others had reached France as refugees. The majority had been born in Poland (*above*), within the area that had now become a part of Greater Germany. One of these first Paris deportees, Israel Chlebowski, had been born in the village of Przytyk, scene of the pogrom of 1936 in which three Jews had died (*page 21*). Another, Henry Eckstein, had been born in London 26 years before. Lazare Mnouchine had been born in Tatarsk, one of the first towns in which the Jews had challenged SS killing squads in the autumn of 1941 (*page 76*). The 41-year-old Moses Schneider had been born in Auschwitz itself, then a market town in the Austro-Hungarian Empire.

The Paris deportation of 27 March 1942 was timed by the SS with precision. The train left Paris at 17.00 hours, reaching the border of Greater Germany at 13.59 on the following day, and arriving at Auschwitz at 5.33 in the morning of March 31.

Even French-born Jews were now subjected to the full rigours of anti-Jewish legislation. On 29 May 1942 all Jews were forbidden access to all public places, squares, restaurants, cafés, libraries, public baths, gardens and sports grounds.

MASS MURDER AND DEATH CAMP DEPORTATIONS, APRIL 1942

Wloclawek

see facing page

Chelmno

Warsaw
at least **4,432** deaths from starvation in April

Leczna
200 to Sobibor
2,225 to Belzec

Lubartow
800 *9-10 April*

Sobibor

Piaski
4,200 to Belzec

Radom **70** *shot*
hundreds deported 28 April

Tomaszow Mazowiecki
100
27 April

Krasnik
2,000
12 April

Uchanie
1,650 *10 April*

Krasniczyn
1,000

Zamosc
3,000
11 April

Radomysl nad Sanem
384

Krasnystaw
1,000

Belzec

Sokal
35 *shot*

Cieszanow
5,000

Lubaczow
2,000

Auschwitz

Biecz
70
30 April

Przemysl
several hundred shot 28-30 April

Grybow
300
30 April

Sniatyn
1,000

Horodenka
1,500
4 April

Tlumacz
1,200
3 April

Peczenizyn
1,000

Kolomyja
1,000
2 April

Zablotow
400

Kuty
950

© Martin Gilbert 1982

0 — miles — 50
0 — kilometres — 80

FURTHER DEPORTATIONS TO IZBICA AND BELZEC, APRIL 1942

GREATER GERMANY

Poppenlauer
14

Schweinfurt
30

Bad Kissingen
23

Bamberg
105 *25 April*

Coburg
27

Piaski

Izbica Lubelska

Nuremberg
650 *24 April*

Hammelberg
13

Karlbach
27

Hassfurt
16

Belzec

BOHEMIA

EASTERN GALICIA

Nordlingen
25

Ceske Budejovice
909
18 April

Krumbach
16

BAVARIA

Landshut
11 *2 April*

SLOVAKIA

Fischach
56

Augsburg
129
3 April

Lindau
3

Memmingen
22

SWITZERLAND
neutral

© Martin Gilbert 1982

0 — miles — 150
0 — kilometres — 200

TEN DEPORTATIONS TO CHELMNO, APRIL 1942

Radzejow **600**

Piotrkow Kujawski **550**

Brzesc Kujawski **200** *30 April*

Lubraniec **100**

Wloclawek **3,000** *22 April*

River Vistula

Gostynin **2,000** *16 April*

Gabin **2,000**

Sanniki **250** *17 April*

WARTHEGAU

narrow gauge railways

River Warta

Kolo

Powierce station
Zawadki mill

Chelmno *death camp*

Chelmno *village*

River Ner

standard gauge railway

River Bzura

Grabow **1,240**

Leczyca **1,700** *10 April*

0 miles 20
0 kilometres 30

© Martin Gilbert 1982

NAZI-DOMINATED EUROPE, APRIL – MAY 1942

North Sea

Baltic Sea

Parafianowo **600**

Krzywicze **350**

German front line

Danzig

Berlin

Warsaw

Dokszyce **600**

Dolhinow **1,000**

Zdzieciol **1,200**

Dobrush **70**

Chelmno

Slavuta **12,000**

Auschwitz

Belzec

Kuty

Brailov **300**

Piryatin **1,530**

Augsburg

Budapest

Berdichev **70**
women and children of mixed marriages 27 April

SWITZ

Bucharest

Black Sea

Adriatic Sea

Rome

Salonica

CRIMEA *declared 'purged of Jews', 16 April*

Tunis

Athens

RHODES

Malta

CRETE

Mediterranean Sea

Derna

Homs

Benghazi

Tobruk

Tripoli

El Alamein

Cairo EGYPT

Giado **562**

LIBYA

5,000 *slave labourers*

0 miles 200
0 kilometres 400

© Martin Gilbert 1982

Throughout April 1942 the eastern killings continued *(right),* as did the deportations to the death camps of Belzec *(opposite, above),* Chelmno *(above),* and Auschwitz.

From Bavaria and Bohemia, the remnants of once flourishing communities were sent to be 'resettled' in the east *(opposite, below).* Their destination was not, however, an eastern labour camp or ghetto, but two transit camps, Izbica and Piaski, from where they were sent the few further miles to Belzec, and its gas chamber. With the deportation of 3 April 1942, the once 1,000-strong Jewish community of Augsburg ceased to exist. Jews had lived in the town since AD 1212, and in the fifteenth century it had been a centre of Jewish culture.

In Warsaw, thousands more Jews died of starvation during April *(opposite, above).*

Two thousand miles to the south *(right),* the 38,000 Jews of Libya, having been briefly under British control at the end of 1941, had come once more under Italian rule in February 1942. Jewish shops were at once plundered, and 2,600 Jews deported to a camp at Giado, for forced labour, building military roads. The death toll was high: in 14 months 562 died of starvation and typhus.

In April 1942 a further 1,750 Jews were taken from Tripoli to forced labour sites at Homs, Benghazi and Derna. Hundreds perished from hunger and the heat. Others, forbidden to use the air-raid shelters, were killed during Allied bombing raids.

DEPORTATION, MASSACRE AND REVOLT, MAY 1942

Werenow 3,000 *11 May*

Radun 2,000 *10 May*

Wolozyn 1,000 *10 May*

WHITE RUSSIA

Iwje 2,500 *8 May*

Wasiliszki 2,000 *10 May*

Lida 12,000 *8 May*
☼ *youths escape to the woods*

☼ *youths escape to the woods*
Stolpce

Szczuczyn 2,060 *9 May*

Zoludek 1,400 *8 May*

Wolkowysk 2,000

Dereczyn 250

BIALYSTOK REGION

REICHSKOMMISSARIAT OSTLAND

● **Warsaw**
at least 3,636
deaths from starvation in May

0 — miles — 40
0 — kilometres — 60

Sobibor

VOLHYNIA

GREATER GERMANY

Miedzyrzecz 1,600 *22 May*

Tyszowce 1,000 *22 May*

Kozin 450 *30 May*

Korzec 2,200 *21 May*

Komarow Osada 1,500 *23 May*

Laszczow 350 *27 May*

Hoszcza 670 *20 May*

Szczebrzeszyn 280 *8 May*

Belz 1,500

Dubno 5,000 *27 May*

Radziwillow 1,500 *29 May* ☼
resistance led by Asher Czerkaski

Belzec

Lvov
over 1,000 *shot* *5 May*

Przemyslany
all inmates of the Jewish hospital murdered

REICHSKOMMISSARIAT UKRAINE

GENERAL GOVERNMENT

SLOVAKIA

Dunajevtsi 3,000 *10 May*

Tlumacz 180 *18 May*

© Martin Gilbert 1982

NEWS OF MASS MURDER REACHES THE WEST, MAY 1942

BRITAIN
London

700,000 *total*
May 1942

Berlin

Chelmno

Warsaw

Sobibor

0 — miles — 200
0 — kilometres — 300

German front line in May 1942

Radom

GREATER GERMANY

Lublin
Majdanek

Belzec

Rowne 15,000

Lvov 30,000

Auschwitz

Tarnow

SOVIET UNION

Cracow 50

Stanislawow 15,000

Tarnopol 5,000

© Martin Gilbert 1982

Map 121

NINETEEN DEPORTATIONS TO SOBIBOR, MAY 1942

Ryki
2,500
7 May

Baranow
1,500
8 May

Lysobyki
500

Parczew forest

Michow
2,500
10 May

Wlodawa
2,000
23 May

River Bug

Deblin
2,500
6 May

Konskowola
3,500
8 May

Lubartow
800
9 May

Sobibor

Pulawy
3,500

Markuszow
1,500
9 May

River Vistula

Wawolnica
500

Lublin

Siedliszcze
1,000
18 May

Opole
3,000

Chelm
4,300
21 May

Jozefow
1,000
7 May

Gorzkow
1,200
14 May

Wysokie
1,000

Zolkiewka
1,000
12 May

Turobin
2,750
12 May

miles   15
kilometres   20

© Martin Gilbert 1982

Throughout May 1942 the killings east of the General Government continued (*opposite, above*). So also did the deportations to Sobibor (*above*), Belzec, Chelmno and Auschwitz (*pages 100-1*). In Przemyslany all the inmates of the Jewish hospital were dragged from their beds and shot. At Dubno 5,000 Jews, judged 'non-productive' for the German war effort, were taken outside the town and killed. At Chelm local Jews, and Slovakian Jews who had been deported there two years before, were deported to Sobibor and gassed.

At that very moment, the first news had reached London (*opposite, below*), smuggled out of Poland by the underground Jewish Socialist Party in Warsaw, telling of the mass murder of 700,000 Jews in Eastern Galicia and the east. Specific figures were given of mass killings in four towns, as well as of other killings in Radom, Lublin, Cracow and Tarnow. Throughout Eastern Galicia, the report stated, 'men, fourteen to sixty years old, were driven to a single place, a square or a cemetery, where they were

slaughtered or shot by machine-guns or killed by hand grenades. They had to dig their own graves. Children in orphanages, inmates in old-age homes, the sick in hospitals were shot, women were killed in the streets. In many towns the Jews were carried off to "an unknown destination" or killed in adjacent woods.'

Only one death camp, Belzec, was named in the report. But it warned that mass killings were still in progress.

Although the victims were weak from hunger and privation, always unarmed against machine-guns and grenades, alone among hostile local populations, and facing vicious torture if they challenged Nazi power, many Jews attempted nevertheless to break out of the SS and local police cordons. In the three examples shown opposite (*above*), some young men and women did succeed in reaching the woods, and in forming, or joining, partisan groups. Some record survives of these particular acts of resistance. Many other such acts went unrecorded.

Map 122

TEN FURTHER DEPORTATIONS, MAY 1942

Gabin
2,150
12 May

Chelmno

Brzeziny
1,700
14 May

Ozorkow
2,000
21 May

Brzeziny Lodzkie
5,000
10 May

Lodz

Pabianice
8,000 deported 16 May
150 murdered on the spot

WARTHELAND

Zloczew
280

GREATER GERMANY

GENERAL GOVERNMENT

Dabrowa Gornicza
630
5 May

Zawierce
2,000

Bedzin
2,000

Gleiwitz
586

Sosnowiec
1,500
12 May

Birkenau ● ● Monowitz
Auschwitz

SILESIA

0   miles   20
0 kilometres 30

SLOVAKIA

© Martin Gilbert 1982

The gassing of more than two million Jews at Auschwitz began on 4 May 1942, first at Auschwitz itself, then at the nearby camp of Birkenau, where four gas chambers and crematoria were built during 1942 and early 1943 for the purpose of mass murder. A few Jews from each deportation were selected to 'live' as slave labourers, some in barracks at Birkenau itself, others at nearby factories, including a synthetic oil and rubber plant later built at Monowitz. While at Birkenau, many Jews, and in particular Jewish women, were selected by SS doctors for medical experiments.

Because Birkenau became known during the war as Auschwitz II, and the slave labour camp in Monowitz as Auschwitz III, most accounts of the deportation of Jews to Birkenau name 'Auschwitz' as the destination, rather than Birkenau, to which they were in fact deported. For nearly two years, all deportees to Birkenau were brought to the railway sidings just outside Auschwitz station, and marched or taken by truck to Birkenau. In April 1944 a direct rail spur was built to Birkenau, almost to the gates of two of the four gas chambers there.

Throughout May 1942 the deportations to Chelmno continued unabated. The map on the left shows six communities destroyed there in one month. Of the Jews of Ozorkow, 2,000 were gassed, while 800 able-bodied men and women were sent to factories in the Lodz ghetto. At Pabianice all 150 patients in the Jewish hospital were murdered on the spot, before the rest of the community was sent to death at Chelmno.

Jewish resistance continued. But the chances of success were remote, as heavily armed SS units moved from town to town. Each Jewish community was unarmed and isolated; forbidden contact with all neighbouring communities, cut off from every normal means of communication, terrified by rumours of slaughter, but having no real knowledge of the fate of the Jews elsewhere.

Sometimes whole villages were able to escape (*opposite, above*). But once they had reached the immediate safety of nearby woods, the families and their leaders had to begin the desperate search for food. Often they were refused food by villagers who were themselves hungry, or even hostile. Then, in their own time, the Germans were able to launch full-scale military attacks: those shown here by heavy black arrows, the first in October 1942, the second in December 1942, were on three separate fronts, supported by artillery, armoured vehicles, grenades, machine-guns, and carried out by armed men who had been trained for military combat and were now being sent to destroy small groups of isolated Jewish families on the verge of starvation.

There was also Jewish defiance in Berlin (*above*). A public display of anti-Nazi posters by a student group led to the capture of one group; all 152 were shot.

As a reprisal for the shooting of the SS chief, Reinhardt Heydrich, in Prague, on May 27, the SS launched 'Operation Reinhardt' against both Czechs and Jews. Some 2,000 Czechs were killed in Prague as well as in the village of Lidice. From the Theresienstadt ghetto, 3,000 Jews were deported to Auschwitz and gassed.

Map 125

ESCAPE, RESISTANCE, DESTRUCTION, MAY - OCTOBER 1942

O miles 35
O kilometres 50

M A Z O V I A and P O D L A S I A

River Vistula

Wyszkow

Treblinka
more than 50 *escape*

several hundred escape

Warsaw

4,000

River Bug

Parczew
4,000

Puszcza Kozienicka

Pulawy
1,000

Lubartow
4,000

Sobibor

Radom

Markuszow

Lublin
Majdanek

Trawniki
slave labour camp

Puszcza Swietokrzyska

Krasnystaw

of whom less than 200 survived the war

Hrubieszow
15,000

Kielce
14,000

100 Janow

Szczebrzeszyn

Zamosc
Puszcza Solska

Bilgoraj

Tomaszow

Vistula River

Dulcza forest

Radomysl

Belzec

Cracow
8,500

Puszcza Niempolomicka

© Martin Gilbert 1982

As the SS continued its drive to deport Jews to death camps and labour camps, the Jews themselves continued to try to escape to the woods and forests *(above)*. These were not escapes of the young and strong, leaving behind the women, children, the old and the sick. Rather, many of the escape leaders sought to save whole families. Once in the woods, survival for more than a few months was virtually impossible. Those who did manage to escape faced full-scale German military campaigns, local peasant hostility and betrayal. The terrible privations of forest life took their toll: no medical help, hardly any food, brackish water, and the ravages of extremes of climate – summer heat and insects, followed by autumn storms and sub-zero winter temperatures. Of more than 100 Jews who escaped from Janow to the Puszcza Solska, for example, no more than ten survived the war.

Nevertheless, the spirit of resistance was strong. These were not 'sheep to the slaughter', but brave men and women, willing, unarmed, to challenge the armed strength of a victorious army. No outside State supported them, while only a few local villagers were prepared to give them haven.

The photographs *(right)*, taken by the author in 1980, show one such forest area: the Parczew forest, the story of which is told on pages 122-3.

DISTANT DEPORTATIONS AND MASSACRES, JUNE 1942

Riga

Smolensk
2,000

Lysa Gora
slave labour camp
400
15 June

Priluki
1,210
15 May-15 June

Duisburg **146** *25 June*

TRANSNISTRIA

Theresienstadt   Auschwitz

Drancy

Paris

SLOVAKIA

Czernowitz
4,000 *deported*
17-27 June
3,500 *perished*
after deportation

52,000
March-June

933 *5 June*
934 *22 June*
999 *25 June*
965 *28 June*

German front line

North Sea   *Baltic Sea*   *Black Sea*

© Martin Gilbert 1982

A GAS VAN ORDERED NORTH, 9 JUNE 1942

Riga
Kaiserwald
Tilsit

Berlin

GREATER   GERMANY
Dresden
Prague

Vienna

Zemun   Belgrade

Baltic Sea   *German front line*   *Black Sea*   *Adriatic Sea*

0   miles   200
0   km   300

© Martin Gilbert 1982

June 1942 saw no relaxation in the SS deportation plan, or in the executions in the east. Hardly had the German army reached the Russian cities of Smolensk and Priluki, than more than 3,000 Jews were murdered. From Czernowitz, in the Bukovina (*pages 72-3*), a further 4,000 were deported eastwards to Transnistria (*above, top*), of whom less than half survived the war. The deportations to Auschwitz continued without pause, with four from Paris, 50 from Slovakia in four months, and five from the Auschwitz region (*opposite*). In Warsaw a further 4,000 Jews died of starvation during June. At Belzec and Sobibor more than 23,000 Jews were gassed.

Among those deported to Belzec, from Cracow, was the 65-year-old Mordechai Gebirtig, a carpenter whose Yiddish songs and melodies were sung throughout Poland. His best known, 'Our town is burning', was written after the Przytyk pogrom (*page 21*). Gebirtig was deported and killed with his wife and two daughters. Another distinguished Cracow Jew, the writer Abraham Naumann, aged 70, was shot in the street during the round-up.

On 9 June 1942 a special gas van, used earlier at Zemun for the murder of Serbian Jews (*page 83*), was sent to Riga (*left*), for the continuing killing not only of Riga's Jews, but of tens of thousands of Jews deported to Riga from Greater Germany six months before. So heavy was its task, that on 15 June 1942 the SS in Riga ordered a second van.

As the killings continued, so did the attempts at resistance: at Dzisna (*opposite*) 2,000 Jews managed to break out of the ghetto. Many were caught, but some reached Russian partisan units, and fought with the Red Army against the Germans.

Map 128

DEPORTATION, MASS MURDER AND REVOLT, JUNE 1942

miles 0 — 60
kilometres 0 — 80

Baltic Sea

EAST PRUSSIA

REICHSKOMMISSARIAT OSTLAND

Druja `1,000` ✶ *revolt*
Miory `1,000`
2 June
✶ *revolt*
Braslaw `3,000` ✶ *revolt*
3 June
Dzisna `4,000`
14 June

Glebokie ✶ *revolt* `2,500`
19 June

Oszmiana `300`
16 June
Ilja *several hundred*
7 June

Lida `1,200` *10 June*
`5,000` *25 June*
Grodek `1,700`
22 June

Molczadz `200`
3 June

Slonim *armed resistance* *29 June* ✶ `10,000`

Dereczyn `100`

Lachowicze `1,200`
10 June

Augustow

Bogusze *slave labour camp* `1,750`

BIALYSTOK REGION

THE GERMAN REICH

卐 **Treblinka** *camp in preparation*

Kobryn `4,000`
6 June

Slawatyce `1,000`

Warsaw *at least* `4,000` *deaths from starvation in June*

Biala Podlaska `3,000`
10 June

Wlodawa *several hundred children under ten years old*
Sobibor

REICHSKOMMISSARIAT UKRAINE

Uchanie `1,650` *10 June*

VOLHYNIA

Krzepice `1,000`

THE GENERAL GOVERNMENT

Cycow `500`

Dubienka `2,670`

Luck `2,000`
June

Pilica `3,000` *to Belzec but several hundred escape*

Krasniczyn `1,000` *6 June*

Hrubieszow `3,049`
2 June

✶ *resistance led by* Joel Szczerbat

Chrzanow `4,000` ✶

Dabrowa Tarnowska `500`

Grabowiec `1,200`
8 June

Olkusz `3,000`

Sosnowiec `2,000`

Tarnow `11,000`

卐 Belzec

Belz `100`
2 June

Bielsko Biala `5,000`
卐 **Auschwitz**

Cracow `2,000` *1 June*
`5,000` *6 June*

WESTERN GALICIA

EASTERN GALICIA

Namestovo `300`

Cadca `500`

Lutowiska `800` *murdered in the market place*

Zilina `2,500`

Liptovsky Svaty Mikulas `1,000`
Poprad `1,000`

Presov `4,600`

Humenne `2,000`

Kolomyja `3,000`

Senica `800`
Handlova `80`
Ruzomberok `950`
Brezno `250`
Sabinov `1,200`
Vranov `1,600`
Medzilaborce `1,500`

Banska Stiavnica `400`
Banska Bystrica
Roznava `1,000`
Kassa (Kosice)
Michalovce `4,500`

Nitra `4,500`
Revuca `500`
Trebisov `2,500`
Krupina `1,250`
Levice

© Martin Gilbert 1982

Map 129

THE JEWS OF HOLLAND ON THE EVE OF DEPORTATION

North Sea

GRONINGEN
4,708
Leeuwarden
● **Groningen**
● Winschoten

FRIESLAND
852
● Assen

Westerbork

DRENTE
2,498
Meppel ●
● Hoogeveen

NORTH HOLLAND
87,566

Alkmaar ●

Zaandam
● Zwolle

Amsterdam
Naarden
OVERIJSSEL
4,385
● Almelo

Bloemendaal
Zandvoort
Haarlem ● Heemstede
Bussum Laren
Apeldoorn
● Deventer
Hengelo ●
Enschede ●

Voorburg
Leiden ●
Hilversum
de Bilt
● Amersfoort
● Zutphen
Lochem

The Hague
SOUTH HOLLAND
25,648
GELDERLAND
6,642
● Winterswijk

Rijswijk ●
Utrecht Zeist
Arnhem

Gouda
Schiedam ● **Rotterdam**
UTRECHT
3,802
Nijmegen

● Dordrecht
● Oss

Hertogenbosch

NORTH BRABANT
2,281
Tilburg

ZEELAND
174

LIMBURG
1,441

Eindhoven

GREATER GERMANY

BELGIUM

● Maastricht

0	miles 30
0	kilometres 50

The figures show the number of Jews in the Dutch Provinces in 1941

● Towns with **300** to **700** Jewish inhabitants
● Towns with **1,000** to **3,000** Jewish inhabitants
● Towns with **8,000** to **14,000** Jewish inhabitants
⬤ Amsterdam: **80,000** Jewish inhabitants

© Martin Gilbert 1982

Since May 1940 the 140,000 Jews of Holland (*above*) had been deliberately cut off from the community around them. On 9 May 1942 the yellow star was made compulsory.

On 14 July 1942 thousands of Dutch Jews were arrested in Amsterdam, and on the following day the first train, with 1,135 Dutch Jews on board, left Holland for an 'unknown destination' (*opposite*). By the end of the month, nearly 6,000 had, in fact, reached Auschwitz, where the majority were gassed.

The photograph shows the special railway spur being built from the internment camp at Westerbork to the main railway line.

From Germany, hundreds of Jews were deported to the Theresienstadt ghetto, and kept there, isolated and starving.

Map 130

DISTANT DEPORTATIONS, JULY 1942

North Sea

Baltic Sea

Danzig

1,135 *15 July*

586 *16 July*

309 *16 July*

931 *21 July*

1,000 *24 July*

1,010 *27 July*

1,007 *31 July*

Westerbork

7 trains left Holland in July

HOLLAND

Padderborn
*all Jewish
orphans deported*

G R E A T E R   G E R M A N Y

Düsseldorf
260
22 July

Boppard
10
27 July

Bacharach
5
26 July

Kempten
200
25 July

Theresienstadt

Auschwitz

*the first 100 women handed
over for sterilization and
other medical experiments,
10 July 1942*

0   miles   100
0   kilometres   150

© Martin Gilbert 1982

Map 131

DEPORTATION, MASSACRE AND REVOLT, JULY 1942

Danzig

GREATER GERMANY

Chelmno

Lutomiersk
700

Kowale Panske
3,000
20 July

Czestochowa

Pilica

Bedzin

Cracow

Bochnia

Bialystok

Treblinka

Warsaw
66,701 deported
and at least
4,000
died of starvation in July

GENERAL GOVERNMENT

Szarkowszczyzna
revolt **600** killed 18 July
900 escape

Molczadz
1,000
15 July

Dereczyn
3,000 24 July

Kosow
1,200 25 July

Antopol
1,100

Kobryn
2,000
25 July

Nieswiez
600
22 July
ghetto
revolt
15 July

Bereza Kartuska
1,000
15 July

Drohiczyn
1,700
26 June

Minsk
25,000
28-30 July

revolt led by
Shalom Cholawsky

Kleck
1,000
21 July
revolt

Byten
840
25 July

Pinsk
all patients in the
Jewish hospital murdered

REICHSKOMMISSARIAT
UKRAINE

Sobibor

Chelm **300**

Jozefow
1,500 shot
13 July

12,000
21–25 July
Tarnobrzeg

Rozwadow

Baranow

Radomysl   Sokolow

Debica   Ropczyce

Pilzno
Wielopole

Strzyzow

Rzeszow
22,000
7–13 July

Zimgrod
1,000 murdered in nearby
woods

Belzec

Brody

Niemirow
500

Sambor
50 shot

Kowel
24,000
mid July

Olyka
5,673
27–28 July

Uhnow
1,000

Rawa
Ruska
2,000 27 July

Sasow
1,000
15 July

Luck
4,000
4 July

Rowne
5,000
14–15 July

Stanislawow
1,000 shot

Tluste
200
mid July

murdered at an
'unknown
destination'
possibly Belzec,
or a nearby
wood

SLOVAKIA

© Martin Gilbert 1982

On 22 July 1942 the Germans embarked upon their most ambitious project: the deportation of more than half a million Jews from the Warsaw ghetto. The death camp prepared for them was at Treblinka, scarcely more than 40 miles from the ghetto. In one month alone, 66,701 Jews were deported from Warsaw to Treblinka, and gassed on arrival.

In an attempt to warn of what was happening, to organize armed resistance, and to link the scattered and isolated ghettos, a Jewish Fighters' Organization, known by its Polish initials ZOB, was set up in Warsaw, Bialystok, Brody, and in five of the ghettos south-west of Warsaw (above).

The deportations to Chelmno and Belzec continued (above). Further east, as the killing squads continued their executions, the last Jews alive in Nieswiez, 600 artisans, fought

with sticks and clubs to resist their killers. Most were murdered. At Kleck a few dozen, fortunate to possess a pistol or two, broke away from the ghetto and were able to join the partisans in the forests.

During August 1942 the Dutch and French deportations continued (opposite, below). Now, for the first time, Jews from Luxembourg and Belgium were deported to Auschwitz.

To prevent the Swedish Government from giving its protection to Dutch Jews, the Germans had decided, on 17 July 1942, to deprive all Jews in Holland of their Dutch citizenship. Two weeks later, to forestall a further Swedish effort to help the Jews of Holland, the Germans decided not to disclose the whereabouts of the deportees. Thus Auschwitz remained an 'unknown destination', 'somewhere in the east'.

THE WARSAW GHETTO DEPORTATIONS, FROM 22 JULY 1942

to Bialystok →

River Narew

River Bug

Malkinia

Treblinka station

Treblinka
death camp

Wyszkow

Lochow

Kosow Lacki

River Bug

Tluszcz

Jadow

River Liwiec

Wegrow

Sokolow Podlaski

Palmiry
execution site

Kampinos forest

River Vistula

Wolomin

Praga

Warsaw

Minsk Mazowiecki

Kaluszyn

Siedlce

0   miles   6
0 kilometres 8

© **Martin Gilbert 1982**

Otwock

DISTANT DEPORTATIONS, AUGUST 1942

1,013
3 August
987
7 August
559
10 August

Westerbork

0   miles   200
0 kilometres 300

Cottbus
12

GREAT BRITAIN
unconquered

Kosel

Auschwitz

English Channel

Malines
5,990

Theresienstadt

Luxembourg
723

GREATER GERMANY

Drancy

Paris
14,000

Pithiviers

Ulm
45
to Theresienstadt

Beaune-la-Rolande

Belfort

SWITZERLAND
neutral

Bay of Biscay

Chalon-sur Sâone

ITALY

Bordeaux Bacalan

Merignac

Zagreb
CROATIA
several thousands

Adriatic Sea

Récébédou

Agde

Les Milles

Noé

Rivesaltes

Mediterranean Sea

SPAIN
neutral

Pyrenees

© **Martin Gilbert 1982**

Map 134

THE JEWS OF BELGIUM AND LUXEMBOURG

North Sea

HOLLAND

Ostend
53

WEST FLANDERS
40

Ghent
197

Antwerp
55,000

Malines
Dossin camp

GREATER

GERMANY

EAST FLANDERS
39

Brussels
35,000

B E L G I U M

HAINAULT
434

Liége
2,000

Charleroi
628

Namur
50

F R A N C E

Wiltz
17

Diekirch
187

LUXEMBOURG
Redange
6

Mersch
63

E
78

C
25

Grevenmacher
79

Remich
99

Esch
470

0   miles   25

0   kilometres   40

© Martin Gilbert 1982

E=Echternach
C=Capellen

Luxembourg
2,111

The Belgian and Luxembourg Jews, now seized and deported, came from many cities, towns and villages *(above)*. The first deportations from Belgium took place on 4 August 1942 *(page 109)*. Henceforth, over a period of two years, a total of 26 trains set off to the 'unknown destination' from the internment camp at Dossin, near Malines. The destination was in fact, Auschwitz.

The Germans ignored protests from the Catholic Church, including one by Jean Hérinckx, a leading right-wing Catholic, and one by Cardinal van Roey, Archbishop of Malines.

The local Belgian population was active in helping Jews, of whom more than 25,000 were hidden in private homes and orphanages, and thereby saved. But of the 25,631 Belgian Jews who were deported, only 1,244 survived the war.

More than 1,000 Belgian Jews fought with the Belgian partisans; 140 of them were killed in action. Other Jews were smuggled across France, to Spain and Switzerland. But on 13 August 1942 the Swiss police began to turn back Jewish refugees who had managed to cross into Switzerland. 'Under current practice', a Police Instruction of 25 September 1942 read, 'refugees on the grounds of race alone are not political refugees'.

From France, the deportations continued without pause. On 17 August 1942, among 997 mainly Polish-born Jews deported from Paris to Auschwitz, 27 were children under the age of four, almost all of whom had been born in France, and most of whom were deported without their parents. Marguerite Jakubovitch was deported with her six brothers and sisters, the oldest of whom was only ten years old: all had been born in Paris, and were deported without their parents. All 27 young children named here *(right)* were gassed within hours of reaching Auschwitz.

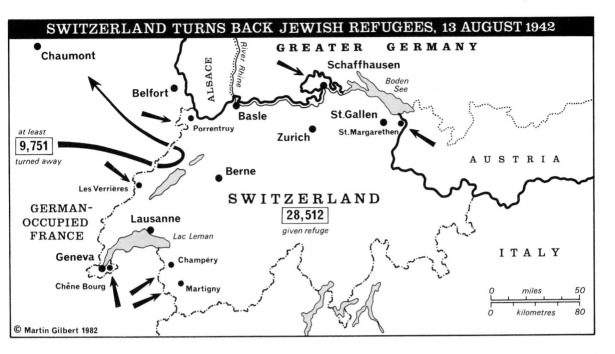

SWITZERLAND TURNS BACK JEWISH REFUGEES, 13 AUGUST 1942

GREATER GERMANY

Chaumont

ALSACE

River Rhine

Schaffhausen

Boden See

Belfort

Basle

St.Gallen

St.Margarethen

Porrentruy

Zurich

AUSTRIA

at least
9,751
turned away

Berne

SWITZERLAND

28,512
given refuge

GERMAN-
OCCUPIED
FRANCE

Les Verrières

Lausanne

Lac Leman

ITALY

Geneva

Champéry

Chêne Bourg

Martigny

0   miles   50

0   kilometres   80

© Martin Gilbert 1982

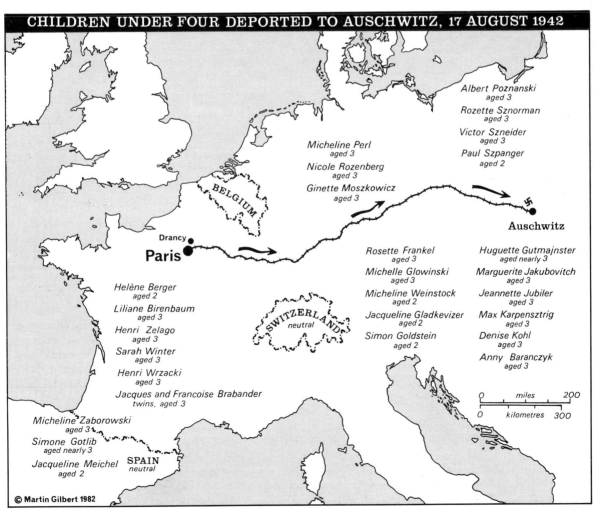

CHILDREN UNDER FOUR DEPORTED TO AUSCHWITZ, 17 AUGUST 1942

Albert Poznanski
aged 3

Rozette Sznorman
aged 3

Victor Szneider
aged 3

Micheline Perl
aged 3

Paul Szpanger
aged 2

Nicole Rozenberg
aged 3

Ginette Moszkowicz
aged 3

BELGIUM

Auschwitz

Drancy

Paris

Rosette Frankel
aged 3

Huguette Gutmajnster
aged nearly 3

Helène Berger
aged 2

Michelle Glowinski
aged 3

Marguerite Jakubovitch
aged 3

Liliane Birenbaum
aged 3

Micheline Weinstock
aged 2

Jeannette Jubiler
aged 3

Henri Zelago
aged 3

SWITZERLAND
neutral

Jacqueline Gladkevizer
aged 2

Max Karpensztrig
aged 3

Sarah Winter
aged 3

Simon Goldstein
aged 2

Denise Kohl
aged 3

Henri Wrzacki
aged 3

Anny Baranczyk
aged 3

Jacques and Francoise Brabander
twins, aged 3

Micheline Zaborowski
aged 3

Simone Gotlib
aged nearly 3

SPAIN
neutral

Jacqueline Meichel
aged 2

0   miles   200

0   kilometres   300

© Martin Gilbert 1982

Map 137

DEPORTATION, MASSACRE AND REVOLT, 1-13 AUGUST 1942

0   miles   60
0   kilometres   80

Radun
500
9 August

Nowogrodek
6,000
7 August

Mir
resistance
9 August
two hundred
escape to the
forests

Zdzieciol
3,000
6 August

three hundred escape
Jewish partisan unit
commanded by
Hirsch Kaplinski

G R E A T E R

G E R M A N Y

Treblinka

Chelmno

Warta
1,000

Lodz
40,000
10·22 August

Warsaw
70,000
1·13 August

Sieradz
1,400
14 August

Belchatow
5,000

Radom
30,000
5·17 August

Zolkiewka
1,000
10 August

Sobibor

Chelm
300

Zamosc
500

VOLHYNIA
over **87,000** killed on
the spot during August
(see page 115)

Szczebrzeszyn
400

Zwierzyniec
300

Bilgoraj
500 9 August

Belzec

Bedzin
5,000
1 August

Sosnowiec
8,000
12 August

Glogow
500

Tarnogrod
1,000
9 August

Krzemieniec

Auschwitz

WESTERN GALICIA
over **69,000** deported and
killed during August
(see page 114)

Przemysl

Lvov

EASTERN GALICIA
over **76,000** deported and
killed during August
(see opposite)

S L O V A K I A

© Martin Gilbert 1982

In the first two weeks of August nearly a quarter of a million Jews were killed at Chelmno, Auschwitz, Treblinka and Belzec (*above*), and by the killing squads in the east. In preparation for a single deportation to Chelmno, Jews were brought to Wielun (*opposite*) from nine nearby communities.

More than 76,000 Jews were deported from Eastern Galicia to Belzec (*opposite, below*). All were killed within a few hours, as were a further 74,000 Jews from Western Galicia (*page 114*). East of Greater Germany, killing on the spot continued, 87,000 Jews being murdered in the Volhynia (*page 115*). Resistance had also led, at both Mir and Zdzieciol, to mass escapes.

JEWS ASSEMBLED FOR DEPORTATION TO CHELMNO, 1-21 AUGUST 1942

miles 0 — 20
kilometres 0 — 30

Chelmno — Dabie

Lodz

Sieradz

922 to Lodz 22 August

Sulmierzyce **990**

10,000 to Chelmno 22 August (see page 114)

Lututow **1,200**

Wieruszow **900**

Kielczyglow **200**

Wielun

Siemkowice **150**

Boleslawiec **474**

Pajeczno **1,800**

Dzialoszyn **1,000**

Praszka **700**

© Martin Gilbert 1982

TWENTY DEPORTATIONS FROM EASTERN GALICIA, AUGUST 1942

miles 0 — 30
kilometres 0 — 50

Belzec

River Bug

Olesko **472** 29 August

Sasow **100** 29 August

Lvov **40,000** 1-10 August

Zloczow **2,700** 28 August

Jezierna **300**

Tarnopol **4,000**

Skalat **500** 31 August

Bobrka **1,260** to Belzec **200** shot 12 August

Mikulince **1,200** 28-29 August

Sambor **4,000** 4-6 August

Truskawiec **100**

Chorostkow **1,500** 24 August

Stary Sambor **1,500** 5-6 August

Drohobycz **2,000** **3,000** 17 August

Czortkow **2,500** 28 August

Turka **5,000**

Boryslaw **2,000**

Dolina **3,000** 3 August

Stanislawow **1,000**

Tluste **300**

© Martin Gilbert 1982

DEPORTATION, MASSACRE AND REVOLT, 14–31 AUGUST 1942

Gostynin 3,500 *15 August*

Minsk Mazowiecki 7,000 *21 August*

Mordy 2,000 *23 August*

Siedlce 15,000 *22 August*

Byten 400 *29 August*

0 miles 50
0 kilometres 80

Lenino 1,000 *14 August*

Warsaw 70,000 *14–21 August*

Chelmno

Losice 6,900 *22 August*

Lomazy 1,700 *shot* *17–19 August*

Antopol 1,000

Sarny

Treblinka

Miedzyrzec 5,000 *25 Aug*

Sadok 405 *14 August*

F
R
Otwock 14,000 *19 August*
resistance

Radzyn 1,500 *20 August*

Lask 3,500 *28 August*

Kock 2,500

Parczew 5,000

VOLHYNIA *see opposite*

Zdunska Wola 12,000 *22–23August*

Jedlinia 300

Wielun 10,000 *22 August*

Garbatka 1,100 *18 August*

Goraj 800 *21 August*

Luck

Warta 1,000 *24 August*

Kielce 21,000 *20 August*

Wloszczowa 4,000 *26 August*

Lezajsk
10,000 **Zolynia**
Lancut
Radymno

Belzec

Tarnopol

WESTERN GALICIA *see below*

Nowy Sacz

EASTERN GALICIA *see page 113*

Czortkow

Stanislawow

F= **Falenica** 6,500 *20 August*   R= **Rembertow** 2,000 *20 August*

SLOVAKIA

© Martin Gilbert 1982

DEPORTATIONS FROM WESTERN GALICIA TO BELZEC, AUGUST 1942

0 miles 25
0 kilometres 40

Bochnia 2,600 *25 August*

Jaslo *and region* 16,000 *mid–August*

Krosno *and region* 5,000 *mid–August*

Belzec

Wieliczka 8,000 *27 August*

Rzeszow 1,000

Auschwitz

Cracow

Tarnow

Frysztak

Blazowa

Skawina 2,000 *28 August*

Niebylec
Jasienica
Brzozow

Przemysl 12,500

Nowy Sacz *and region* 16,000 *24–28 August*

Biecz 700

Makow

Rabka

Dukla

Zagorz
Ropienka
Olszanica

Rymanow 500

Zaslaw 4,000 *to Belzec* 7,000 *shot in nearby forests*

Szczawnica

Krynica

Szczawne *transit camp*

Nowy Targ *and region* 2,500 *28–30 August*

Stary Sacz 700 *17 August*

Gorlice 700 *14 August*

© Martin Gilbert 1982

Map 142

MASSACRE. RESISTANCE AND ESCAPE IN THE VOLHYNIA. AUGUST 1942

Lubieszow 15

Pohost 2,000
16 August

Ratno 1,000 500 escape

Kamen Kashirski 2,400 10 August 600 escape

Dabrowica 2,800 1,500 escape
28 August

Wlodzimierzec 2,400 600 escape

Bereznica 1,000

Tomaszgrod 150

Niesuchojeze 350

Rafalowka 1,600 800 escape
28 August

Klesow 50

Sarny 10,500 3,500 escape

Rokitno 900 700 escape

Kowel over 5,000

VOLHYNIA

Stepan 2,000 500 escape

Maciejow 1,500

Kostopol all 700 escape

Berezne 1,800 200 escape

Turzysk 1,000

Rozyszcze 3,000

Zofiowka 1,500

Derazno 500

Siedliszcze 500

Torczyn 2,000

Luck 14,700 2,000 escape

Tuczyn 2,000

PODOLIA

Polish – Soviet border 1921–1939

River Bug

EASTERN GALICIA

Szumsk over 1,000

Krzemieniec over 3,000

Lanowce over 400

Wiszniewicze 1,000
30 August

Sarny: resistance led by Mendel Tendler

Zofiewka: resistance led by Chaim Wodchin Gad Rosenblatt

0 miles 20
0 kilometres 40

© Martin Gilbert 1982

During the last two weeks of August, more than 200,000 Jews were murdered in German-occupied Poland, most of them deported to the three death camps of Chelmno, Treblinka and Belzec. These deportations were dominated by the relentless rounding up and deportation of Jews from Warsaw to Treblinka.

For every deportation, a precise time-table was devised, and copies sent to every station en route. After the deportees had been taken off, the trains were cleaned, and returned empty along the same routes, and with the same careful planning.

Resistance also continued: at Treblinka itself, on 26 August 1942, a young deportee fom the town of Kielce, having been forbidden by one of the Ukrainian guards to say farewell to his mother, attacked the guard with a knife. Hardly had he done so, than the whole trainload of deportees was machine-gunned.

In the Volhynia (above) over 87,000 Jews were murdered in August 1942. As German units came to kill them, as many as 15,000 managed to escape. But less than 1,000 of the escapees, who included men, women and children, were able to survive nearly two years of intense hunger, severe winter cold, sickness, and repeated German and Ukrainian attacks. Some of the men later joined the small Soviet partisan units which were later parachuted into the Volhynia.

Between May and December 1942 more than 140,000 Volhynia Jews were murdered. Some, who had been given refuge in Polish homes, were murdered together with their Polish protectors in the spring of 1943, when, of 300,000 Poles living in the Volhynia, 40,000 were murdered by Ukrainian 'bandits'. In many villages, Poles and Jews fought together against the common foe.

Map 143

DEPORTATION AND MASS MURDER, 1-5 SEPTEMBER 1942

Serniki
500 killed
500 escape

Wysock
700 killed
300 escape

Trojanowka
50

Poworsk
20

Mielnica
700

Maniewicze
800 killed
200 escape

Lublin
2,000
2 September
Majdan Tatarsky

Uscilug
2,000

Wlodzimierz Wolynski (Ludmir)
13,500 500 escape
killed

Piatydni

Horochow **2,500** killed
500 escape

Poryck
1,000

Belzec

Druszkopol
500

Beresteczko
1,000

VOLHYNIA

Poczaje
700

GREATER GERMANY

River Bug

resistance led by
Moshe Skoczylas and
Michael Majtek
in nearby forest

Dzialoszyce
1,000 shot in the town
8,000 deported to Belzec
3 September

Bochnia
600 shot in the town
2,000 deported to Belzec
3 September

GENERAL GOVERNMENT

Lvov

Mikolajow
500
4 September

Rozdol
1,000
4-5 September

Sambor
2,000
2 September

Brzozdowce
500 3-5 September

Stryj
3,000
1 September

Skole
2,000
4 September

Chodorow
2,000
4 September

Zydaczow
500
5 September

Zurawno
500
5 September

Bolechow
2,000
3-5 September

EASTERN GALICIA

Zbaraz
'hundreds'
1 September

© Martin Gilbert 1982

Throughout September 1942, deportation to the death camps continued. For the Wloszczowa deportation (opposite) an intricate timetable, typical of hundreds more, was devised:

Wloszczowa		depart 16.38
Kielce	arrive 19.06	depart 19.55
Skarzysko	arrive 21.41	depart 22.43
Radom	arrive 0.03	depart 0.13
Deblin	arrive 2.00	depart 3.10
Łukow	arrive 5.17	depart 6.08
Siedlce	arrive 6.58	depart 8.34
Treblinka	arrive 11.24	(depart empty) 15.59

Following the empty train's despatch from Treblinka, an equally intricate timetable was devised, to return it to the next deportation point.

East of the border of Greater Germany, the killings continued to take place, as shown above, in or near the towns themselves: at Wlodzimierz Wolynski 4,000 Jews were shot in the prison courtyard, and 14,000 driven to the gravel pits at Piatydni, and machine-gunned. Even inside the General Government, as at Warsaw (opposite) and Dzialoszyce (above), thousands were shot in the streets while the deportations were in progress.

Map 144

DEPORTATIONS TO TWO DEATH CAMPS, 1 AND 6-16 SEPTEMBER 1942

Treblinka

Dobre
500
15 September

Siedlce

Warsaw
54,069
deported
3,047
shot in the streets 6-16 September

Lukow

Biala Podlaska
1,000
6 September

Grojec
3,000

Deblin

River Bug

Radom

G E N E R A L

Skarzysko Kamienna

Wloszczowa
5,000
I September

Kielce

G O V E R N M E N T

Zamosc
400

Radziechow
1,400
15 September

Checiny
4,000
13 September

Belzec

Jedzejow
6,000 *16 September*

Wolbrom
8,000
6 September

River Vistula

Pustkow
slave labour camp opened 16 September

Kamionka Strumilowa
1,500
15 September

Lvov

Brzesko
500

Tuchow
3,000

Tarnow
8,000

WESTERN GALICIA

Sanok
8,000
10 September

E A S T E R N GALICIA

S L O V A K I A

Stanislawow
5,000
12 September

© Martin Gilbert 1982

0   *miles*   40
0   *kilometres*   60

At Treblinka, there was a further act of resistance on 11 September 1942, by a young Jew from the Argentine, who had been trapped in Warsaw at the outbreak of war. The young man, Meir Berliner, having been deported in one of the daily September transports to Treblinka, stabbed an SS officer to death with his penknife.

Meir Berliner's action saved no lives. But it was an act of considerable courage. So too was the decision of a number of Jews from Dzialoszyce (*opposite*) to try to break out on the eve of deportation to Belzec, and make for the forests. Some of them succeeded. Led by Moshe Skoczylas and Michael Majtek, they formed two small but effective partisan units. Majtek helped to organize resistance in Pinczow (*page 131*). Within three months, however, both had been hunted down and destroyed by German troops.

Map 145

NINE DEPORTATIONS TO BELZEC, 7 SEPTEMBER 1942

Belzec

REICHSKOMMISSARIAT UKRAINE

GENERAL GOVERNMENT

Lvov

Janowska
slave labour camp

GREATER GERMANY

EASTERN GALICIA

Zablotow 250

Kolomyja 8,700

Sniatyn 2,000

Jablonow 800

Roznow 100

RUTHENIA

Kosow 600

Kuty 800

HUNGARY

Pistyn 500

Zabie 200

BUKOVINA

© Martin Gilbert 1982

TRANSYLVANIA

miles 0 — 30
kilometres 0 — 40

The map above shows nine deportations to Belzec in a single day. The only Jews not sent to their deaths were a group of young people from Kuty. While the rest of their community was sent to Belzec, they were sent to the Janowska slave labour camp in Lvov: a camp where brutality was so savage that almost no-one survived.

In the east (*opposite, above*), German troops had reached the Caucasus. Killing squads at once rounded up the local Jews, murdering them on the spot, or deporting them to nearby execution sites.

In the west (*opposite, below*), the deportations to Auschwitz continued with eight trains from Holland, five from

Belgium, and 13 from Paris. The French deportees included many German Jews who had been deported to the Pyrenees two years before (*page 48*). Deportations also continued to Theresienstadt; there, as in the Polish ghettos, tens of thousands died of starvation and disease. Of 533 Jews deported from Nuremberg in September 1942, only 27 survived the war.

Resistance also continued: at Lachwa, where all 820 Jews fought against the 'liquidation', most were killed, but a few managed to escape and join a Soviet partisan unit. At Stolin local Ukrainians handed over to the SS the two leaders of the revolt, who were then shot.

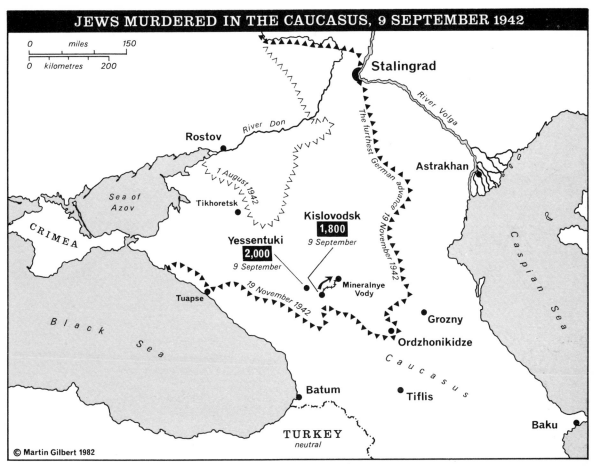

JEWS MURDERED IN THE CAUCASUS, 9 SEPTEMBER 1942

0 — miles — 150
0 — kilometres — 200

Stalingrad

River Don

River Volga

Rostov

The furthest German advance

Astrakhan

1 August 1942

Sea of Azov

Tikhoretsk

CRIMEA

Kislovodsk
1,800
9 September

Yessentuki
2,000
9 September

19 November 1942

Mineralnye Vody

Tuapse

19 November 1942

Grozny

Ordzhonikidze

Black Sea

Caucasus

Caspian Sea

Batum

Tiflis

Baku

TURKEY
neutral

© Martin Gilbert 1982

DISTANT DEPORTATIONS, MASSACRE AND REVOLT, SEPTEMBER 1942

Leningrad

Moscow

led by
Dov Lopatin
700 *killed*
120 *escape*

HOLLAND
6,675
in 8 trains

Vitebsk
8,350

Lachwa
revolt
2 September

Baltic Sea

led by Moses Glazer
and Asher Shapira

GREATER GERMANY

Stalingrad

BELGIUM
5,750
in 5 trains

Stolin
7,000
11 September resistance

Rostov
18,000

Lille
1,000
in 1 train

Paris
13,000
2·30 September

Krzemieniec
armed resistance
9 September

Theresienstadt

Auschwitz

Bamberg
300
9 September

Belfort

Noe

Gurs
Rivesaltes

Les Milles

Nuremberg
533
10 September

Piatygorsk
300

SPAIN
neutral

Black Sea

Yessentuki
2,000

Shaumyan
114

Kislovodsk
1,800

Caspian Sea

TURKEY
neutral

0 — miles — 400
0 — kilometres — 600

© Martin Gilbert 1982

Map 148

THE HIRSCHSPRUNG FAMILY DEPORTED, 15 SEPTEMBER 1942

North Sea

Baltic Sea

Amsterdam
their children
Nelly Hirschsprung born 8 June 1933
David Hirschsprung born 21 April 1938

Lille

Malines
The Hirschsprung family
among more than a thousand
Jews deported to Auschwitz
15 September 1942

Cracow

Auschwitz
Helene Hirschsprung
born 22 August 1909
in the Austro-Hungarian Empire

married to

Mozes Hirschsprung
born 16 October 1901
in the Austro-Hungarian
Empire

0   *miles*   150

0   *kilometres*   200

© **Martin Gilbert 1982**

The map above tells of a single family deported from Belgium in September 1942. Hélène Hirschsprung, born in Auschwitz itself, had married a man from Cracow, and then had emigrated to Holland, where both their children were born. With the coming of war they had fled for refuge to Lille, in north-eastern France. But on 15 September 1942 they were among 1,000 Jews who were seized by the SS, transferred to Malines, and then deported to Auschwitz.

The deportees of September 15 *(opposite, above)* included many Jews born in the Polish provinces of Tsarist Russia, and others from the former Austro-Hungarian Empire.

The SS deportation lists from Paris record a total of 25 Auschwitz-born Jews, deported back to Auschwitz between 1942 and 1944. Among them was Frajdla Leiber, who had left Auschwitz with her parents shortly after her birth in September 1932, but was deported back to Auschwitz and gassed, when she was only 11 years old.

The Lille deportation of September 15 included the 21-year-old Bernice Winer, born in neutral Switzerland *(page 144),* and the 28-year-old Fanny Yerkowski, born in London. On the following day, from Paris, a further deportation to Auschwitz contained 40 Bulgarian-born Jews who had been seized in the French capital. The fact that no Jew had yet been deported to Auschwitz from Bulgaria itself could not save them. The names and ages of 14 of them are given opposite. Also deported was the 42-year-old Flora Landsman, born in Britain, and the 28-year-old Londoner, Lea Cohen, as well as Jews with Dutch, Estonian, Lithuanian, Latvian, Yugoslav, and even neutral Turkish citizenship.

BIRTHPLACES OF POLISH-BORN JEWS DEPORTED FROM LILLE, 15 SEPTEMBER 1942

Ciechanow

Inowroclaw

River Vistula

0 — miles — 50
0 — kilometres — 80

Wegrow

River Bug

Kutno

Warsaw

Kaluszyn

Siedlce

Ozorkow

Zyrardow

Zgierz

Lodz

Mszczonow

**TSARIST
EMPIRE**
to 1914

Kalisz

Pabianice

Lubartow

**GERMAN
EMPIRE**
to 1914

Warta

Zdunska
Wola

Tomaszow

Piotrkow

Radom

Chelm

Radomsko

Konskie

Szydlowiec

Izbica

Krzepice

Gidle

Kielce

Zamosc

Czestochowa

Koniecpol

Daleszyce

Tyszowce

Szczekociny

Jedrzejow

Wolbrom

Baranow

Rawa
Ruska

Bedzin

Stopnica

River Vistula

Kolbuszowa

Olkusz

Radomysl

Rzeszow

Auschwitz

Cracow

Tarnow

Debica

Tyczyn

Biala

Wielpole

Strzyzow

Przemysl

Rymanow

River San

Gorlice

Krynica

Dukla

AUSTRO-HUNGARIAN EMPIRE
to 1914

© Martin Gilbert 1982

BULGARIAN-BORN JEWS DEPORTED FROM PARIS TO AUSCHWITZ, 16 SEPTEMBER 1942

0 — miles — 75
0 — kilometres — 90

River Danube

Ruschuk (Ruse)
*Anna Mayer aged 45
Djamba Mayer aged 21
Djoia Mayer aged 14*

Varna
*Bellina Mitrani aged 47
Rebecca Ninio aged 34
Elizer Papo aged 45*

*Jacques Sabetai aged 41
Jeanne Tadger aged 42
Marcel Mayer aged 15
Avram Ninio aged 40
Daniel Ninio aged 37
Esther Ninio aged 37
Moshe Ninio aged 16*

Sofia

BULGARIA

*Black
Sea*

Kustendil
David Alkali aged 33

Plovdiv
*Leon Seliktar aged 37
Joseph Illel aged 53
Israel Cohen aged 40*

TURKEY
neutral

borders of 1940

GREECE

© Martin Gilbert 1982

*Sea of
Marmara*

Map 151

DEPORTATIONS AND REVOLT, 17-20 SEPTEMBER 1942

Treblinka

Byten
50
19 September

0   miles   50

0   kilometres   80

River Bug

Parczew
5,000
19 September
'Altana' and 'Tabor'
*family camps
hideout and
resistance group led by*
Yehiel Grynszpan

Sokal
2,500
17 September

Belzec

*mass break out from
deportation train;
almost all the would-
be escapees machine
gunned*

Brody
3,000
19 September

EASTERN
GALICIA

Zaleszczyki
2,000
20 September

© Martin Gilbert 1982

In only three days, over 10,000 Jews were deported to Belzec and Treblinka *(left)*. All were murdered. The photograph shows a group of Jews being deported from Eastern Galicia; their bundles contained everything they were allowed to take with them. At Belzec all these belongings were taken from them, sorted, and sent to Germany.

As the Parczew round-ups were in progress, several thousand Jews managed to break through the cordon, escape southwards to the hamlet of Makoszka *(opposite),* and reach the dense woods, thickets and swamps of the Parczew forest *(photographs on page 103).* Most of them were hunted down by German armed units, and shot. Three particular German hunts, one in November and two in December 1942, led to hundreds of Jewish families being massacred in the forest itself. Others died of starvation, cold and disease. Those few hundred who survived the repeated searches, and the ravages of winter, remained hidden in the forest, in two family camps.

One particularly unpleasant and unexpected hazard for the Jewish families hiding in the Parczew forest was the activity of a group of former Red Army soldiers, prisoners-of-war who had formed their own partisan unit. These Russians promised to give the Jews guns in return for money and jewelry, but simply took the money and disappeared. Others raped the Jewish women, one of whom, Sarah, from Parczew, was murdered by a Russian partisan when she resisted his attempt to rape her. Her murderer was killed by a Jewish partisan.

Only 200 Jews of the family camps survived the war in the Parczew forest, emerging in July 1944 as the Red Army liberated the region.

Map 152

THE 'FAMILY' CAMPS IN THE PARCZEW FOREST, 1942-1943

to Siedlce

Jasionka

Przewloka

0   miles   2

0   kilometres   3

Koczergi

Parczew

Chmielow

Brudno

to Lublin

Bednarzowka

Sowin

Stepkow

Lejtno

Laski

Bojki

Zmiarka

Plebania

Debowa Kloda

Pogulanki

Lake Obradowskie

Makoszka

Uhnin

Buradow

Parczew   forest

Tysmienica

'Altana'

Sojki

Ochoza

and

Marsh

Tabor

Prokop

family camps

Bialka

Borki

Lake Biala

Rudka

New

Lake Czarna

Jedlanka

Ostrow

Old

© Martin Gilbert 1982

During the final year of the war, a Polish partisan battalion, commanded by a Jewish officer, Alexander Skotnicki, was also to make the Parczew forest its base of operations, attacking German military trains on the Lublin-Siedlce railway line. Under his command, Skotnicki had one entirely Jewish company, led by Yehiel Grynszpan. At first, Grynszpan's company had only two rifles and one pistol: but by a series of raids on German military posts, he managed to acquire seven rifles, ammunition, and even a number of grenades. About 150 of these Jewish partisans survived the war.

Map 153

DEPORTATION, MASSACRE AND REVOLT, 21-22 SEPTEMBER 1942

Baranowicze
3,000

WHITE RUSSIA

Pripet

marshes

River Pripet

Treblinka

Jadow
1,000

Sterdyn
2,000

Wegrow
10,500

Sokolow
7,000

Warsaw
2,196

River Bug

Stoczek
2,000

Serokomla
200

UKRAINE

Aleksandrija
1,000

Kamionka Strumilowa
600

Radziechow 600

Jozefow
1,500

Belzec

EASTERN GALICIA

Cholojow

Busk
1,000

Bursztyn
200

Narajow
1,400

Rohatyn
1,000

Brzezany
1,000

Bukaczowce
200

Podhajce
1,000

Bolszowce
1,000

0   miles   60

0   kilometres   100

© Martin Gilbert 1982

The Day of Atonement, the holiest day in the Jewish calendar, fell in 1942 on September 21. During that day and the following day, more than 30,000 Jews were murdered in eastern Europe. From Wegrow and Sokolow hundreds managed to escape to nearby woods but most were quickly hunted down and shot. In the following week (*opposite, above*) thousands more were killed or deported. At Tuczyn 2,000 Jews managed to escape. At Korzec 50 Jews who escaped built up a small partisan unit.

On September 25 the SS seized more than 700 Rumanian-born Jews in Paris, and deported them to Auschwitz. The deportees had been born throughout Rumania (*opposite, below*), among them the 46-year-old Estera Bercovici and her six children. Many children were deported without parents or relatives, among them two 8-year-olds, Suzanne Sloim and Raymond Toutman. Sarah Sepolghi, aged 33, was deported with her ten-month-old baby, Paul. Of the 1,594 deportees on this single train, only 15 able-bodied men, who had been among those 'selected' for slave labour, survived the war.

DEPORTATION, MASSACRE AND REVOLT, 23-30 SEPTEMBER 1942

| 0 | miles | 50 |
| 0 | kilometres | 80 |

Pripet marshes

Ivanova
1,000
24 September

Serniki
850 *killed*
150 *escape to the forests*
29 September
only **10** *survive the war*

River Bug

VOLHYNIA

Miedzyrzec
1,500

resistance led by
Misha Gildenman

1,000 *killed*
2,000 *escape to the forests*
23 September
only **15** *survive the war*

Tuczyn
revolt led by
Gecel Schwarzman
Meir Himmelfarb
Tuwia Czuwak
23 September

Korzec
2,000
30 September

Hoszcza
500

GREATER

GERMANY

Belzec

REICHSKOMMISSARIAT

UKRAINE

Zborow
1,000

from
Skala Podolska
1,500
26 September

EASTERN GALICIA

Pomorzany
1,000

Tarnopol
1,000
30 September

© Martin Gilbert 1982

RUMANIAN-BORN JEWS DEPORTED FROM PARIS, 25 SEPTEMBER 1942

| 0 | miles | 80 |
| 0 | kilometres | 60 |

TRANSYLVANIA

Czernowitz

TRANSNISTRIA

River Bug

UKRAINE

Sighet
(Marmarosszighet)

BUKOVINA

Dorohoi
Botosani

Balti

Satu Mare

Campulung

Falticeni

Stefanesti

MOLDAVIA

Jassy

River

Dubossary

Nikolaiev

Kishinev

Odessa

Oradea

Targu Neamt

Piatra Neamt

Roman

BESSARABIA

Dniester

Bendery

Bacau

Barlad

River Pruth

Cetatea Alba

RUMANIA

Focsani

Tatarbunary

Galati

Braila

Sulina

Tulcea

Black Sea

Ploesti

Bucharest

Calarasi

© Martin Gilbert 1982

DEPORTATIONS TO CHELMNO AND TREBLINKA, 23 SEPTEMBER-5 OCTOBER 1942

WARTHEGAU

River Vistula

Chelmno

Lodz
16,000
23-30 September

Warsaw

see map 157

Treblinka

Siedlce

Biala Podlaska
4,000
26 September

River Bug

Zelechow

Kozienice
13,000
27 September

Szydlowiec
10,000
23 September

G E N E R A L
G O V E R N M E N T

River Vistula

Czestochowa
39,000
23 September - 5 October

© Martin Gilbert 1982

SEVEN FURTHER DEPORTATIONS TO TREBLINKA

Treblinka

River Bug

Kosow Lacki
5,000
23 September

Stanislawow
700 *25 September*

Kaluszyn
2,000
25 September

Warsaw

River Vistula

Kolbiel
1,000
27 September

Parysow
4,000
30 September escape

Siedlce
2,000
26 September

Zelechow
10,000
30 September

© Martin Gilbert 1982

In the middle of September the SS, having decided to make the Lodz ghetto an entirely 'working' ghetto, launched the 'Gehsperre' action, aimed at deporting to Chelmno all children up to the age of 10, all men and women over 60, and all who were sick or emaciated. In all, 16,000 Jews were deported and gassed within two weeks (*above*). East of Warsaw (*left*) more than 24,000 Jews were deported to Treblinka and killed.

The deportations from the General Government also continued on a massive scale (*above*). From one town, Zelechow, a few hundred young Jews managed to escape into the woods and form a partisan group. But most Jews were trapped by the overwhelming German military might.

From Paris the deportations to Auschwitz continued, bringing to the gas chambers Jews born throughout Asia (*opposite, above*), the Dutch East Indies and North Africa (*opposite, below*); men and women who had sought a new life in Paris before 1939.

JEWS BORN IN AFRICA & ASIA, DEPORTED FROM PARIS TO AUSCHWITZ

RUSSIA

German front line, October 1942

Auschwitz

Paris

German front line October 1942

Sahara desert

Lake Baikal

Chita
Pinchas Reznik aged 36

Samarkand
Henrietta Fiess aged 45

CHINA

Tashkent
Moise Rubin aged 42

Tientsin
*Gerda Hecht aged 32
Eva Niwesz aged 40*

AFGHANISTAN

Bukhara
Piena Slama aged 33

Kabul
Abraham Kaufmann aged 63

Calcutta
Murad Gubbay aged 68

Hong Kong
Henry Ullman aged 60

INDIA

Bombay
Louise Andjel aged 43

Bay of Bengal

South China Sea

BELGIAN CONGO

Stanleyville
Rosette Kadaner aged 19

Indian Ocean

DUTCH EAST INDIES
Batavia
Dick Prins aged 24

Bandoeng
Rubin Zonge aged 51

Surabaja
Jacob Prins aged 28

Kimberley
Bertha Tint aged 36

SOUTH AFRICA

© Martin Gilbert 1982

JEWS BORN IN NORTH AFRICA, DEPORTED FROM PARIS TO AUSCHWITZ, 1942-1944

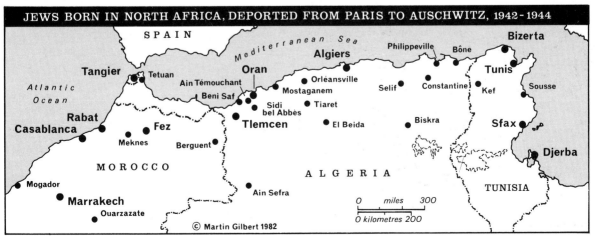

SPAIN

Mediterranean Sea

Bizerta

Philippeville   Bône

Algiers

Tunis

Tangier   Tetuan

Aïn Témouchant

Oran

Orléansville

Selif   Constantine   Kef

Sousse

Atlantic Ocean

Beni Saf

Mostaganem

Sidi bel Abbès   Tiaret

Rabat

Fez

Tlemcen

El Beida

Biskra

Sfax

Casablanca

Meknes

Berguent

MOROCCO

Marrakech

Mogador

Ouarzazate

Aïn Sefra

ALGERIA

Djerba

TUNISIA

0   miles   300

0 kilometres 200

© Martin Gilbert 1982

127

DEPORTATIONS AND REVOLT, 1-14 OCTOBER 1942

Z = Zarki
800
6 October

K = Koniecpol
1,600
7 October

Treblinka

Radzymin
3,900
2 October

Wolomin
2,400
4 October

Miedzyrzec
6,000
6 October

Kobryn
4,000
14 October

Siedlce

Biala Podlaska
1,200
6 October

Sobienie
Jeziory
4,000
2 October

Ludwisin
1,000
4 October

Lukow
7,000

Radzyn
1,000
1 October

Firlej
317

Sobibor

Konskowola
2,000

Lubartow
4,500
11 October

Luboml

Resistance group 'Lions' led by
Julian Ajzenman
sabotage
railway line

Opoczno

Opole
3,000

Gorzkowice
1,500

Przedborz
4,500

Konskie
9 October

Skarzysko
2,200

Belzyce
3,000

Majdanek

U

Radomsko
14,000
10-12 October

Ostrowiec
11,000
11 October

A   D

Zakrzowek
1,176 to Belzec

K

Lagow
2,000
7 October

Modliborzyce
2,202 to Belzec

Z

from
Holland
1,014 2 October

Chmielnik
8,000
6 October

Belzec

2,012 5 October

Wislica
3,000
3 October

Busko
Zdroj
2,000
1 October

A = Annopol
1,943 to Belzec

U = Urzedow
500 to Belzec

D = Dzierkowice
146 to Belzec

1,703 9 October

1,711 12 October

Auschwitz

0   miles   40
0   kilometers   60

© Martin Gilbert 1982

MORE KILLINGS, SEPTEMBER - OCTOBER 1942

0   miles   100
0   kilometres   150

Baltic
Sea

Koziany
400 30 September

Korzeniec
2,000
9 Sept

Kobylnik
150 29 September

Grodek
1,600 11 September

Danzig

Wolozyn
1,000 29 September

Rakow
112 21 September

GREATER
GERMANY

Warsaw

Janow
2,000
24 August

Kiev

CZORTKOW
REGION
Jezierzany
900
Kopyczynce
1,500
Korolowka
700
Mielnica
1,000
Probuzna
1,500

Belzec

to Belzec

Buczacz
1,500

Horodenka
1,500 8-10 September

© Martin Gilbert 1982

Among the Jews murdered in September 1942 *(left)* were 1,000 from the town of Wolozyn, formerly a centre of Jewish spiritual learning. In Eastern Galicia Jews had been deported to Belzec from seven communities, some of them small villages in the Czortkow region.

Throughout October 1942 the deportations continued. From Holland *(above)* and Belgium *(opposite, above)*, Jews were brought to Auschwitz *(see also page 130)*. From central Poland and Theresienstadt they were deported to Treblinka, with as many as 30 deportations during the last two weeks of October *(opposite, below)*; and from eastern Galicia to Belzec *(opposite, above)*. East of Greater Germany, the Jews were killed in the streets, or in nearby woods and quarries, including 10,000 in the Volhynian town of Luboml.

DEPORTATION, MASSACRE AND REVOLT, 1-31 OCTOBER 1942

Baltic Sea

GREATER

GERMANY

from Belgium

German front line

Bystrzycza *hundreds*

Kiemieliszki *hundreds*

Oszmiana 406 *23 October*

Nowogrodek 50 Jews escape to join resistance led by *Tobias Bielski*

Bielsk Podlaski 11,000 *2 October*

Treblinka

Siedlce

Ryki | Parczew 108

Kosow 300 *14 October*

Antopol 1,000

Drohiczyn 2,500 *15 October*

Szack 150

Kamen Kashirsky 300 *14 October*

Luboml | Warkowicze

Zdolbunow 1,000

Mizocz | Ostrog

999 *10 October*
675 *16 October*
995 *20 October*
476 *24 October*
822 *31 October*
875 *31 October*

Belzec

EASTERN GALICIA

Auschwitz

Theresienstadt
1,000 *5 October*
1,998 *15 October*
2,018 *22 October*
1,000 *8 October*
1,984 *19 October*

Czortkow 500

Tluste 1,000 *5 October*

Kolomyja 4,500 *3 October*

Bar 12,000

Luboml 10,000 *1 October*
hundreds escape but later hunted down

Warkowicze 400 *killed* | 1,600 *escape*

Mizocz 850 | 850

Ostrog 2,200 | 800 *escape*

0 miles 150
0 kilometres 200

© Martin Gilbert 1982

THIRTY DEPORTATIONS TO TREBLINKA, 15-31 OCTOBER 1942

to Treblinka

Koluszki 3,000

Biala Rawska 4,000

Rawa Mazowiecka 4,000

Ryki 2,000

Ujazd 800

Tomaszow Mazowiecki 7,000

Drzewica 2,000

Przytyk 1,000

Deblin 1,500

Przyglow 2,000

Opoczno 3,000

Gnielniow 250

Przysucha 4,000

Ciepielow 600

Chotcza Nowa 4,000

Lublin

Sulejow 1,500

Zarnow 2,000

Ilza 2,000

Sienno 2,000

Kamiensk 500

Konskie 4,500

Starachowice 4,500

Tarlow 10,000

Cmielow 900

Ozarow 4,500

Opatow 6,000

Iwaniska 1,600

Klimontow 4,000

Koprzywnica 1,600

Pinczow *see page 135*

Osiek 500

0 miles 25
0 kilometres 40

© Martin Gilbert 1982

129

Map 164

DEPORTATIONS TO AUSCHWITZ, 15–31 OCTOBER 1942

NORWAY

Oslo
209
25 October 1942

930
escape

Skagerrak

Kattegat

SWEDEN

neutral

North Sea

DENMARK

Baltic Sea

HOLLAND

Stettin

1,170
16 October
1,327
19 October
988
23 October
841
26 October
659
30 October

Sachsenhausen
several thousand
17 October 1942   *revolt*

Berlin

Frankfurt-on-Oder

0   *miles*   100

0   *kilometres*   150

BELGIUM

to Auschwitz

G R E A T E R   G E R M A N Y

Leipzig

Dresden

Liegnitz

Breslau

Bebra

Buchenwald
10,000
17 October 1942

Oppeln

Auschwitz

Offenbach
759

Theresienstadt
1,866
26 October 1942

Prague

Moravska Ostrava

Prerov   SLOVAKIA

© Martin Gilbert 1982

The map above shows ten of the deportations from western Europe and Norway to Auschwitz in the second half of October 1942. In addition to these deportations, and four from Belgium (*page 129*), the Auschwitz calendar records a further train reaching the camp from Slovakia on October 23.

Within six months of the German occupation of Norway in April 1940 (*page 45*), Jews had been forbidden to participate in professional life. Forcible registration of

Map 165

FURTHER DEPORTATIONS, MASSACRE AND REVOLT, 15-31 OCTOBER 1942

0 miles 40
0 kilometres 60

Ciechanowiec **3,000** *15 October*

Bereza Kartuska **3,500** *16 October*

Pinsk **10,000** *28 October*

Treblinka

Latowicz **800** *15 October*

Siennica **700** *18 October*

for the other Treblinka deportations 15-31 October 1942 see page 129

Brest-Litovsk **25,000** *resistance led by* Hana Ginsberg *15 October*

Przytyk

Wlodawa **2,000**

Sobibor

REICHSKOMMISSARIAT UKRAINE

Leczna **1,000**

Siedliszcze **1,000**

Lublin **1,800**

Chelm **3,300**

Demidowka **500**

Opole **2,000**

Krasnystaw **10,000**

Izbica

Hrubieszow **2,000**

Targowica **700** *killed* **200** *escape*

Mlynow **500**

Zawichost **5,000**

Krasnik **1,000**

Sokal **2,500**

Dubno **3,000**

Murawica **150**

Szczebrzeszyn **1,000**

Zamosc **4,000**

Radzwillow **1,800** **600** *escape*

Sandomierz **3,200**

Ulanow **500**

Bilgoraj **500** Belzec

Lopatin **400**

Zbaraz **1,000**

resistance led by Michael Majtek Zalman Fajnsztat

Pinczow **3,000**

GENERAL

Kamionka Strumilowa **500**

Auschwitz

Skalat **3,000**

Cracow **6,000** *deported* **300** *children killed on the spot 28 October*

GOVERNMENT

Sambor **3,000** *deported naked to prevent revolt*

Podhajce **1,500**

Drohobycz **2,300**

Stryj **2,000**

Monasterzyska **2,500**

Buczacz **1,500**

SLOVAKIA

© Martin Gilbert 1982

all Jews took place in June 1942, and the confiscation of all Jewish property in October 1942. Then, on October 25, all Jewish men and boys over the age of sixteen, some 209 in all, were seized throughout the country, sent by sea from Norway to Stettin, and then on by rail to Auschwitz. A further 531 women and children were seized on November 25 *(page 133)*, and likewise sent to their deaths. Only 12 of the 740 deportees survived the war.

Helped by the Norwegian people, often at the risk of their own lives, as many as 930 Norwegian Jews succeeded in escaping into neutral Sweden. About 60 were imprisoned or interned inside Norway itself.

The map above shows some of the deportations to the eastern death camps during the same two-week period. Before the deportation from Drohobycz, nearly 200 old and sick Jews were shot in the streets of the town. Among the executions on the spot was the killing of 25,000 Jews in Brest-Litovsk. Almost all the other Jews of Brest, some 5,000, had been murdered in June 1941 *(page 67)*. Most of the few hundred Jews still alive managed to join partisan units.

Among the deportations during these two weeks was one from Przytyk to Treblinka *(page 129)*. It was the murder of three Jews in Przytyk before the Second World War *(page 21)* that had created such alarm among Polish Jewry, reviving memories of the Tsarist pogroms. But in the autumn of 1942 the deportation and immediate murder of 1,000 Jews from the same village, deaths horrific in themselves, were dwarfed by the total number of deaths in only two weeks, in eastern Poland alone, of more than 100,000 men, women and children.

Map 166

DEPORTATION AND RESISTANCE, 1-6 NOVEMBER 1942

Ciechanow
1,000

Bielsk

BIALYSTOK REGION
over **110,000**
see map opposite

Plonsk
12,000
1 November - 5 December

Treblinka

Gowarczow
1,000

Tomaszow Mazowiecki
7,000
3 November

Miedzyrzec
1,500
7 November

Sobibor

Skarzysko-Kamienna
slave labour camp

Chelm
10,000
6 November

Radoszyce
4,000
3 November

Krasnik

resistance led by
Abraham Braun
Eduard Forst

Frampol
600

Jozefow
600 *2 November*

Belzec

Zloczow
2,500
2 November including the poet
S.J.Imber

Konskie
6,000
6 November

Stopnica
5,000
5 November

Krzeszow
500 *shot*
2 November

Tarnogrod
3,000
2 November

Szczucin

GENERAL

GOVERNMENT

Bilgoraj
4,000
2 November

Lvov
8,000

Komarno
2,000

Brzezany
1,000
4 November

Auschwitz

Boryslaw
600
5 November
deported naked to prevent revolt

0 — miles — 50
0 — kilometres — 80

SLOVAKIA

© Martin Gilbert 1982

In November 1942 the Dutch, French and Norwegian deportations continued (*opposite, above*). Further east, Jews were slaughtered at Slutsk; and at Proskurov, where 1,700 Jews had been killed in 1919 (*page 15*), the last 7,000 Jews were murdered.

On November 2 one of the most carefully organized and intensive round-ups of the war took place throughout the Bialystok region (*opposite, below*), where more than 20,000 Jews had already been murdered during the first two months of the German invasion (*pages 67 and 68*). The remaining 110,000 Jews, who had been strictly confined to their towns and villages, were now seized and sent to camps at Zambrow, Wolkowysk, Bogusze and Kielbasin, before being taken

by train to Treblinka and Auschwitz. When the Jews of Marcinkance resisted deportation, all were shot in the village.

At Siemiatycze a few dozen Jews managed to escape to nearby forests and to form a small resistance group. Most were then killed by Polish partisan bands.

Further south, at Stopnica (*above*), 1,500 men were sent to the slave labour camps at Skarzysko Kamienna, while 400 children and old people were shot in the town cemetery. The remaining 3,000 Jews were marched to Szczucin, many being shot on the way, and the survivors sent on by train to Treblinka, at which, with Belzec and Auschwitz, more than 170,000 Jews were killed within one week (*above*).

DISTANT DEPORTATIONS AND MASS MURDER, NOVEMBER 1942

Bergen
531 *women and girls*

North Sea

Baltic Sea

HOLLAND
5,199

Leningrad

Moscow

Grodno
6,000
14 November

German front line, November 1942

GREATER GERMANY

Slutsk
5,000
11 November

Stalingrad

Paris
4,000

Auschwitz

Proskurov
7,000
30 November

Caucasus

0 — miles — 400
0 — kilometres — 500

© Martin Gilbert 1982

SIXTY-FIVE DEPORTATIONS FROM THE BIALYSTOK REGION, 2 NOVEMBER 1942

to the Leningrad front

to Konigsberg and the Baltic

360 *killed on the spot*

Marcinkance

Porzecze **1,000**

Augustow **2,000**

Sopockinie **2,000**

Druskieniki **500**

GREATER EAST PRUSSIA

Bogusze *slave labour camp*

Rajgrod **400**

Dabrowa Bialostocka **1,000**

Grodno **4,500**

Ostryna **2,000**

Grajewo **2,500**

Jeziory **2,000**

Szczuczyn **1,500**

Suchowola **5,100**

Kuznica **1,000**

Skidel **3,000**

Wasosz **50**

Goniadz **1,280**

Sidra **350**

Kielbasin *slave labour camp*

Lunna **1,500**

River Niemen

Stawiski **60**

Janow **950**

Korycin **1,000**

BIALYSTOK

Mosty **350**

GREATER

Radzilow **22**

Sokolka **8,000**

Indura **2,500**

Krynki **5,000**

Wolpa **1,500**

Jedwabne **30**

Trzcianne **1,200**

Knyszyn **1,300**

Wasilkow **1,180**

Suprasl **170**

REGION

Ros **1,000**

to the Moscow front

Nowogrod **36**

Lomza **7,000**

Zawady **180**

Bialystok

Wolkowysk **7,000**

GERMANY

Rutki **20**

Choroszcz **440**

Grodek **1,300**

Michalowo **750**

Swislocz **3,000**

Sniadowo **650**

Zambrow **2,000**

Lapy **600**

Zabludow **2,000**

Rozana **3,000**

Wysokie **3,700**

Sokoly **850**

Narew **400**

Jalowka **850**

Porozow **1,000**

Lyskow **600**

Lubotyn **174**

Czyzew **200**

Bielsk **5,000**

Orla **2,000**

Klukowo **68**

Malkinia Junction

River Bug

Bransk **2,600**

Bocki **756**

Treblinka

Ciechanowiec **700**

Milejczyce **1,000**

Kleszczele **1,000**

Pruzana **3,000**

resistance led by Herschl Shabbes

GENERAL GOVERNMENT

Siemiatycze **6,000**

Drohiczyn **500**

to Germany

0 — miles — 20
0 — kilometres — 30

© Martin Gilbert 1982

Map 169

JEWS DEPORTED FROM PROVINCIAL FRANCE, 3 NOVEMBER 1942

English Channel

St.Quentin
37

to Auschwitz

Rouen

Caen
5

Drancy

Châlons
sur Marne
52

Nancy
234

Paris

Melun
69

Troyes
3

Rennes
36

GERMAN-OCCUPIED

FRANCE

Angers
296

Poitiers
617

Bay

of

Biscay

VICHY

FRANCE

Lyons

Angoulême
9

Merignac

Bordeaux
135

0   miles   100

0   kilometres   140

© Martin Gilbert 1982

Among the deportations to Auschwitz in November 1942 was one, from Paris on November 3, which included several hundred Jews who had been seized in provincial France *(above)*.

Of the 1,000 Jews deported on that day, 200 were children, deported with their parents or grandparents; including the 4-year-old twins, Annie and Lydia Kirzner, the 2-year-old Jacques Wlademirski, the 4-year-old Daniel Szulc, and the Zajdenwerger children, David aged 4 and his sister, Solange, aged 3. All were gassed.

The map opposite *(top)* shows some of the other birthplaces of those deported from Paris to Auschwitz on November 3. Some were old people, such as Gabriel Erlich, from Warsaw, aged 70, deported with his wife, and his two daughters, aged 36 and 38.

Many of the deportees, like the Erlich daughters, were in the prime of life: Magalta

Poulios, from the Greek island of Chios, was 35; Jean Blumenthal, from Berlin, was 27; so also was Joseph Rozio from the Turkish port of Smyrna; Robert Geyer from Metz was just 20; Gabrielle Bruski from Budapest was only 18. Deported all alone was a boy, the 4-year-old Jankiel Ciesielski, who had been born in Lodz.

The two smaller maps *(opposite, below)* give the birthplaces and names of some of the hundreds of Jews deported from Paris to Auschwitz between 1942 and 1944 who had been born in the Americas. At least 10 were still United States citizens at the time of their deportation. Between the wars all had chosen to come to Europe; to teach, to work, to marry and to bring up children.

The photograph was taken during one of the Paris deportations; more than 80,000 Jews were deported from Paris to Auschwitz in little over two years.

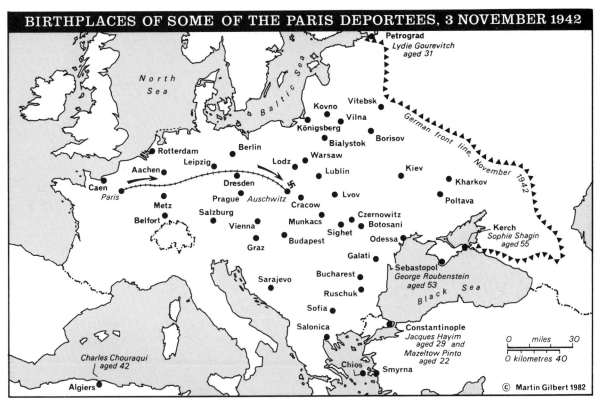

BIRTHPLACES OF SOME OF THE PARIS DEPORTEES, 3 NOVEMBER 1942

North Sea

Baltic Sea

Petrograd
Lydie Gourevitch aged 31

German front line, November 1942

Kovno
Vitebsk
Vilna
Königsberg
Borisov
Bialystok
Berlin
Warsaw
Rotterdam
Leipzig
Lodz
Aachen
Lublin
Kiev
Dresden
Caen
Paris
Prague *Auschwitz*
Kharkov
Metz
Cracow
Lvov
Poltava
Salzburg
Munkacs
Czernowitz
Belfort
Vienna
Sighet
Botosani
Kerch
Sophie Shagin aged 55
Graz
Budapest
Odessa
Galati
Sebastopol
George Roubenstein aged 53
Sarajevo
Bucharest
Ruschuk
Black Sea
Sofia
Salonica
Constantinople
Jacques Hayim aged 29 and Mazeltow Pinto aged 22

Charles Chouraqui aged 42

Chios
Smyrna

0 miles 30
0 kilometres 40

Algiers

© Martin Gilbert 1982

AMERICAN-BORN JEWS DEPORTED TO AUSCHWITZ

0 miles 400
0 kilometres 600

Chicago
Robert Schillio aged 48

Port Chester
Erna Abelson aged 24

New York
Yetta Flater aged 35
Clara Kahn aged 81
Pola Modiano aged 81
Michel Feldman aged 55
Morris Churinski aged 74
Paul Francfort aged 53
Fanny Goldberg aged 33

St Louis
Hety Baum aged 72
Louis Haas aged 51
Benjamin Bloch aged 38

Williamstown
Zadie Abraham aged 89

Texarkana
Berthe Francfort aged 48

© Martin Gilbert 1982

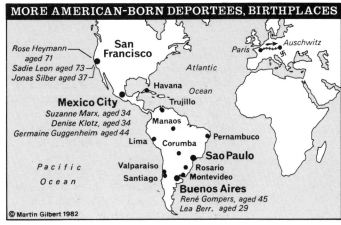

MORE AMERICAN-BORN DEPORTEES, BIRTHPLACES

Rose Heymann aged 71
Sadie Leon aged 73
Jonas Silber aged 37

San Francisco

Paris Auschwitz

Atlantic Ocean

Havana
Trujillo

Mexico City
Suzanne Marx, aged 34
Denise Klotz, aged 34
Germaine Guggenheim aged 44

Manaos

Lima
Corumba
Pernambuco

Sao Paulo

Pacific Ocean

Valparaiso
Santiago
Rosario
Montevideo

Buenos Aires
René Gompers, aged 45
Lea Berr. aged 29

© Martin Gilbert 1982

135

Map 173

DEPORTATION, MASSACRE AND REVOLT, 7-30 NOVEMBER 1942

Mlawa | 6,300 | *10 November*

Makow | 500 | *14 November*

Treblinka

Wyszogrod | 2,700 | *19 November*

Warsaw

Miedzyrzec Podlaski | 1,500 | *7 November*

Serokomla | 200 | *shot* | *22 November*

Lukow | 3,000 | *7 November*

Wisznice | 120 | *shot* | *20 November*

Danilowicze | 900 | *21 November*

Szydlowiec | 10,000 | *23 November*

Gniewoszow | 1,000 | *15 November*

Leczna | 1,000 | *11 November*

Komarow Osada | 1,000 | *10 November*

Konskie | 4,500 | *7 November*

Zwolen | 10,000 | *29 November*

Majdanek

Piaski | 4,000 | *9 November*

Wlodzimierz Wolynski | 2,500 | *13 November resistance*

Szczekociny | 1,500 | *21 November*

Suchedniow | 4,000 | *21 November*

Zamosc | 4,000 | *15 November*

Goraj | 30 | *shot* | *30 November*

Belzec

Brody | 250 | *to Belzec* | 20 | *shot* | *26 November*

Sedziszow | 1,000 | *21 November*

Staszow | 6,000 | *7 November*

Kolbuszowa | 2,500

Lubaczow

Zolkiew | 2,500 | *22 November*

Busk | 1,000 | *shot*

Zbaraz | 1,000 | *8 November*

Ksiaz Wielki | 500 | *shot*

Cracow

Rzeszow | 2,000

Przemysl | 4,000 | *18 November*

Sasow | 400 | *25 November*

Bochnia | 570 | *10 November*

Tarnow | 3,000 | *15 November*

Rudki | 800

Lvov | 5,000 | *18 November*

Skalat | 1,100 | *9 November*

Zakliczyn | 500

'Amsterdam' Jewish resistance group active, November 1942 – November 1944

Stryj | 1,500 | *to Belzec*

Buczacz | 2,750 | *27 November*

SLOVAKIA

Jaworow | 1,500 | *7 November*

Szczerzec | 600

Tlumacz | 2,000 | *27 November*

Mosciska | 2,500 | *28 November*

© Martin Gilbert 1982

0 — miles — 50
0 — kilometres — 80

During the last three weeks of November more than 50,000 Jews were deported to the death camps of Treblinka and Belzec, sent to the concentration camp at Majdanek, now a death camp; or, as in Wlodzimierz Wolynski, massacred in the streets *(above)*.

In the course of a few hours ancient communities were totally destroyed: the Jews of Wyszogrod could trace their first settlement in the town to the early fifteenth century, those of Buczacz to the late sixteenth century.

It was in Buczacz that the author S. Y. Agnon, a Nobel prizewinner, had been born in 1907; at the age of 20, he had emigrated to Palestine. After a visit to Buczacz in 1930, he published a nightmarish picture of his home town, its synagogues empty, its society collapsed, its people shattered: a 'city of the dead'.

In Buczacz, following the first killings in August 1941 *(page 69),* and the deportations of October 1942 *(page 131),* young men and women had searched for arms, and tried to

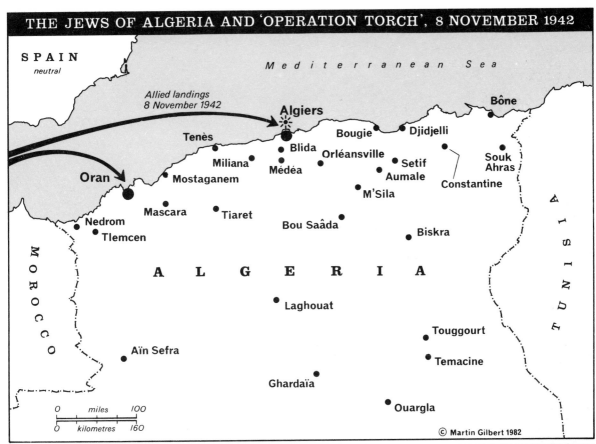

THE JEWS OF ALGERIA AND 'OPERATION TORCH', 8 NOVEMBER 1942

SPAIN
neutral

Mediterranean Sea

Allied landings 8 November 1942

Algiers

Bône

Tenès · Bougie · Djidjelli

Blida · Orléansville · Souk Ahras

Miliana · Médéa · Setif · Aumale

Oran Mostaganem · M'Sila · Constantine

Mascara · Tiaret · Bou Saâda · Biskra

Nedrom · Tlemcen

MOROCCO

A L G E R I A

Laghouat

Aïn Sefra · Touggourt · Temacine

Ghardaïa · Ouargla

T U N I S I A

0 miles 100
0 kilometres 160

© Martin Gilbert 1982

train themselves for a breakout. In mid-1943 (*page 161*), when the SS liquidated the ghetto, some Jews managed to escape to the forest. But most were murdered near the Jewish cemetery on the outskirt of the town.

It was not only in Europe, but also in North Africa (*above*) that Jews were at risk. Jews were active throughout the Algerian resistance, and it was a Jew, Jose Abulker, who led the uprising in Algiers, tying down the Vichy French and 'neutralizing' the capital, as the Allies carried out 'Operation Torch', the landings of 8 November 1942. For the 117,000 Jews of Algeria, the Allied landings brought security from deportation.

With the almost simultaneous German defeats at Stalingrad and El Alamein (*right*) the Allied landings in North Africa marked a major turning point of the war. But a full year and a half were to pass before the Red Army reached the first of the death camps on Polish soil, Majdanek (*page 200*), or the western Allies landed on the Normandy beaches (*page 201*). During those eighteen months the deportation of Jews continued without respite throughout Nazi-dominated Europe.

STALINGRAD, EL ALAMEIN, 'TORCH'

0 miles 400
0 kilometres 800

North Sea

Baltic Sea

Leningrad *besieged*

SOVIET RUSSIA

Atlantic Ocean

GREATER GERMANY Warsaw · Cracow

Stalingrad *relieved*

Black Sea

Oran Algiers
Allied landings

Mediterranean Sea

EGYPT

El Alamein
Germans defeated

© Martin Gilbert 1982

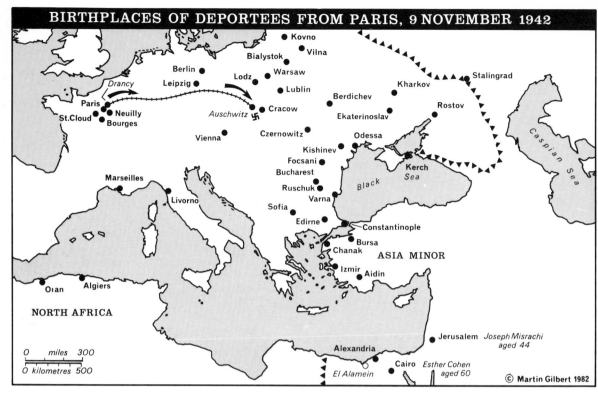

BIRTHPLACES OF DEPORTEES FROM PARIS, 9 NOVEMBER 1942

© Martin Gilbert 1982

GREEK-BORN DEPORTEES FROM PARIS

© Martin Gilbert 1982

On 9 November 1942 it was the turn of Jews who had been born in Greece to be seized in Paris and deported to Auschwitz. More than 800 of these deportees had been born in Salonica (*above*): nearly 100 or them were children under 12. Among those from the ancient town of Drama were Jacques and Nicoula Benveniste, and their daughter Liza, aged 19. From Canea, in Crete, had come the 67-year-old Moise Cohen.

As with each of the previous Paris deportations, there were Jews who had been born throughout Europe (*above*), North Africa and Asia Minor. Esther Cohen had been born in Cairo 60 years before, Joseph Misrahi in Jerusalem 44 years before, Solomon Moscowitz in the port of Kerch in 1877.

In the General Government several thousand Jews, from four communities, had been in hiding in the forests since the spring (*opposite, above*). On November 10 a German promise of the security of a new ghetto led more than 6,000 of them to agree to come out in return for safe conduct. Starving and freezing, they were taken to Sandomierz: but two months later, on 10 January 1943, almost all of them were deported to Treblinka and gassed, only a few hundred being sent to labour camps at Skarzysko Kamienna and Sandomierz itself.

In the province of Zamosc (*opposite, below*) it was Poles who faced Nazi brutality. To enable SS men, ethnic Germans and Ukrainians to settle in the province's rich pastureland, tens of thousands of Poles were driven from their homes, and hundreds killed. At the same time, thousands of Polish children were deported to concentration camps. In all more than 100 villages were emptied of their inhabitants, and more than 40,000 Poles expelled.

ESCAPE, DECEPTION AND DEPORTATION, 10 NOVEMBER 1942

POLES EXPELLED AND MURDERED, 27 NOVEMBER - 31 DECEMBER 1942

DEPORTATION, MASSACRE AND REVOLT, DECEMBER 1942

O miles 40
O kilometres 60

Dworzec

Slonim
300
and 500 escaped to
join the partisans

Baranowicze
3,000
17 December

3,000 killed
slave labour camp
19 December

to Treblinka
4,000
8 December
to Auschwitz
1,500
6 December

Makow

Treblinka

Minsk
Mazowiecki
slave labour camp
218
24 December

Nowy Dwor
and

Czerwinsk
2,000
12 December

Karczew
slave labour camp
400
1 December

Miedzyrzec
500

Biala Podlaska
231 shot
17 December

Pinsk
150
23 December
the last artisans
murdered

Radzyn
1,500
20 December

Sobibor
4 escape, betrayed in
a nearby village and shot
25 December

Kruszyna
slave labour camp
557 killed
17 December

Kielce
ghetto resistance
organized

Trawniki
slave labour
camp

Luck
500

slave labour camp
remnant murdered
12 December

Czestochowa
ghetto resistance
organized

Stalowa Wola
slave labour camp
2 Jews shot for mutiny
28 December

Parczew
forest
resistance groups
active

Belzec

Rawa Ruska
several thousands
7-11 December

Brody acts of
resistance led by

Jakub Linder

Samuel Weiler and

Solomon Halberszstadt

Auschwitz

Cracow
attacks on Gestapo officers
20 Jews killed including
the resistance leader
Adolf Liebeskind
24 December

Krosno
600
4 December

Rohatyn
1,250
8 December

Bursztyn

Bolszowce

Bukaczowce

Buczacz

Czortkow
acts of resistance led by

Meir Waserman

Ryuwen Rosenburg

Heniek Nusbaum

Mundek Nusbaum

© Martin Gilbert 1982

THREE DEPORTATIONS, THREE MASSACRES

North
Sea

Baltic Sea

Westerbork

Postawy
2,500
25 December 1942

Iwje
150
31 December 1942

Berlin

Korelicze
1,000

Auschwitz

HOLLAND GREATER
GERMANY

817 4 December
927 8 December
757 12 December 1942

O miles 300
O kms 400

Black
Sea

© Martin Gilbert 1982

From western Europe the deportations from
Holland to Auschwitz continued (*left*). But
by the end of 1942 the deportation of Polish
Jews to Belzec and Treblinka had almost
ended, and in many regions (*above*) only the
remnants of communities now remained. In
slave labour camps Jews were also murdered.

Throughout German-occupied Poland, as
in the Parczew forest, Jewish resistance had
become more organized. In Buczacz the Jews
were preparing to break out of the ghetto. In
Cracow the Jewish Fighters' Organization, set
up in July 1942, carried out acts of sabotage.
Elsewhere, acts of resistance, escape to the
forests, preparation for uprisings, and even
escape from the death camps, continued,

Map 182

GYPSY DEPORTATIONS, MASSACRES, AND REVOLT, 1939-1945

NORWAY
60

ESTONIA
1,000

LATVIA
2,500

LITHUANIA
1,000

REICHSKOMMISSARIAT
OSTLAND
30,000

HOLLAND
500

BELGIUM
500

POLAND
35,000

Bialystok
2,600

Nieswiez
revolt

Bergen
Belsen

Ravensbrück
Sachsenhausen
Chelmno

Treblinka

Babi Yar
hundreds

GREATER

Sobibor

VOLHYNIA
4,000

Gross
Rosen

Majdanek

Buchenwald

revolt
Auschwitz

Belzec

Lierenfeld
sterilization

GERMANY
15,000

Dachau

Nikolaiev

Valogne
sterilization

LUXEMBOURG
200

Natzweiler

SLOVAKIA
1,000

Tiraspol

Mauthausen
AUSTRIA
6,500

HUNGARY
28,000

BOHEMIA
6,500

RUMANIA
36,000

Simferopol
800

FRANCE
15,000

SWITZ.

CROATIA
28,000

ITALY
1,000

Zemun

Jasenovac

ALBANIA
thousands

SERBIA
12,000

Black Sea

Baltic Sea

© Martin Gilbert 1982

0   miles   200
0   kilometres   300

against formidable odds.

Like the Jews, Europe's Gypsies were marked for destruction by the Nazis (*above*). Following a decree of 16 December 1942, all German Gypsies were deported to Auschwitz. On 29 March 1943 the order was given to deport all Dutch Gypsies to Auschwitz. All over Europe, as shown above, Gypsy communities were destroyed. Several Gypsy revolts are recorded. But like the Jews, the Gypsies had to face a combination of artificially intensified 'race' hatred, meticulous planning, continual deception, and overwhelming military power.

Many Gypsies were deported to Jewish ghettos. In Lithuania the Gestapo locked 1,000 Gypsies in a synagogue until they died of starvation. Hundreds were killed alongside Jews, as at Babi Yar. At Valogne, Lierenfeld and Ravensbrück, hundreds of Gypsy women were sterilized. By 1945 more than 220,000 of Europe's 700,000 Gypsies had been murdered by the Nazis. The photograph is of a Gypsy family in Volhynia.

Map 183

DEPORTATION, MASSACRE AND REVOLT, JANUARY 1943

During January 1943, as the deportation of the remaining Jews of Poland continued, many were murdered on the spot, such as the last 200 in Sokolka (*above*) who had been working in a boot factory, the last 27 Jews in Bilgoraj, and the last 17 craftsmen of Dzisna (*opposite*). Deported to Auschwitz (*opposite, above*) were more than 10,000 Jews from

Holland, Theresienstadt and Belgium, as well as 2,000 from Berlin. The last Dutch transport contained 869 invalids and children; all were gassed on arrival.

Jewish resistance was also growing in scale and confidence. In Czestochowa a Jewish resistance group killed 25 German soldiers. But as a reprisal, the SS shot 250 old

142

DISTANT DEPORTATIONS TO AUSCHWITZ, JANUARY 1943

THE LAST SEVENTEEN CRAFTSMEN OF DZISNA, MURDERED

people and children. Reprisals on this scale made acts of resistance all the more perilous. At Pruzana a small group of Jews made contact with nearby Polish partisans, but even this course of action was not free from danger. When the three Sabatkowski brothers, Hayyim, Mordekhai and Herzke, finally reached the forests near Konskie, they were murdered by Polish partisans. While fleeing many Jews were killed by anti-semitic Poles, many other Jews were saved when Poles risked their lives to shelter them.

As the sealed trains reached Treblinka, the Ukrainian guards drove the starving, frightened passengers with whips and rifle butts along the short road to the gas chamber. The road itself was flanked by bogus shops, and the station disguised as a transit point. But by January 1943 it was no longer fear of the unknown but fear of death which filled the deportees, and when one of the trains from Grodno reached Treblinka late in the evening, 1,000 Jews turned on the guards and attacked them with wooden clubs torn from a nearby fence, with knives and with razors. The fight lasted several hours. In the morning all the Jews and the guards were found dead in the snow, killed by SS machine-gun fire and grenades aimed indiscriminately at both.

BIRTHPLACES OF SOME WHO DIED AT DRANCY DURING 1943

Paris
Max Bybeleser aged 28
Ernest Fernbach aged 73
Daniel Halphein aged 62
Yvette Menasse aged 10

Warsaw
Jacob Altglass aged 62
Alexander Imbryezeck aged 67
Ida Prussak aged 88
Mrs Maltz aged 23

Petrograd
Simon Gordon
aged 71

0   miles   200
0   kilometres   300

North Sea

Baltic Sea

Gulf of Finland

Vilna
Hirsch Linkever
aged 81

Poltava
Olga Apostol
aged 71

Warsaw

Pinsk
Nicolas Piekmann
aged 78

Amsterdam
Louis Voorzanger
aged 47

Kalisz
Abraham Szymkiewiecz
aged 61

Radom
Lazare Berman
aged 62

Kiev
Samuel Bistritzky
aged 71

Brody
Mathilde Barbasch
aged 76

Odessa
Sarah Dimonte aged 66
Abraham Lichtenstein aged 71

Drancy
Paris

Reims
Maxime Hirtz aged 57

Nancy
Lucien Weill aged 67

Vienna
Richard Treibb
aged 57

Bacau
Rosa Moscovitch
aged 70

Orleans
Octave Lion
aged 67

Mulhouse
Jean Dreyfus
aged 64
Marcel Bloch
aged 53

Black Sea

Lyon
the widow Weil
aged 71

Adriatic Sea

Dardanelles
Isaac Capsuto
aged 51

Isaac Beressi aged 66
Isaac Emram aged 60
Hugo Mosseri aged 65

Salonica

Constantinople
Bernard Brittman aged 72
Abraham Mires aged 44

New York
Henry Weille aged 60

© Martin Gilbert 1982

EIGHT SWISS-BORN JEWS DEPORTED FROM PARIS TO AUSCHWITZ, 1942-1944

English Channel

FRANCE

Drancy
Paris

GREATER GERMANY

Auschwitz

Betty Rubin aged 37
Lucie Lucas aged 65
Rose Malinsky, aged 37

Bernice Winer, aged 23

Zurich Max Liskin, aged 24

Basle

St. Gallen Isidor Selczer, aged 21

SWITZERLAND

Coire

Geneva **Berne**
Jenny Levis, aged 66

David Weill, aged 65

0   miles   200
0   kilometres   300

© Martin Gilbert 1982

THE JEWS OF TUNIS AT RISK

Bizerta
Mateur · Utica
Souk el Arba · Béja · Tunis
Chemtou · Menzel Bou Zelfa
Testour
Soliman · Nabeul
Lekef
Ebba-Ksour · Sousse
Thala · Monastir
Kairouan · Moknine
Hadjeb-el-Aioun · Mahdia
Sbeitla

under Axis military control

Gafsa · Sfax
El Guettar
Nefta · Tozeur
El Hamma · Hara Kebira
Djerba Island
Gabès · Hara Sghira
Kebili
Zarzis
Médenine
Foum Tatahouine · Ben Gardane

TUNISIA

ALGERIA · LIBYA

0 miles 100
0 kilometres 160

© Martin Gilbert 1982

n preparing to deport Jews from Paris, the Gestapo confined them at Drancy, where conditions were primitive. More than 100 Jews died there during 1943, including many old people (*opposite, above*) who could not stand the continuous privation. Henry Weille had been born in New York in 1883, and Ida Prussak had been born in Warsaw at the time of the Crimean War. Some young people also died in the camp, including the 10-year-old Yvette Menasse.

The photograph was taken by the Germans at Drancy detention camp in 1942.

Even Jews who had been born in neutral Switzerland were not immune from deportation. The Gestapo's own lists of those deported fom Paris record 39 Swiss-born Jews deported to Auschwitz between March 1942 and May 1944: their birthplaces are shown on the map opposite (*below*): both Max Liskin from Zurich and Bernice Winer from Berne were in their early twenties at the time of their deportation.

The Jews of Tunis (*right*) suffered five months of confiscation of property, plunder, forced labour, ill-treatment and execution under German rule. More than 4,000 of them had been sent to labour camps near the front lines, and many had died from ill-treatment, disease, and even during Allied aerial bombardments. Shown here are the principal towns in which more than 50,000 Tunisian Jews lived. Their suffering came to an end in May 1943, as the Allied armies drove the Germans from North Africa.

THE ADVANCE OF THE ALLIES

Mediterranean Sea

ITALY
GREECE
CORFU
SICILY
MALTA

Algiers
Allied landing
8 November 1942

Tunis
captured
7 May 1943

battle area
January-April 1943

Tripoli
captured
23 January 1943

Benghazi
captured
20 November 1942

ALGERIA

LIBYA

0 miles 200
0 kilometres 300

© Martin Gilbert 1982

Map 190

SOME CHILDREN DEPORTED TO AUSCHWITZ, 11 FEBRUARY 1943

GREAT BRITAIN

North Sea

Amsterdam

| Miriam Sluizer | aged 5 |
| Abel Sluizer | aged 2 |

Antwerp

| Joseph Skoulsky | aged 10 |
| Augusta Skoulsky | aged 5 |

Straits of Dover

English Channel

Luxembourg

| Gaston Kahn |
| aged 9 |

Rouen

| Leon Eskenazi |
| aged 6 |

Metz

Anna Checinski	aged 7
Elise Checinski	aged 12
Simon Checinski	aged 14

Le Havre

| Claire Leibel | aged 6 |
| Nelly Leibel | aged 4 |

Paris

| Pauline Leibel |
| aged 9 |

Nancy

| Joseph Haber | aged 8 |
| Samy Gryn | aged 9 |

St. Nazaire

| Maxime Borenheim |
| aged 3 |

Angers

| Mina Sternchuss | aged 10 |
| and her sisters |
| Lola | aged 6 |
| Simone | aged 4 |

Mulhouse

| Pierre Roth | aged 3 |
| Germaine Roth | aged 7 |

SWITZERLAND *neutral*

Bay of Biscay

Angoulême

| Joseph Wapniarz | aged 11 months |
| Frieda Reiss | aged 11 months |

Bordeaux

Henri Ayzenberg	aged 3
Helene Zavidowitcz	aged 8
Simone Zavidowitcz	aged 6

| 0 | miles | 100 |
| 0 | kilometres | 160 |

Gulf of Lions

SPAIN *neutral*

Pyrenees

Mediterranean Sea

© Martin Gilbert 1982

Map 191

OLD PEOPLE DEPORTED TO AUSCHWITZ, 11 FEBRUARY 1943

As the deportations from France to Auschwitz continued, neither children nor old people were spared. Among 1,000 Jews deported on 11 February 1943, of whom only 10 survived the war, were several hundred children and old people who were gassed immediately the deportation train reached the camp.

The children whose names and birthplaces are shown opposite were deported together with their parents, except for Joseph and Augusta Skoulsky who were deported alone, and the two Leibel sisters who were deported with their sister Pauline, aged 9, who had been born in Paris.

The young Maxime Borenheim was deported with his 19-year-old mother, who had been born in Warsaw. The three Sternchuss sisters were deported with their 74-year-old grandmother, also born in Warsaw. The Zavidowitcz sisters were deported with their father, who had been born in Brest-Litovsk.

In addition to the old people in their eighties and nineties whose birthpalces are given in the above map, a further 15 old people in their seventies were deported in this particular train: all were likewise gassed on arrival at Auschwitz.

On February 12 the Gestapo reported that three Jews had tried to escape from the train at the French frontier. But each had been caught and forced to continue the journey.

The photograph shows a group of Jewish children from Beregszasz and Bilke arriving at Auschwitz in 1944 (page 197).

Map 192

DISTANT DEPORTATIONS AND THE 'FACTORY ACTION', FEBRUARY 1943

890	2 February
1,184	9 February
1,108	16 February
1,101	23 February

Baltic Sea

HOLLAND

Hamburg
1,000

also 952 | 3 February
1,000 | 19 February
913 | 26 February

Berlin
7,000

GREATER

Treblinka

Essen
Cologne
1,000

Sobibor

FRANCE

Frankfurt

Theresienstadt
1,000
1 February

Majdanek

Bedzin
Auschwitz

GERMANY

1,000
9 February
998
11 February
1,000
13
February

Munich
1,000

SWITZERLAND
neutral

0   miles   150
0   kilometres   200

© Martin Gilbert 1982

In February 1943 transports reached the eastern death camps from Holland, Berlin, Theresienstadt and Paris (*above*). Among those deported fom Paris to Auschwitz on February 13 was Gisele Lustiger, who had been born in Bedzin. Her son, Aaron, who had converted to Catholicism before the war, survived the war; in February 1981 he was appointed Archbishop of Paris.

At the beginning of 1943 more than 10,000 Jews were working in factories throughout Germany. On February 27 the SS put into operation the 'Factory Action', deporting these workers to the east (*above*), where few survived. The photograph, taken in 1980, shows some of the fences and watchtowers at Majdanek.

The destruction of slave labour camps also continued, 1,000 labourers being sent from Chrzanow to Auschwitz (*opposite*).

In Eastern Galicia the deportations to Belzec had ceased: those Jews still alive were killed in local cemeteries or nearby woods.

At Bialystok eight SS men were killed

Map 193

DEPORTATION, MASS MURDER, AND REVOLT, FEBRUARY 1943

Rakow `1,000`
2 February Maly Trostenets

Minsk
`1,500`
1 February

*bringing the total
number of Jews
murdered in Minsk
since July 1941 to*

`86,632`

*according to Nazi
calculations*

Nowogrodek
`450`
4 February

resistance led by
`Eliyahu Boraks`
Eight S.S. men killed

Bialystok
`10,000` `1,000`
*deposited   killed on
5 February   the spot
to Treblinka   5 February
and
Auschwitz*

Treblinka
guards attacked

River Vistula

River Bug

V O L H Y N I A

*hundreds of Jews hiding in the
woods since August 1942
hunted down and shot. Of*
`40,000` *in hiding in February
1943 more than* `37,000`
*were killed, or died of hunger
during 1943.*

Belzec

Chrzanow *slave labour camp*
`1,000`   *18 February*

Auschwitz

Boryslaw
`600 men`
15 February

`600 women
& children`
16 February

**E A S T E R N
G A L I C I A**
River

Chodorow
`200`
5 February

Buczacz
`2,000`
1 February

Tluste
`40`
12 February

Stryj
`2,000`

Dniester

Fedor Hill

*Szeparowce
forest*

Kolomyja
`1,500`

Stanislawow
`10,000`
22 February

resistance led by `Oskar Friedlender`
`Anda Luft`

0   miles   50

0   kilometres   80

© Martin Gilbert 1982

when members of a Zionist youth movement
resisted deportation. Captured and deported,
the remnants of the group then attacked the
guards at Treblinka, using one, possibly two,
remaining pistols. But they were quickly
killed: at Treblinka the 150-strong SS and
Ukrainian garrison had a large armoury of
machine-guns and grenades. They also
wielded their whips and clubs without
mercy against men, women and children
staggering from the trains. Even then,
individuals resisted, as when a young
women, stripped naked, snatched a rifle
from a Ukrainian, shot dead two Nazis and
wounded a third, before being overpowered
and viciously tortured until she was dead.

Map 194

THE JEWS OF MACEDONIA AND THRACE DEPORTED, 3-22 MARCH 1943

SERBIA
under German military occupation

YUGOSLAVIA

Nis

4 barges

Lom Palanka
left 20-22 March

River Danube   RUMANIA

0   miles   40
0   kilometres   60

Pirot
185

Sofia

BULGARIA

Radomir
labour camp

Pristina
249

Kriva Palanka
5

Kumanova
13

Dupnitsa
internment camp 18-19 March
Gorna Dzhumaia
internment camp 18-19 March

Skopje
3,351

Tobacco factory camp 11-31 March

Veles
18

Stip
551

Didimoticon
867

Nea Orestia
194

Drama
589

Paranestion
19

M A C E D O N I A

occupied by Bulgaria

Ziliahovo
18

Xanthi
526

EASTERN THRACE

Bitola
3,315

Komotini
878

Souflion
32

Gevgelija
11

Seres
471

T H R A C E

Kavalla
1,484

Sarzhshaban
12

Dedeagatch
137

Salonica

Thasos
16

Samothrace
3

Aegean

GREECE

Mount Athos

Sea

Dardanelles

TURKEY
neutral

© Martin Gilbert 1982

Map 195

After the Bulgarian occupation of the Greek province of Thrace in April 1941, the Germans imposed direct German rule on Eastern Thrace, which lay along the Turkish border *(left)*. In this zone were some 1,250 Jews, most of them in the town of Didimoticon, where the Jewish community could trace its origins back to 1542, to the arrival of refugees from Spain. After 300 years these 'Sephardi' (or Spanish) Jews still spoke a Spanish dialect, Ladino.

On 3 March 1943 the Germans seized the Jews of Eastern Thrace, including the three Jews living on the island of Samothrace. Five days later they were deported by train to Treblinka. Other than 40 who managed to escape the round-up at Nea Orestia, and 33 who evaded deportation from Didimoticon, none of the Jews of Eastern Thrace survived the war.

A day after the round-up in Eastern Thrace, the Jews of Bulgarian-occupied Thrace and Bulgarian-occupied Macedonia were likewise seized, taken to internment camps at Skopje, and inside Bulgaria, and then deported in a total of 20 trains *(right)*, some direct to Treblinka, others to the Danube town of Lom, where they were transferred first by barge through the Iron Gates to Vienna, and then by train.

Within three weeks 23 communities had been destroyed. The Bitola community had been established shortly after the expulsion of the Jews from Spain in 1492.

The photographs were taken on board one of the barges *(left)* and at a deportation centre.

TWENTY BALKAN TRAINS, MARCH 1943

Pirot 2 trains
Radomir 4 trains
Dupnitsa 3 trains
Gorna 3 trains
Skopje 5 trains
Bitola 3 trains

one deportation barge sank several hundred drowned

© Martin Gilbert 1982

Map 196

THE SALONICA DEPORTATIONS, FROM 15 MARCH 1943

GREATER GERMANY

Auschwitz

SLOVAKIA

Vienna

Graz
Maribor

Zidani Most

Trieste

Zagreb

C R O A T I A

0   miles   150

0   kilometres   200

Belgrade

SERBIA

Adriatic Sea

Nis

Sofia

ITALY

Skopje

BULGARIA

ALBANIA

Salonica
43,850

Kastoria
655

Veroia
424
1 May

GREECE

Aegean Sea

© Martin Gilbert 1982

Within two weeks of the deportation of the Jews of Thrace and Macedonia to Treblinka, the Jews of Salonica were being seized, interned, and deported to Auschwitz (*left*). The photograph shows the preliminary indignities to which they were subjected: compulsory drills until they collapsed.

Jews had lived in Salonica since the time of St Paul. In the twelfth century they had their own mayor. In 1430 their rabbis were placed on the same footing as the spiritual heads of the Greek Church. In the fifteenth and sixteenth centuries, both German and Spanish Jews found in the city a safe haven from persecution. In the nineteenth century the Jews of Salonica were active as artisans, traders, shopkeepers and dock workers. Between the wars many emigrated to Palestine, France and the United States. Others stayed as part of a flourishing community: doctors, lawyers, teachers, and above all stevedores and dock workers.

The first deportation of Salonica Jewry began on 15 March 1943, when 2,800 Jews were forced into 40 cattle trucks and told that they were to be 'resettled' in Poland. Five months later, on 7 August 1943, the last train left Salonica for Auschwitz, where more than 43,000 of Salonica's 56,000 Jews had been killed (*pages 154, 157 and 160 to 162*).

The insanity of the German policy towards the Jews was clearly shown in Salonica, where the Jewish dock workers and port labourers were essential to the efficient operation of the port. But even this practical consideration was of no interest to the Nazis: nothing was to be allowed to stand in the way of the destruction of every

Map 197

THE SAVING OF THE JEWS OF BULGARIA, 17 MARCH 1943

GERMAN-OCCUPIED SERBIA

RUMANIA

DOBRUDJA

Vidin

Lom

Silistra

Ruse

Dobrich

River   Danube

Samovit *labour camp*

Razgrad

Sumen

Varna

Provadiya

YUGOSLAVIA

BULGARIA

Sofia

Radomir *labour camp*

Kazanlik

Sliven

Karnobat

Stara Zagora

Nova Zagora

Yambol

Burgas

Black Sea

Pazardzhik

Plovdiv

Khaskova

Stanimaka

BULGARIAN-OCCUPIED MACEDONIA

Kirdzhali

TURKEY *neutral*

EASTERN THRACE

© Martin Gilbert 1982

BULGARIAN-OCCUPIED THRACE

Sea of Marmara

GREECE

0 miles 20

kilometres 40

Salonica *under German occupation*

Aegean Sea

one of Europe's Jewish communities.

North-east of Salonica, the Jews of Bulgaria (*above*) were likewise marked out by the Nazis for deportation. In 1934 there were 48,398 Jews in Bulgaria, out of a total Bulgarian population of six million. On 22 January 1941 a 'Law for the Defence of the Nation' gave Jews one month to leave all public posts, and forced almost all Jewish doctors, dentists and lawyers to give up their practices. In addition, a special tax was imposed on all Jewish homes, shops and other property, amounting to a quarter of its value. By the end of 1941, there were some 400 Bulgarian Jews serving in local Bulgarian partisan units.

On 10 March 1943 the SS demanded the deportation of all Bulgarian Jews to Poland, on the same pattern as the deportation from Thrace, Macedonia and Salonica. The Bulgarian Government had already bowed to the demand that 12,000 Jews under Bulgarian occupation in Thrace and Macedonia should be deported. But the demand for the deportation of the 49,000

Jews of Bulgaria proper was resisted by the Bulgarian people: by the King, the Parliament, the intellectuals, and the farmers. The farmers, indeed, were said to be ready to lie down on the railway tracks to prevent any such deportations, and on 17 March 1943 the Bulgarian Parliament voted unanimously against the deportation order.

Not only the King, but the Archimandrite Cyril, and the Papal Nuncio in Turkey, Angelo Roncalli (later Pope John XXIII) protested strongly against the proposed deportations.

As a result of these protests, no Bulgarian Jews were deported to the gas chambers from Bulgaria itself. A few, who were living in Paris at the time of the outbreak of war, has already been deported to Auschwitz (*page 121*). Others were sent to labour camps at Samovit and Radomir. But these were not punitive camps, as in Germany.

Bulgaria was the only country under German influence or control whose Jewish population actually increased during the war years, from 48,565 in 1934, to 49,172 in 1945.

DISTANT DEPORTATIONS, MASSACRE AND REVOLT, MARCH 1943

North Sea

Baltic Sea

resistance

Braslaw
'thousands'

Soviet forces advancing

Radoszkowicze
the last 300

Orel

Minsk
'thousands'

Kursk

Westerbork
5,679
to Sobibor
5 trains

Berlin 7,752
5 trains

Treblinka

Sobibor

fifty escape, and
join the ' Revenge'
partisan group

Poltava

Majdanek
Auschwitz

Khmelnik
1,300
5 March

Calais

Luxembourg

Drancy

Prague

Paris

Tours

Mosbach

Munich
113
13 March

FRANCE

Lausanne

Montauban

Les Milles
1,400

Zagreb

Belgrade

0 miles 200
0 kilometres 300

Gurs

Marseilles
997 23 March
1,000 25 March

Rome

Adriatic Sea

Black Sea

888
4 March
926
6 March

Salonica
10,002
in 4 trains

THRACE

© Martin Gilbert 1982

DEPORTATION, MASSACRE AND REVOLT, MARCH 1943

Czestochowa
127 'intelligentsia'
20 March

River Vistula

River San

Plaszow *slave
labour camp*

Borek
forest

Auschwitz

Cracow
2,000 *to Auschwitz*
700 *shot*
13-14 March

Zolkiew
2,000
25 March

Lvov
1,500
17 March

Szebnie
*slave labour camp
opened*

Sambor
900
14 March

escape organized by
Artur Sandauer

0 miles 35
0 kilometres 60

© Martin Gilbert 1982

154

Map 200

During March 1943 five trains left Holland for Sobibor, one train left Paris for Auschwitz and two trains left Paris for Majdanek (*opposite, above*). Among the deportees to Majdanek was the German Jewish painter, Hermann Lismann, who had studied in Lausanne, Rome and Paris. A post-impressionist, he had emigrated to France in 1933. At first he had lived near Tours. Then he escaped to Montauban, from where he was deported.

From Gurs were deported to their deaths all but two of the 51 Jews of Mosbach, who had been deported from Germany to Gurs more than two years before (*page 48*).

Also deported to Majdanek from Paris in March 1943 were Nathan Lewinsztejn, aged 29, and Lajwa Krysztal, aged 40, who had both been born in Lublin, in a suburb of which the Majdanek concentration camp and gas chamber was situated.

From the General Government (*opposite, below*), 10,000 Jews were seized, deported from Cracow to Auschwitz, sent to the slave labour camp in the suburb of Plaszow, or shot in the streets. At Sambor 900 Jews were shot in the town's main square, many mothers being forced to watch their children being shot first. Resistance plans, carefully nurtured, were cut short by the 'liquidation'. At Braslaw (*opposite, above*) the resistance fighters fell at their posts. During the slaughter at Minsk, while thousands were shot, only 50 were able to break out of the armed cordons and reach the partisans.

Among those deported from France in March 1943 were 4,000 Jews from the Marseilles region (*right*), most of whom had been seized two months earlier during 'action Tiger'. Sent to Drancy, they were deported on 23 March 1943 to Sobibor. All the deportees, were gassed on arrival. A second train left Drancy for Sobibor two days later, with 1,000 Jews. All but 15 were gassed. Only five survived the war.

Among the Jews in these two trains were Vidal Farhi and Lea Klauser, both of whom had been born in Jerusalem, Dick and Jacob Prins from the Dutch East Indies (*page 127*) and the 18-year-old twins, Jean and Victor Nerver, who had been born in Calais.

At Les Accates, in the Marseilles region, 16 Jewish children were sheltered, and saved. But the 30 orphans from La Rose, photographed by the author in 1976, were deported to Auschwitz, together with their guardian, Alice Salomon, who insisted on sharing their fate.

THE JEWS OF MARSEILLES AND AIX

Aix-en-Provence
55 Jewish properties confiscated

Meyreuil
labour camp
20

les Milles
detention camp
1,400
deported

Calas
Jewish families emigrate

Bouc-Bel-Air
Jews deported

Gardanne
Jewish families emigrate

Cabriès
Jewish property confiscated

Biver coal mines
labour camp

Plan-de-Cuques
Jewish property confiscated

Allauch
Jewish property confiscated

Port

La Rose
30 orphans deported

Vieux Port

les Accates
16 Jewish and 27 Spanish children sheltered

les Camoins
a Jew deported

Marseilles

4,000
deported

Mediterranean Sea

0   miles   4
0   kilometres   6

© Martin Gilbert 1982

Map 201

DEPORTATION, MASSACRE AND REVOLT, APRIL 1943

Wlodawa
2,000
30 April

On arrival at the unloading ramp,
Jews in the transport from
Wlodawa attacked the S.S.
All the Jews were killed by
S.S. machine-gun fire and
grenades

Sobibor

0   miles   5
0   kilometres   8

Leczna
slave labour camp
the last
300
slave labourers
killed
29 April

Izbica
300
28 April

River Bug

REICHSKOMMISSARIAT

UKRAINE

GREATER

GERMANY

Belzec

VOLHYNIA

Leszniow
100

Jaworow
3,489
18 April

Zloczow
5,000
5 April

Przemysl
revolt

Rudki
1,700
9 April

EASTERN

GALICIA

Komarno
500
9 April

resistance led by
Michael Glanz

Sambor
1,000
14 April

Brzezany
2,000
12 April

Kozowa
1,000
9, 17 April

Skalat
750
7 April

© Martin Gilbert 1982

The killings in Eastern Galicia continued during April 1943 (*above*), as did the distant deportations to Auschwitz and Treblinka (*opposite, above*): nine from Salonica, four from Holland, one from Belgium and one from France.

The 300 Jews of Soly and Smorgonie (*opposite, above*) were brought by train to Vilna, having been told that they were to be resettled in the Kovno ghetto. But instead of going to Kovno, the train stopped at nearby Ponary. A 15-year-old Vilna schoolboy, Yitskhok Rudashevski, noted in his diary the story that reached Vilna within a few hours: 'Like wild animals before dying, the people began in mortal despair to break the railroad cars, they broke the little windows reinforced by strong wire. Hundreds were shot to death while running away. The railroad line over a great distance is covered with corpses.'

All who survived the rail-side massacre of April 5 were shot in the pits at Ponary by the German and Lithuanian SS men. A few hours later 4,000 Jews reached Ponary station from Swieciany, where the ghetto had been virtually unmolested since the Polygon slaughter of September 1941 (*page 77*). They too resisted, with revolvers, knives and fists. A few dozen managed to escape to Vilna. The rest were shot down on the spot.

From Jaworow (*opposite, below*), the Jews already expelled from six nearby village communities, and held in the town, were murdered on 18 April 1943, the Jews of Jaworow itself having already been killed at Belzec the previous November (*page 136*).

From Jaworow, most of those who reached the forests fell in battle against the Germans. There was also resistance in Skalat and Przemysl (*above*), in Belgium (*opposite, above*) and, on a massive scale, in Warsaw (*page 158*).

DISTANT DEPORTATION, MASSACRE AND REVOLT, APRIL 1943

HOLLAND

2,020 *6 April*
1,204 *13 April*
1,166 *20 April*
1,204 *27 April*

Brussels
1,400
19 April

Berlin
938
19 April

Baltic Sea

Kovno
5,000

Widze
1,800

Moscow

Soviet forces advancing

April 1943

Soly
Smorgonie

Vilna
Ponary

Oszmiana
2,500

Swieciany
4,000

Westerbork

derailment

Warsaw
ghetto revolt
19 April

Treblinka

Sobibor

Drancy

Paris

Auschwitz

EASTERN
GALICIA

Siedlce
*slave labour
camp liquidated
14 April*

Trembowla
800
7 April

Borszczow
800 *19 April*

Kopyczynce
600
15 April

Buczacz
2,000
13 April

Avignon
20
17 April

Black Sea

24,921
in 9 trains
Salonica

0	miles	300
0	kilometres	400

© Martin Gilbert 1982

SIX COMMUNITIES DESTROYED, 18 APRIL 1943

Lubaczewski forest

Wielkie Oczy
547

Skolin
7

EASTERN
GALICIA

Jaworow
3,489 *shot*

*acts of resistance
led by*
Artur Henner *and*
Henry Gleich

Krakowiec
529

River San

Szklo
53

Lvov

Przemysl

Mosciska
2,328

Sadowa Wisznia
25

0	miles	10
0	kilometres	15

© Martin Gilbert 1982

157

Map 204

THE WARSAW GHETTO REVOLT, 19 APRIL 1943

© Martin Gilbert 1982

On 18 January 1943 the Jewish underground in Warsaw had resisted a new wave of deportations. In four days 6,000 Jews had been deported and 1,000 murdered in the streets (*page 142*). But so fierce was the Jewish resistance and street fighting that the deportations had been suspended.

The Jewish underground, led by Mordecai Anielewicz, prepared to resist any further attempt to renew the deportations.

On 19 April 1943 a German military force, equipped with tanks and artillery, entered he ghetto in order to resume the death camp deportations. The Jewish units fought back, and the Germans were driven out of the ghetto altogether.

Within a few hours the Germans returned, no longer seeking open conflict with Jewish armed units, but systematically burning down houses in the ghetto street by street, while at the same time killing or driving out with smoke and hand grenades those who were hiding in bunkers or sewers.

On 8 May 1943 the German forces reached the Jewish underground headquarters. In the ensuing battle Anielewicz, and more than 100 of his fighters, were killed. A week later the German commander, General Stroop, reported to his superiors: 'The Warsaw ghetto is no more.'

During the fighting more than 56,000 Jews had been burned alive, shot as they emerged from the burning buildings, or rounded up and deported to Treblinka.

The map shows the municipal boundary of Warsaw, the original extent of the ghetto, and, in solid black, the three much smaller areas to which the ghetto had been reduced following the massive deportations between July and September 1942. The photograph on the left, taken in 1980, shows two of the very few buildings in the ghetto area which survived the otherwise total destruction.

The photographs on the right are both taken from the special album prepared by General Stroop to celebrate his 'victory'. The upper photograph shows a Jewish fighter being brought out of a bunker. The lower photograph shows German officers and soldiers, and (left), two captured Jewish fighters, a man (sitting) and a woman (standing).

As many as 15,000 Jews escaped to the 'Aryan' part of Warsaw. Some were later caught or betrayed. But most, sheltered by the Poles, survived the war, and many were to fight in the Warsaw uprising in August 1944 (*pages 206–207*).

Map 205

SEVEN DEPORTATIONS, MASSACRE AND RESISTANCE, 4-25 MAY 1943

HOLLAND
1,187 4 May
1,446 11 May
2,511 18 May
2,862 25 May

Baltic Sea

Nowogrodek
the last **370**
7 May

Bryuchovo
• **40**

The Red Army
advances, May 1943

Germans capture headquarters
bunker of Ghetto revolt
The commander of the revolt
Mordechai Anielewicz
killed 8 May

Warsaw
56,000

Berlin
at least **395** 17 May

Sobibor

Brody **2,500** 1 May
Jewish resistance
against German army
and Ukrainian police, 17 May

Auschwitz

GALICIA

Skalat
660
9 May

Sokal
2,500

Busk
1,000
21 May

Tluste
3,000
27 May

Stryj
1,000
22 May

27 May

CROATIA

Black Sea

0 — miles — 250
0 — kilometres — 400

Zagreb
at least **1,000** 7 May
at least **1,000** 13 May

from Salonica
10,930
in four trains

© Martin Gilbert 1982

At the very moment when the Warsaw ghetto uprising was being crushed, and 56,000 Warsaw Jews were being burned to death, shot, or deported, the deportations continued from outside Greater Germany: four from Holland and two from Croatia.

In the Eastern Galician town of Brody, as well as in Warsaw, Jewish resistance had led to German deaths: but with Soviet forces still more than 300 miles to the east, the Germans were able to devote considerable strength and efforts during May and June 1943 to wiping out the remaining Jewish communities of Eastern Galicia, as seen above and in the map opposite (below).

The photograph is of a mother and her three children at the moment of deportation. Most of those marked out to die in Galicia were now taken, not to one of the death camps, but to local forests or gravel pits, or, as at Tluste, to the Jewish cemetery. Here, the executions were carried out with savagery and sadism, a crying child often being seized from its mother's arms and shot in front of her, or having its head crushed by a single blow from a rifle butt. Hundreds of children were thrown alive into pits, and died in fear and agony under the weight of bodies thrown on top of them.

Throughout June the Dutch and French deportations continued (opposite, above). On

NINE EASTWARD DEPORTATIONS, JUNE 1943

HOLLAND
3,006 *1 June*
1.266 *children* 5 June
3,017 *8 June*
2,397
8 June

Baltic Sea

Bialystok

Berlin

Brest-Litovsk

Sobibor

Bamberg
16 *18 June*

Breslau

Belzec

Auschwitz

GALICIA

434,329

Jews deported to Belzec between June 1942 and June 1943, or killed in their towns, according to an S.S. report

Drancy

Nuremberg
70
18 June

Würzburg
57
17 June

sterilization rate reported to Berlin on 7 June as 1,000 women a day

Paris
1,002
23 June

SWITZ.
neutral

from Salonica
880 *8 June*

Soviet forces June 1943

0 miles 200
0 kilometres 300

© Martin Gilbert 1982

Black Sea

DEPORTATION, MASSACRE AND REVOLT, JUNE 1943

0 miles 40
0 kilometres 60

Warsaw
the last resistance crushed

Minsk Mazowiecki
Rudzi factory
all 150 *shot*
5 June

Wlodawa
1,000

Sobibor

B = **Brzezany**
100 *12 June*

K = **Kozowa**
400 *4 June*

T = **Trembowla**
900 *3 June*

Borszczow
700 *5 June*

Skala Podolska
800
9 June

SILESIA

Czestochowa
armed resistance 25 June
1,000 *deported*

Belzec
the corpse-burning squad deported to Sobibor, revolted on arrival, and shot

Rawa Ruska
100 *shot*
8 June

Dabrowa Gornicza
2,000
26 June

Sosnowiec
resistance led by
Zevi Dunski

GALICIA

Lvov
13,000
21 - 27 June

armed resistance 25 June

Tarnopol
4,000
20 June

T

Auschwitz

Drohobycz
all Jewish workers in the municipal factories murdered 21 June

Rohatyn
1,000
6 June

B

K

Podhajce
300
6 June

Moravska Ostrava
all residents of the Jewish old peoples home deported 23 June

Buczacz
ghetto liquidated escape and resistance

Tluste
1,000 *6 June*

© Martin Gilbert 1982

June 5 a total of 1,266 children under the age of 16 were deported from Holland to Sobibor. All were gassed on arrival. Among 1,000 Jews deported from Paris to Auschwitz on June 23, more than 100 were likewise under 16 years. There were also 13 babies and many mothers with young children, all of whom were murdered on arrival, including the eight-months-old Henry Kaminka deported with his mother Salomée, born in Bialystok, and his father Vital, born in Brest-Litovsk.

In Galicia and Silesia as the killings continued, so too did the resistance (*above*). But with arms almost impossible to obtain, and the local population often unwilling to give shelter, both defence and escape were equally hopeless. But both continued.

Map 208

DEPORTATION, MASSACRE AND REVOLT, JULY 1943

Leningrad

Moscow

Soviet front line in July 1943

Riga · Lida

Shavli · Vitebsk

North Sea

Nowo-Wilejka
*slave labour camp
liquidated
28 July*

Kovno

Vilna
☼ *resistance
24 July*

BELGIUM
1,553
31 July

Baltic Sea

Minsk

Berlin

20 July
2 *escape*

Treblinka ☼

Miedzyrzec
200 *slave labourers*
18 July

Sobibor 卐

Kamionka Strumilowa
5,000 *slave labourers*
10 July

HOLLAND **2,209** *20 July*
2,417 *6 July*
1,988 *13 July*

Malines

Drancy

Auschwitz

Skalat
400 *slave labourers*
28 July

Czestochowa
500 *slave labourers*
20 July

Bolechow
300
13 July

Paris
1,000
18 July
1,000
31 July

Natzweiler · Strasbourg 卐

Black Sea

Jasenovac
800 *15 July*

Adriatic Sea

GREECE

Salonica
1,800
28 July

Aegean Sea

miles 200
kilometres 300

© Martin Gilbert 1982

CRETE
Heraklion
6 *Jews shot 6 June 1943*

As the Red Army began its advance westward in the summer of 1943, the Nazis murdered several thousand Jews who had not been deported to the death camps earlier, but who had been kept alive in order to serve as slave labourers in factories and labour camps. At the same time, the deportations to Auschwitz continued from the furthest extremities of German rule (*above*), including two from Paris, one from Belgium, three from Holland, and the remaining Jews in Salonica (*page 152*).

Six eastern ghettos had escaped 'liquidation' by the Nazis during 1942: Vilna, Kovno, Shauliai (known to the Jews as Shavli), Riga, Minsk and Lida.

In Vilna (*above and opposite*), where 20,000 Jews lived in the ghetto, a group of 21 young men and women who had been active in the Jewish underground movement decided to try to make contact with the Soviet partisans who were now increasingly active behind the German front line.

The escape of the 21 was successful, but they were ambushed by German soldiers at the Mickun bridge, and nine were killed in the ensuing fighting.

Three days after the ambush at the bridge,

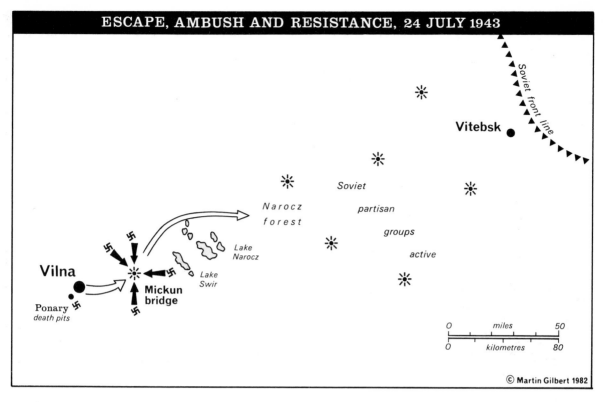

Map 209

32 relatives of the nine Jews who had been killed were seized by the Gestapo in Vilna, taken to Ponary, and executed.

Those who survived the ambush continued eastwards to the Narocz forest where they joined the Soviet partisans, and were active in disrupting German military supplies and communications with the front line.

In Vilna itself, the execution of the 32 relatives proved a tragedy for all those who remained in the ghetto. To prevent any further such escapes, the head of the Gestapo in the city, Bruno Kittel, at once made it known that in future the whole family of anyone who escaped to the forest would be killed as a reprisal, while if the man who got away had no family then those who shared his room, or even lived in the same tenement building, would likewise be executed. The Gestapo also decreed that if, from any of the labour gangs of 10 Jews sent out of the ghetto, even a single man failed to return, the remaining nine would be shot. Escapes to the forest ceased. But inside the ghetto the Jewish resistance groups continued to make plans, and to collect arms.

In 1940 the SS had set up a concentration camp at Natzweiler, in Alsace, with 20 satellite labour camps. Between the first executions on 18 September 1942 and the liberation of Natzweiler on 31 August 1944,

at least 25,000 prisoners, Jews and non-Jews, died there of starvation and ill-treatment, or were murdered.

Many Jewish and non-Jewish women, active in the French resistance, were executed in Natzweiler, as well as many Russian and Polish prisoners. The meticulous camp records show, for example, eight civilians from Luxembourg shot in the camp on 19 May 1944.

On 6 November 1942 Heinrich Himmler had given his support to a plan to establish a collection of Jewish skulls and skeletons at the Reich Anatomical Institute in Strasbourg, near Natzweiler. On 21 June 1943, 73 Jews and 30 Jewesses were selected in Auschwitz, and sent to Natzweiler, where they were measured, weighed and gassed, and their corpses sent on to the Anatomical Institute in Strasbourg. On 15 October 1944, as Allied forces approached Strasbourg, Himmler ordered the skeleton collection to be destroyed. But all the documents relating to it survived the war.

At Auschwitz itself, medical experiments (*page 107*) continued, and led to the deaths of hundreds of people, especially women. Many hundreds were maimed for life by sterilization and other experiments. Others were deliberately murdered so that the SS doctors could study their bone structure.

Map 210

DEPORTATION, MASSACRE AND REVOLT, AUGUST 1943

Baltic Sea

Koziany ●
100
20 August

revolt ☀

Glebokie ●
3,000
20 August

Vilna ●
1,000
deported to Estonia dozens who resisted deportation killed, 6 August

☀

REICHSKOMMISSARIAT OSTLAND

Stutthof ⚡

revolt led by Mordecai Tenenbaum *and* Daniel Moszkowicz

slave labour camp revolt led by Rabbi Joshua Aaronson

Bialystok ●
40,000
revolt 16·23 August
☀

⚡ ☀
Konin

Treblinka
☀ ⚡
revolt 2 August

River Vistula

among the leaders, Dr. Julian Chorarzycki *a physician who worked in the camp hospital, and was killed before the revolt* Engineer Alfred Galewski *and* Zelo Bloch

from Holland
1,001 *26 August*
1,004 *21 August*

River Bug

Sobibor ⚡

members of the corpse-burning squad dig a tunnel to escape. Their tunnel came out in the camp minefield. All **150** *members of the squad were executed.*

Sosnowiec
15,000

Bedzin
many thousands

● Krychow
☀ *slave labour camp revolt 16 August*

Dabrowa Gornicza
'thousands'
3 August

River Vistula

revolt ☀
Sasow
slave labour camp 'liquidated'

Borszczow
360 *shot*
14 August

⚡
Auschwitz

armed resistance ☀
Lackie Wielkie
slave labour camp 'liquidated'

armed resistance
☀ **Jaktorow**
slave labour camp 'liquidated'

SLOVAKIA

0   *miles*   60

0   *kilometres*   80

© **Martin Gilbert** 1982

In August 1943 more than 2,000 Jews were deported from Holland to Auschwitz *(above)*, while several slave labour camps in the General Government were 'liquidated', and their inmates murdered.

The deportation of 40,000 Jews from the Bialystok ghetto to Treblinka led to two major revolts: inside Bialystok itself, when the Germans used artillery and tanks to crush the rebellion, and at Treblinka *(above)*,

JEWISH PARTISAN ACTIVITY IN THE BIALYSTOK REGION, 1943

THE KILLING OF 1,260 CHILDREN OF BIALYSTOK

where several hundred prisoners battled with guards, and tried to break out across the minefields. But at Treblinka, as elsewhere, all acts of resistance were brutally suppressed. After the Bialystok revolt more than 1,000 Jewish children were seized in the city and deported, first to Theresienstadt, and then to Auschwitz *(right)*, while at Glebokie 3,000 Jews who tried to resist being taken out to the nearby woods were massacred in a single day. But those Jews who did manage to escape built up small but active networks of partisan activity. Throughout the Bialystok region *(above)* Jews who had managed to escape from the deportations of 2 November 1942 *(page 133)* did whatever they could to disrupt German rail communication with the Leningrad and Moscow fronts: the arrows show the main partisan attacks.

Map 213

THE JEWS OF DENMARK RESCUED, SEPTEMBER 1943

SWEDEN
neutral

Skagerrak

Kattegat

Aalborg

Nibe

Viborg

Randers

Aarhus

DENMARK

Hälsingborg

Helsingor

Hillerod

Horsens

Copenhagen

Roskilde

Malmö

Fredericia

Middlefart

Ringsted

Odense

Slagelse

Haderslav

Nyborg

Nestved

The Baelts

Assens

Svenborg

escape of	
5,919	*Jews*
1,301	*half-Jews*
686	*Christians married to Jews*

Nakskov

Baltic Sea

Kiel

Stralsund

GERMANY

Lübeck

0	*miles*	40
0	*kilometres*	60

© Martin Gilbert 1982

Hamburg

Map 214

Following the German occupation of Denmark in the spring of 1940, the Germans had embarked on a policy of cooperation and negotiation with the Danish authorities, as embodied in the Danish-German Agreement of 9 April 1940. As a result, the Jews had been left unmolested. But on 28 August 1943, as Danish resistance to the German occupation undermined any chance of continued cooperation, the Germans abolished the Agreement, and declared martial law.

The SS hoped to use this opportunity to deport all Denmark's 7,200 Jews, most of whom lived in Copenhagen, a few hundred in each of the towns and villages shown opposite. Forewarned, however, of the planned deportation, Danes and Jews plotted to ensure that, on the eve of the deportation, Danish sea captains and fishermen ferried 5,919 Jews, 1,301 part Jews (designated Jews by the Nazis), and 686 Christians married to Jews, to safety in Sweden, a country where, between 1933 and 1943, more than three thousand European Jews, including many from Germany itself, had already found refuge *(right)*.

On 1 October 1943 the Germans found only 500 Jews still in Denmark. All were sent to Theresienstadt; 423 survived the war.

The photograph is of Danish Jews waiting in a cellar for the moment of rescue.

SWEDEN AND THE JEWS, 1939-1945

NORWAY
SWEDEN *neutral*
North Sea
DENMARK
Goteborg
Stockholm
Nordkopping
Malmö
Karlskrona
LITHUANIA
GERMANY
CZECHO SLOVAKIA
AUSTRIA

0 miles 200
0 kilometres 300

© Martin Gilbert 1982

A SLAVE LABOUR CAMP ESTABLISHED, 30 SEPTEMBER 1943

Baltic Sea

Vilna

Nowo-Wilejka

Minsk

Koldyczewo

GREATER GERMANY

Dworzec

WHITE RUSSIA

Hancewicze

Orel

Kursk

Karczew

Miedzyrzec

Borki

Poniatowa

Krychow

Trawniki

Kamionka Strumilowa

Funfteichen

SILESIA

Sosnowiec

Rozwadow

Pustkow

Mielec

Kiev

UKRAINE

Kharkhov

Soviet forces advancing

Plaszow

Szebnie

Lvov

Sasow

Skalat

Dnepropetrovsk

Auschwitz

GALICIA

SLOVAKIA

Kirovo

Mariupol

Sered

Novaky

Balta

Odessa

Sea of Azov

0 miles 150

0 kilometres 200

CRIMEA

Black Sea

front line on 1 September 1943

© Martin Gilbert 1982

SLAVE LABOUR CAMPS, 1943–1944

North Sea

Vaivara

Klooga

Baltic Sea

Kaiserwald

WHITE RUSSIA

Neuengamme

Ravensbrück

Stutthof

Sachsenhausen

Warsaw

Poniatowa

RUHR

Lodz

Borki

Krychow

Buchenwald

Funfteichen

SILESIA

Pustkow

Sasow

Auschwitz

Flossenbürg

GALICIA

Natzweiler

Novaky

Dachau

Sered

Szebnie

Skalat

Bor

Alderney
deaths include:
Chayim Goldin
7.12.1943
Robert Perlestein
22.12.1943
Seib Becker
30.12.1943
Lucien Worms
7.1.1944
Isaac Stekovsky
8.2.1944
Wilfred Gordeson
26.2.1944
Henry Lippman
2.3.1944
Szmul Kirschenblatt
26.4.1944

Adriatic Sea

0 miles 300

0 kilometres 400

© Martin Gilbert 1982

As Soviet forces advanced westwards more and more Jews were taken to slave labour camps in White Russia and Greater Germany. With the disbanding of a Krupp armaments works at Mariupol (above), it was relocated at Funfteichen in Silesia. Jews who had just been deported from Sosnowiec to Auschwitz were sent by train to work at Funfteichen, where many died.

In all labour camps, deaths from brutality were a daily occurrence. The map on the left names eight of the 100 Jews who died on Alderney, a British island captured by the Germans in 1940.

One use of slave labour was to obliterate all trace of earlier mass murders. At Himmler's instigation, a series of special units, known collectively as 'Unit 1005', were being forced to dig up the corpses of those slain, to burn them, and to scatter the ashes. This work took nearly two years and involved exhuming more than two million corpses (opposite, above).

One such unit was at work at Babi Yar (opposite). Others, working at different times at the murder sites shown above, were

Map 217

HIMMLER ORDERS THE EVIDENCE OF MASS MURDER DESTROYED

Leningrad

Moscow

Klooga

Riga
Kaiserwald

REICHSKOMMISSARIAT
OSTLAND

Kovno

Ponary
58,000

front line in November 1942

840,000

North
Sea

Baltic Sea

Treblinka

Chelmno
360,000

Sobibor

250,000

Berlin

front line in September 1943

Borki

Majdanek

600,000

Babi Yar
33,771

GREATER
GERMANY

Plaszow
9,000

Belzec

Janowska

and
1,500 *Poles*
who helped Jews

Natzweiler

| 0 | miles | 200 |
| 0 | kilometres | 300 |

© Martin Gilbert 1982

Black   Sea

themselves murdered once their work was done. The SS wanted no trace to survive either of their crimes, or of the slave labourers who were being forced to hide them. Nevertheless, a few did manage to escape. The Janowska unit, which had begun its grim work in July 1943, revolted four months later *(page 174)*. Even from Borki, where there was an equal number of armed guards as of prisoners, three prisoners survived an attempted break-out.

At Plaszow, in January 1945, a 'unit 1005' was forced to exhume 9,000 bodies from 11 mass graves. At Ponary more than 58,000 bodies were exhumed and cremated between September 1943 and April 1944. The Ponary unit, made up of 70 Jews and 10 Soviet prisoners-of-war who were suspected of being Jewish, was chained while working, and kept at night in a deep pit, access to which was by a wooden ladder which was withdrawn each evening. After digging an escape tunnel for three months with hands and spoons, 40 escaped on the night of 15 April 1944 *(page 181)*. Twenty-five were caught and killed; 15 eluded their pursuers.

The photograph is of a group of prisoners at the slave labour camp at Plaszow.

Map 218

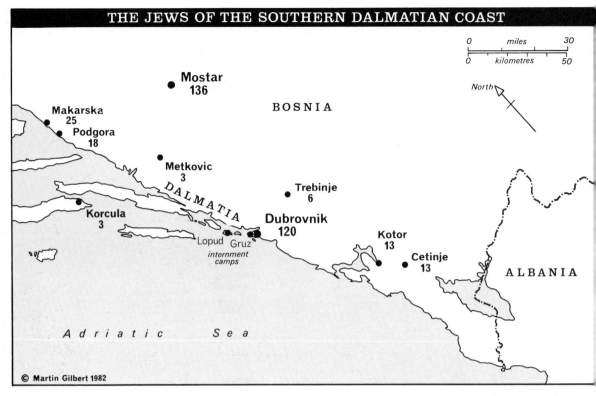

THE JEWS OF THE SOUTHERN DALMATIAN COAST

Mostar
136

BOSNIA

Makarska
25

Podgora
18

Metkovic
3

Trebinje
6

DALMATIA

Korcula
3

Dubrovnik
120

Lopud Gruz

internment
camps

Kotor
13

Cetinje
13

ALBANIA

Adriatic   Sea

© Martin Gilbert 1982

North

0   miles   30
0   kilometres   50

In April 1941 the Italian army had occupied Dalmatia, whose small Jewish communities *(above)* dated back to the fourteenth century. The numbers shown are according to the Yugoslav census of 31 March 1931. In November 1942, following German pressure, the Jews of Dalmatia were interned at Gruz and Lopud. In June 1943 they were transferred to the island of Rab *(opposite, above)*. With Italy's withdrawal from the war in September 1943, many escaped, and joined the Yugoslav partisans. But the old, the sick, and women with children, were deported to Zemun, and killed.

From France, Belgium, Holland and the north of Italy, newly occupied by Germany, *(opposite, above)* more than 5,000 Jews were deported to Auschwitz, as were Jews from Theresienstadt, Moravia and Galicia. Before the deportation from Tarnow to Auschwitz *(opposite, below)*, hundreds of Jews were murdered in the streets, then 5,000 forced into a single train, with an average of 160 in each sealed truck. The train stopped at Bochnia, where more trucks were added, containing a further 3,000 Jews. When it reached Auschwitz, only 400 of the deportees were still alive. The 'survivors' were sent to the gas chambers.

In the east *(opposite, above)*, with the deportation of more than 7,000 Vilna Jews to the slave labour camps of Estonia at the end of August and in early September, several hundred Jews managed to escape from Vilna to the forests, and to join the partisans.

Meanwhile, as the Soviet army advanced steadily westward, and the Allied armies were on European soil south of Rome, 2,000 Jews were deported from Minsk to Sobibor.

At Miedzyrzec, and at Sobibor itself, virtually unarmed Jews challenged German troops and SS. At Treblinka, on 2 September 1943, a group of 13 Jewish slave labourers killed their Ukrainian SS guard with a crowbar while working just outside the camp wire. The leader, an 18-year-old Polish Jew, Seweryn Klajnman, put on the dead guard's uniform, took his rifle, and 'marched off' his fellow prisoners as if to a new work detail further off, cursing and bellowing at them as they went, as befitted an SS guard. Guided by one of their number, a carter, who knew the area well, they escaped their pursuers and evaded capture.

Near Kiev, on 30 September 1943, a work unit of 325 Jewish and Soviet prisoners who were being forced, in chains, to dig up and burn victims of the Babi Yar massacre *(page 76)* resisted when they too were about to be killed. The SS overseers opened fire with machine-guns and grenades. Only 14 of the prisoners survived the revolt.

DISTANT DEPORTATIONS, ESCAPE AND REVOLT, SEPTEMBER 1943

NORWAY

SWEDEN
neutral

Leningrad

Klooga

ESTONIA

*North
Sea*

7,906
escape

Moscow

DENMARK

Baltic Sea

Riga

Soviet front line

Dvinsk

7,130
deported

HOLLAND
987 7 September
1,005 14 September
979 21 September

Vilna

hundreds escape

Minsk
2,000
18 September

GREATER   **GERMANY**

Treblinka

13 *escape*

Sobibor

Jews attack the
S.S. with stones
and bottles.
All attackers
killed.

Kiev

*revolt of
Jewish & Soviet
prisoners-of-war
29 September*
311 *killed*
14 *escape*

BELGIUM
631 *both
on*
794 *20
September*

MORAVIA

Auschwitz

GALICIA

Miedzyrzec
*Jewish youths attack
Germans. 2 Germans
killed.* **5** *Jews shot
10 September*

Vilna
escape organized by
Izik Wittenberg
Joseph Glazman
Abba Kovner

Paris
1,000
2 September

0   *miles*   200

0   *kilometres*   300

Merano
24
16-18 September

ITALY

Zemun

RAB

*Adriatic
Sea*

Split **500**
Dubrovnik

Rome

*under
Allied
control*

*Black
Sea*

© Martin Gilbert 1982

FIVE DEPORTATIONS TO AUSCHWITZ, 2-8 SEPTEMBER 1943

Theresienstadt
5,007
8 September

0   *miles*   80
0 *kilometres* 100

Auschwitz

Tarnow
5,000
2 September

resistance

Przemysl
3,500
2 September

MORAVIA

**Moravska
Ostrava**
3,442
8 September

WESTERN

GALICIA

Bochnia
3,000 *3 September*

© Martin Gilbert 1982

Map 221

THE JEWS OF ITALY DEPORTED, 9 OCTOBER – 21 NOVEMBER 1943

Auschwitz

Moravska Ostrava

SLOVAKIA

GREATER

GERMANY

Vienna

HUNGARY

SWITZERLAND
neutral

Merano

Bolzano

Villach

Milan
9 November

Trieste
9 October

La Risiera di San Sabba

Vercelli

Verona   **Padua**

`3,000` *Italian prisoners-of-war
murdered by the S.S.
and Ukrainian guards,*

Turin

Venice
9 November

`620` *of Trieste's* `1,920` *Jews
also murdered*

Asti
Alessandria

Mantua

Fossoli

Ferrara
14 September

Parma

Bologna

Genoa
3 November

Modena

`85`

La Spezia

Florence
9 November

San Remo

Pisa

Livorno

A d r i a t i c

D A L M A T I A

Borgo San Dalmazzo

`325`

21 November

Sienna

NORTHERN
ITALY
*occupied by
Germany
16 September
1943*

S e a

Termoli

Rome
`1,015`
18 October

Foggia

under

The front line on 15 November

The front line on 12 October

Naples

Allied

Salerno

control

T y r r h e n i a n

S e a

0   *miles*   80

0   *kilometres*   120

**Ferramonte
di Tarsia**

© Martin Gilbert 1982

Map 222

DEPORTATIONS, MASSACRE AND REVOLT, OCTOBER 1943

On 16 September 1943 more than 37,000 Italian Jews had come under Nazi rule. Some escaped to Switzerland. Several thousand found refuge in Catholic homes. On 16 October 1943, 1,000 Jews were seized in Rome and deported to Auschwitz. Within a month 8,360 Italian Jews, mostly from the towns shown opposite, had been deported to Auschwitz, where 7,749 were murdered.

The deportations from Holland and France to Auschwitz continued. From Kovno 3,000 Jews were sent to the Klooga slave labour camp in Estonia (above).

In September (page 171) 2,000 Jews and Soviet prisoners-of-war had been deported from Minsk to Sobibor: 80 had been selected to work as carpenters and joiners. The rest had been gassed. One of the 80, Alexander Pechersky, a Soviet officer and also a Jew, together with other prisoners, planned a break-out. On October 14 the revolt took place: 11 or 12 SS men, and more than a dozen Ukrainian SS guards, were killed. Of the 600 Jews then in the labour camp, 200 were shot while escaping, or were blown up in the camp minefields; 400 escaped, of whom 100 were subsequently captured and killed; others joined Soviet partisan units, and were mostly killed fighting; others died of typhus, or were killed by hostile Polish gangs. Only 64 survived the war, including Pechersky.

Map 223

DEPORTATION, MASSACRE AND REVOLT, NOVEMBER–DECEMBER 1943

Riga
several thousand
3 November

Kovno
150 Jewish
partisans escape
23 November

Rudnicka

forest

Baltic Sea

Berlin more than **100**
Jewish mental home
patients deported
22 November

from
Holland
1,149
15 November
995
16 November

resistance
by a former
Hebrew teacher
Szosznik
hundreds killed
10 escape

Lublin
Lipowa Street camp
2,500
3 November

Trawniki
slave labour camp
8,000
November

Majdanek
18,000
3 November

Borki
corpse-burning
squad revolt
50 killed
3 survived

Poniatowa
slave labour camp
14,000
5 November

Theresienstadt
2,504
15 December
2,503
18 December
also **300** die
during an all-day roll call
11 November

Funfteichen
slave labour camp
the first deaths
November

Sosnowiec
1,000 November

Krychow
slave labour camp
1,500
5 November

Auschwitz

Rzeszow
1,000

Lvov
Janowska camp
uprising
19 November
leaders included
Leon Weliczker

Szebnie
slave labour camp
2,800 to Auschwitz
4 November
500 shot
6 November

Drohobycz
200 shot
14 December

212
from Milan and Verona
6 December

0 miles 80
0 kilometres 100

© Martin Gilbert 1982

During November and December 1943 the deportations to Auschwitz continued from Italy, Holland and Theresienstadt (*above*). At Majdanek 18,000 prisoners were murdered in a single day of slaughter, called by the SS the 'harvest festival'. Elsewhere, the SS continued to destroy slave labour camps. Jews tried to resist execution, as at Majdanek, Janowska and Poniatowa (*above*).

Many of the Jews who had managed to escape the ghettos and camps joined Soviet partisan groups, or formed small units of their own. The map opposite shows 35 towns and villages from which Jews had managed to escape to the forests. From Kovno almost all who tried to escape were killed.

Map 224

ESCAPE AND RESISTANCE, JULY - DECEMBER 1943

0   *miles*   40

0   *kilometres*   60

REICHSKOMMISSARIAT
OSTLAND

Russo-Polish border, 1921 - 1939

Lake Narocz

Miadziol

Kovno

24 December 1943
Sixty-four escape
from the Ninth Fort
45 *caught and
killed.*
19 *survive*

Vilna

*Narocz
forest*

Wilejka

Krasnoe

Horodok

Olkieniki

*Rudnicka
forest*

Minsk

Werenow

Iwje

Lida

Wasiliszki

Bielce

Nowogrodek

Korelicze

Stolpce

Grodno

Zoludek

Mir

Szczucin

Nowojelnia

River

Dworzec

Nieswiez

Slutsk

Dereczyn

Baranowicze

Kleck

Niemen

Zelwa

Slonim

Lachowicze

**GREATER
GERMANY**

Hancewicze

**BIALYSTOK
REGION**

**BARANOWICZE
REGION**

95,000 *executed*

6,000 *escape
in August 1942*

Lenino

Pruzana

Brest-
Litovsk

Kobryn

Drohiczyn

Janow

Pinsk

Russo-Polish border, 1921 - 1939

River Bug

**REICHSKOMMISSARIAT
UKRAINE**

*Pripet
marshes*

© Martin Gilbert 1982

Map 225

JEWS DEPORTED TO AUSCHWITZ AND GASSED, JANUARY-FEBRUARY 1944

North Sea

SWEDEN
neutral

Baltic Sea

Narva
86
22 February

Westerbork
687 *27 January*
800 *10 February*

Stutthof
1,000 *12 January*

Berlin
26 *23 February*

Lodz
95
12 January

Malines
417
17 January

Drancy

Auschwitz

Buczacz
300 *Jews in hiding in the forests for over six months, surrounded by German tanks, and killed, 18 January*

Paris
1,068 *20 January*
985 *3 February*
1,229 *10 February*

Vienna
37
25 January

Sosnowiec
54 *26 February*

Bay of Biscay

SWITZ
neutral

Verona

563 **Milan**
30 January

Trieste
23 *12 January*

Fossoli
462
22 February

Adriatic Sea

SPAIN
neutral

Soviet front line

0 miles 200
0 kilometres 300

Black Sea

© **Martin Gilbert 1982**

BIRTHPLACES OF TWENTY-FOUR OF THOSE DEPORTED TO AUSCHWITZ, 22 JANUARY 1944

0 miles 400
0 kilometres 600

North Sea
Baltic Sea

Vilna
Jankel Lewin,
aged 51

Bialystok
Riwka Golombek, aged 19
Anna Golombek, aged 15

Manchester
Maurice Braunstein,
aged 39

Drancy

Auschwitz

London
Joseph Terasfeld,
aged 28
Rebecca Gabay,
aged 29

Paris
Jean Navon, aged 19
Odette Navon, aged 6

Bordeaux

Black Sea

Jacqueline Dray, aged 4
Michel Dray, aged 1

Nice
Rachael Haim, aged 14
Fanny Haim, aged 13
Renée Haim, aged 5

Bursa

Albert Navon, aged 45
Sol Navon, aged 37
Mordechai Haim, aged 40
Esthera Haim, aged 37

Baghdad
David Somekh
aged 37

Mediterranean Sea

Tunis
Albert Dana
aged 62
Nina Dana
aged 62

Damascus
Isaac Saal,
aged 59

Casablanca
David Dray, aged 11
Leon Dray, aged 8

Cairo
Jacques Menache
aged 23

© Martin Gilbert 1982

The map opposite shows the deportations to Auschwitz during January and February 1944. The dates are those of the arrival of each train at Auschwitz; the figures show the actual numbers gassed, according to the records kept by the SS in Auschwitz itself. In all, the SS recorded 13 deportations for these two months, from the Baltic to the Adriatic.

The map above shows the birthplaces, and ages, of 24 of the deportees in one of these 13 deportations, that which reached Auschwitz from Drancy on 22 January 1944. It had left Paris two days earlier, with 632 men, 515 women and 221 children under the age of 18. Of these 1,368 Jews, 749 were gassed on arrival at Auschwitz. As well as those named on the map, the deportees included Jews who had been born in every country in Europe.

Among the Jews deported from Paris to Auschwitz were more than 1,000 who had been born in Turkey, but whose nationality was no protection, despite Turkish neutrality. Some of their birthplaces are shown on the right-hand map.

The photograph is of children in the Dutch deportation centre of Westerbork, on the eve of deportation.

TURKISH-BORN JEWS DEPORTED FROM PARIS

BULGARIA

Black Sea

Edirne

TURKEY
-IN-
EUROPE

Istanbul

EASTERN THRACE

Silviri

Izmit

Gallipoli

Sea of Marmara

Adapazari

Chanak
(Canakkale)

Bursa

Pazarcik

TURKEY
neutral

Bergama

Aegean Sea

Manisa

Izmir
(Smyrna)

0 miles 60
0 kilometres 80

Aydin

© Martin Gilbert 1982

BIRTHPLACES OF THIRTY OF THOSE DEPORTED TO AUSCHWITZ, 3 FEBRUARY 1944

Petrograd
Salomon Rakcine, aged 46
Alexandre Scheffer, aged 55

Moscow
Maurice Liss, aged 53

Astrakhan
Jacques Gantcherelsky, aged 58

Warsaw
Simon Zamber, aged 21
Chaim Zamber, aged 46
Marcel Warszawiak, aged 19
Abraham Szajnsalc, aged 18

London
Betty Zilberstein aged 35
Mary Fajwlewicz aged 33

Drancy

Kharkov
Joseph Brussilovski, aged 77

Paris
Roger Fajwlewicz, aged 6
Robert Moucatel, aged 16

Auschwitz

Odessa
Nathalie Steinberg, aged 52
Hetty Abrahams, aged 68

Marseilles

Barcelona
Max Stammreich, aged 8

Istanbul
Esther Toledano aged 41

Ankara
Isaac Moucatel, aged 39

Chios
Isaac Leon, aged 57

Aleppo
Guarez Chalom, aged 60
Jourad Chalom, aged 75

Casablanca
Maurice Benarrosch, aged 44
Roger Benarrosch aged 7

Tunis
Victor Cohen aged 52

Jaffa
Pauline Blann, aged 44
Maier Wulff, aged 61

Jerusalem
Frida Kaleschmann, aged 22
Suzanne Kaleschmann, aged 20

Alexandria
Isaac Engros, aged 53
Eliassof Gattegno, aged 40

North Sea
Baltic Sea
Atlantic Ocean
Caspian Sea
Black Sea
Mediterranean Sea

0 miles 500
0 kilometres 700

© Martin Gilbert 1982

THE JEWS OF NORTHERN DALMATIA

GREATER GERMANY

AUSTRIA

Lake Balaton

HUNGARY

SLOVENIA

Trieste

ISTRIA

Kraljevica 2
Crikvenica 30

Jasenovac

Senj 6
Rab 4

C R O A T I A

DALMATIA
Gospic

Obrovac 1
Bencovac 1
Drnis 1

Knin 1

B O S N I A

Sibenic 28
Split 210

Dalmatian Coast

Adriatic Sea

ITALY

0 miles 60
0 kilometres 80

© Martin Gilbert 1982

On 3 February 1944 yet another train left Paris for Auschwitz. It was the 67th such deportation in nearly two years. The map above shows the names, birthplaces and ages of 30 of the deportees. Also deported, and gassed on arrival at Auschwitz, was the 39-year-old Chief Rabbi of Strasbourg, René Hirschler, who had been born in Marseilles, and his 32-year-old wife Simone. In 1939 Hirschler had been chaplain to those Jewish refugees who had joined the French Foreign Legion in order to fight against Germany. In March 1943 he had become chaplain of all foreign-born Jews in the detention camps in France. He and his wife had been arrested in Marseilles in December 1943.

In all, 1,214 Jews were deported in this one train. Fourteen of the deportees were over 80. More than 100 were under 16 years old. Only 26 survived the war.

The deportees of February 3 included four American-born deportees, the 89-year-old Zadie Abraham, the 81-year-old Clara Kahn, the 81-year-old Pola Modiano, the 57-year-old Michel Feldman *(page 135)*, Murad Gubbay, born in Calcutta *(page 127)*, and the 17-year-old Raymond Strauss, born in the Brazilian city of Sao Paulo.

The Jewish communities, and individual Jews, of northern Dalmatia, according to the Yugoslavia census of 31 March 1931, are shown in the map opposite (below). The Jews of Split could trace their Jewish predecessors to the third century AD.

On 11 March 1944, 300 women and children from northern Dalmatia, having been interned at Gospic, were deported to the Croat concentration camp at Jasenovac (right, below). Not a single one survived. The men had already been deported to the Sajmiste death camp near Belgrade five months earlier (page 173).

In 1941, following the Italian occupation of Dalmatia, the island of Rab which in 1931 had been the home of a single Jewish family, became the centre of a large refugee population, of Jews from Austria, Croatia and Bosnia. Many had been able to join the Yugoslav partisans in September 1943: others mostly women and children, were seized in March 1944, and deported to Auschwitz (right, below).

The Jews of Albania had survived unmolested under Italian rule. The first Jews to settle in Albania had been refugees from the Spanish expulsions of 1492. Other refugees had joined them in the sixteenth century from Sicily and southern Italy. By 1927 most of Albania's Jews were living in Koritza (right, top). After 1938 several hundred Jewish refugees from Germany and Austria took refuge in Tirana and Durazzo. Following the collapse of Italy in September 1943, they were, at first, unmolested. Then in April 1944, at German insistence, they were interned at Pristina, and consequently deported to Bergen-Belsen. Of 400 Albanian deportees, only 100 survived the war.

These deportations of March and April 1944 took place as the Allied armies in southern Italy were approaching Rome, and after Soviet forces had already crossed the eastern border of Greater Germany and were approaching Lvov.

Meanwhile in Warsaw, on 7 March 1944, the historian Emanuel Ringelblum, who had struggled to collect and preserve as much material as possible about the Warsaw ghetto, and who had managed to hide in 'Aryan' Warsaw after the ghetto revolt, was discovered by the Gestapo, and, together with his family, tortured and killed. Elsewhere in 'Ayran' Warsaw, Polish families, at the risk of their own lives, gave shelter to several thousand Jews, most of whom survived the war.

THE JEWS OF ALBANIA INTERNED

THREE DEPORTATIONS, MARCH – APRIL 1944

© Martin Gilbert 1982

Map 232

GREEK JEWS DEPORTED TO AUSCHWITZ, 23 MARCH - 2 APRIL 1944

On 15 March 1944 the German authorities assembled trucks and guards throughout mainland Greece, and began a systematic search for more than 10,000 Greek Jews. Half were able to flee into the mountains to find shelter with local peasants, to join Greek partisan units, or to escape across the Aegean to neutral Turkey. Many survived as a result of an instruction issued by Archbishop Damaskinos to all monasteries and convents in Athens and the provincial towns to shelter any Jew who knocked on their doors. But over 5,000 Greek Jews were caught, and deported to Auschwitz. It was an eight-day journey in sealed cattle trucks. Hundreds died during the journey itself.

From the west the French and Dutch deportations continued (*opposite*): there were Jews on these two Paris trains from Hong Kong, Senegal, Liverpool and Samarkand.

In the east there were two rebellions. On 22 March 1944, at Koldyczewo, 10 SS guards were killed, and hundreds of prisoners escaped to join the partisans. Twenty-five escapees were caught, including the leader, who committed suicide. On 15 April 1944

(*see also page 169*) a group of prisoners whose task was to destroy the evidence of mass murder, tried to escape from Ponary. Twenty-five were killed; 15 got away. Five days later, the remaining 40 members of the unit were killed.

Thousands of individual Jews served and fought in the French resistance, and in Yugoslav and Greek partisan units (*above*). More than 300 Jewish soldiers from the Greek Army, and 1,000 other Jews, joined Greek partisan units. A group of 40 Jewish partisans took part in the blowing up of the Gorgopotamo Bridge, breaking German rail communications between Greece and the north. The main Greek national resistance organization in the Trikala, Larisa and Volos region was commanded by Moses Pesah, a Greek rabbi.

Jews also served in Soviet partisan forces which were parachuted behind the German lines in order to disrupt German troop and munition movements. In the Lublin region, by March 1944, were many Jews who had been parachuted into Poland as members of Soviet partisan units. Among these Jews

Map 233

DEPORTATION, MASSACRE AND REVOLT, MARCH-APRIL 1944

were the commander of the Special Soviet Parachute Battalion, Lieutenant Colonel Henryk Torunczyk, from Lodz; his deputy commander, Joseph Kratko, from Chelm; and the only woman officer in the battalion,

Lieutenant Lucyna Herz, who was killed in action while leading a company against a German position on the Vistula. For her bravery she was posthumously awarded the rank of Captain in the Red Army.

SLAVE LABOUR CAMP EVACUATIONS, MARCH 1944

© Martin Gilbert 1982

As Soviet forces advanced further and further westward, the Germans began the systematic evacuation of the slave labour camps in their path (*above*). From the camp at Plaszow, many hundreds were sent to Auschwitz, others westward to Mauthausen and Flossenbürg, some northward to the concentration camp at Stutthof.

Majdanek itself was evacuated on 20 March 1944, when all sick prisoners were sent direct to Auschwitz to be gassed, while the rest were sent to Gross Rosen, and the women to Ravensbrück and Natzweiler.

The photograph, taken in 1980, shows some of the hundreds of thousands of shoes which the Germans had collected from their victims at Majdanek between 1942 and 1944, hoping to find a technical process which would enable used shoe leather to be turned to some practical or even military purpose. But no such process had been discovered before the camp was evacuated. The shoes remained in their original storehouse.

Even while the first westward evacuations were in progress, the eastward deportations were continuing. Those from Holland, Italy and Paris are shown on the two small maps (*opposite*). More than half of the Dutch Jews sent to Bergen-Belsen and Theresienstadt survived. But most of those sent to Auschwitz perished.

182

FIVE DUTCH DEPORTATIONS

North Sea

Baltic Sea

Bergen-Belsen   [101] 5 April
[232] 19 May

HOLLAND

Theresienstadt
[289]
5 April

Auschwitz
[240]
5 April
[453]
19 May

0   miles   300
0   kilometres   500

© Martin Gilbert 1982

FOUR FURTHER DEPORTATIONS

North Sea

Treblinka

0   miles   200
0   km   300

Warsaw

Auschwitz

Paris
[1,500] including Simone Jacob
13 April   (Simone Veil)
[1,004] including Itzak
29 April   Katznelson

Fossoli
[518]
16 May

Backa
Topola
[3,000]
29 April

Adriatic Sea

© Martin Gilbert 1992

Among those deported from Paris on 13 April 1944 were several hundred Jews who had been born in Alsace, the French province annexed by Germany, first in 1870 and again in 1940. The map on the far right shows some of the towns, villages and hamlets in which these deportees were born, many of them during the period of German rule before the First World War.

In all, 1,500 Jews were deported from Paris to Auschwitz on 13 April 1944, among them 148 children under 12, and a 16-year-old girl, Simone Jacob, who had been born in Nice. Miss Jacob was one of 100 deportees from this particular train who survived Auschwitz. Later, as Simone Veil, she became Minister of Health in the French Government, and, in July 1979, President of the European Parliament at Strasbourg.

From the second Paris deportation that month, on 29 April 1944, those killed included the Yiddish poet from Warsaw, Itzak Katznelson. His wife and most of his family had already been killed at Treblinka.

ALSACE-BORN DEPORTEES, 13 APRIL 1944

Niederbronn

Oberbronn

Struth

Ingwiller

Mertzwiller

Neuwiller

Ringendorf

Haguenau

Phalsbourg

Mommenheim

Schwindratzheim

Saverne

Brumath

Wingersheim

Romanswiller

Küttolsheim

Strasbourg

Quatzenheim

Molsheim

Lingolsheim

Urmatt

Düttlenheim

Duppingheim

Rosheim

Fegersheim

Wishes

Eschau

Ottrott

Obernai

Rhine

Westhausen

Benfeld

Gerstheim

ALSACE

Muttersholz

River

Bergheim

BADEN

Grussenheim

Colmar

0   miles   10
0   kilometres   15

© Martin Gilbert 1982

Map 238

THE JEWS OF HUNGARY AND THE GERMAN OCCUPATION, 19 MARCH 1944

GREATER GERMANY

FELVIDEK
78,000
annexed from Czechoslovakia
2 November 1938

MORAVIA

AUSTRIA

SLOVAKIA

Kassa
(Kosice)

EASTERN GALICIA

RUTHENIA
72,000
annexed from Czechoslovakia
2 November 1938 and
15 March 1939

Munkacs
(Mukacevo)

River Danube

Budapest

Lake
Balaton

HUNGARY
444,567

Kolozsvar
(Cluj)

R U M A N I A

CROATIA

BACSKA
20,000
annexed from Yugoslavia
7 April 1941

Novi Sad
(Ujvidek)

B A N A T

SREM

NORTHERN
TRANSYLVANIA
149,000
annexed from Rumania
30 August 1940

© Martin Gilbert 1982

0 — miles — 100
0 — kilometres — 160

On 19 March 1944 German control was imposed on Hungary. Suddenly more than three quarters of a million Jews who had hitherto seemed safe from Nazi terror, and in particular from deportation, came under Nazi dominance.

More than a quarter of a million of these Jews lived in areas which Hungary itself had annexed between 1938 and 1941, as shown on the map above. One such area was the Bacska, whose Jewish communities are shown on the map opposite, according to the Yugoslav census of 1931.

In the autumn of 1941 more than 10,000 Jews whose Hungarian citizenship was in doubt had been deported to Kamenets Podolsk, and murdered (*page 68*). A few months later, in January 1942, 1,000 Jews had been massacred in the Bacska (*page 87*).

In January 1943, after more than 50,000 Hungarian Jews had been forced to serve in labour battalions on the eastern front as part of Hungary's war effort against Russia, at least 40,000 had been killed during the fighting or had died after the Soviet army's

victory on the River Don (*page 143*).

Despite the deaths of so many Jews, the Hungarian Government had adamantly rejected two German requests for the deportation of Hungarian Jews to Greater Germany in 1943, and had even begun to institute court proceedings against those responsible for the Bacska killings of 1942.

Hitler himself had protested twice to the Hungarian Government about what he called its 'irresolute and ineffective' handling of the Jewish question, and on 12 March 1944, a week before the German occupation of Hungary, the SS began to plan the complete destruction of Hungarian Jewry.

Within a few weeks of the imposition of German control over Hungary, tens of thousands of Jews were driven from their towns and villages, and forced into ghettos and special camps (*page 186*).

The photograph shows a deportation from a town in the Felvidek region, which Hungary had annexed from Czechoslovakia in November 1938.

Map 239

THE JEWISH COMMUNITIES OF THE BACSKA, INTERNED

RUMANIA

HUNGARY

River Danube

Baja
5

Bacsalmas
5

Horgos
42

Martonos
17

Stare
Kanjiza
40

Subotica
3,758

Senta
1,457

Bajmok
131

Cantavir
78

River Tisza

Stanisic
80

Ada
342

Bezdan
74

Conoplja
49

Topola
411

B A C S K A

Petrovo Selo
282

BANAT

Monostor
22

Sombor
1,175

Feketic
48

Stari Bečej
500

Kupusina
7

Prigrevica
13

Kula
88

Nadalj
2

Gradiste
4

Apatin
94

Sonta
47

Srbobran
50

Curug
72

Bogojevo
10

Odzaci
16

Dubrava
20

Temerin
92

Zabalj
41

Y U G O S L A V I A

Karavukovo
16

Mosorin
10

Bac
14

Kac
25

Titel
67

Novi Sad
2,445

River Danube

SREM

0   miles   15

0   kilometres   20

© Martin Gilbert 1982

Map 240

JEWS ASSEMBLED FOR DEPORTATION, 16 APRIL-23 MAY 1944

GREATER GERMANY

EASTERN GALICIA

SLOVAKIA

Kassa (Kosice)
12,000
11 May

Ungvar
14,000
6 May

Havasko
3 May

Nevicke
3 May

Munkacs
26,000
15·22 May

RUTHENIA

Iza
3,000

BUKOVINA

Satoraljaujhely
15,000
11 May

Csap

Beregszasz
10,000

Huszt
10,000 *11 May*

Miskolc
21,000
11 May

Kisvarda
2,000 *15 May*

Nyiregyhaza

Maramarossziget

Vad

Petrova

NORTHERN TRANSYLVANIA

Eger
9,000

Nagykallo
23 May

Szatmarnemeti
24,000

Nagybanya
3,500

Felsoviso
8,000
5 May

HUNGARY

Monostor-Kapolnok
3 May

Bethlen
3 May

Szekelyhid
3 May

Szilagysomlyo
7,000
3 May

Des
10,000
3 May

Beszterce
8,000 (Bistriza)
3 May

Nagyszollos
8,000 *15 May*

Nagyvarad (Oradea Mare)
36,000
3 May

Kolozsvar (Cluj)
22,000
3 May

Szaszregen
8,000
3 May

Szamosujvar
1,600

Marosvasarhely
6,000
3 May

RUMANIA

Sepsiszentgyorgy
3 May

0 — miles — 50
0 — kilometres — 80

© Martin Gilbert 1982

Beginning on 15 April 1944, tens of thousands of Hungarian Jews were forced to leave their homes, and to move into specially designated ghetto areas. The map above shows some of these ghettos, with the approximate numbers held in them.

On entering each Hungarian town or village, one Gestapo method was to seize several leading citizens, and then threaten to kill them unless the community agreed to a punitive ransom. In this way, the Jews of the town were impoverished overnight, without even the money to buy railway tickets. The ransom exercise also made the SS seem plausible: they had said they would release the hostages as soon as the money was paid, and they had kept their word. When the SS then said: 'we have orders to put you in brick factories and timber yards *and no harm will come to you*', it could be believed. 'Quite soon', the SS told those who had been thus

confined, 'you will go east to help with the harvest.'

On 15 May 1944 *(opposite, above)* the deportations to Auschwitz began. By mid June a total of 289,357 Jews had been deported to Auschwitz from Ruthenia and northern Transylvania *(see also pages 196-201)*.

The map opposite, gives the approximate number of Jews known to have been deported to Auschwitz and then gassed there, from 63 towns and villages in eastern Hungary. The places shown here amount to no more than half of the towns and villages in this region alone from which Jews were deported. At Miskolc and Satoraljaujhely hundreds of Jews were shot as they tried to resist boarding the trains.

An indication of the size of the destruction elsewhere in Hungary during the summer months of 1944 can be seen from the maps on pages 196 to 201.

DEPORTATIONS FROM EASTERN HUNGARY, 15 MAY - 7 JUNE 1944

© Martin Gilbert 1982

SOME HUNGARIAN JEWISH COMMUNITIES DESTROYED, 15 MAY - 7 JUNE 1944

© Martin Gilbert 1982

THE PARIS DEPORTATIONS OF 15 MAY 1944

FINLAND

North Sea

Reval
arrived 19 May

Leningrad

Baltic Sea

Kovno
arrived 18 May

Soviet forces

Stutthof

Proyanovska
slave labour camp

Soviet forces

Drancy

Paris
878
15 May

Auschwitz

including Israel Kopelov, aged 38 born in Kovno

| 0 | miles | 200 |
| 0 | kilometres | 300 |

© Martin Gilbert 1982

BIRTHPLACES OF SOME OF THE PARIS DEPORTEES OF 15 MAY 1944

also Moses Algaze – Razon, born in Havana, Cuba, aged 23

North Sea

Reval

Petrograd (Leningrad)

Riga

Moscow
Jacob Boguslavski aged 26

Baltic Sea

Dvinsk

Atlantic Ocean

London

Kovno

Vilna

Molczacz

Amsterdam
Brussels

Berlin

Warsaw

Kobryn

Kiev

Drancy

Lodz

Lublin

Paris

Frankfurt

Cracow

Lvov

Strasbourg

Sokal

Dijon

Vienna

Brno

Zurich

Budapest

Kishinev

Odessa

Bordeaux

Lyons

Geneva

Szombathely

Mako

Jassy

Caspian Sea

Avignon

Pecs

Ismail

Sulina

Sevastopol

Belgrade

Bucharest

Adriatic Sea

Varna

Black Sea

Baku
Abraham Jakoubovitch aged 22

Marseilles

Rome

Edirne

Salonica

Constantinople

Bursa

Aegean Sea

Smyrna
Aidin

Algiers

Tunis

Oran

Constantine

Baghdad
Arnold David aged 32

Emmanuel Cohen aged 54

Rabat
Simon Kadosh aged 20

Tlemcen

Georges Quaziz aged 19

Mediterranean Sea

Safed

Damascus

Jaffa

Jerusalem
Haim Epstein aged 39

Georges Sirkis, aged 37

| 0 | miles | 500 |
| 0 | kilometres | 800 |

© Martin Gilbert 1982

Map 245

BIRTHPLACES OF SOME OF THE PARIS DEPORTEES TO AUSCHWITZ, 20 MAY 1944

Chita — Pinchas Reznik, aged 36
Liverpool — Jaffa Hermann, aged 55
Baghdad — Lily Haim, aged 48
Mogador — David Dahan, aged 60
Cairo — Allegra Cori, aged 31
Havana — Dorothée Salomontchik, aged 29
Jerusalem — Tobias Salomon, aged 49
Lima — Rosita Lindow, aged 59
Sao Paulo — Denise Levy, aged 34
Buenos Aires — Sigismund Syskind, aged 30

© Martin Gilbert 1982

On the very day that the first deportations took place from Hungary to Auschwitz, a train left Paris with 878 Jews locked into its 15 cattle trucks. All were men. Their destination was not Auschwitz, but Kovno.

After three days and three nights, on 18 May 1944 they reached their destination, and were sent to the Proyanovska slave labour camp. There, 160 of them were shot and the rest evacuated with other Jews from Kovno six weeks later *(page 200)*.

Nearly 260 of the deportees had been sent on to Reval. Six days after their arrival, 60 were taken for work but never seen again. The rest worked on airfield repairs, 60 being taken to a nearby forest and shot on July 14. On August 14 a hundred of the sick were sent to an 'unknown destination'. Four days later the 34 survivors were evacuated to Stutthof *(page 206):* 15 survived the war.

The lower map *(opposite)* shows some of the birthplaces of the May 15 deportees; the map above shows the birthplaces of 10 of the deportees in the train sent from Paris to Auschwitz five days later. Like several thousand of those murdered at Auschwitz, they had emigrated to western Europe between the wars. The photograph is of a Jew at the moment of departure from Paris.

Map 246

JEWS EXECUTED IN FRANCE FOR RESISTANCE, 1 JANUARY-5 JUNE 1944

London
Dover
North Sea
BRITAIN
Portsmouth
English Channel
NORMANDY
BELGIUM
Cologne
GREATER
GERMANY
LUX.
LORRAINE
ALSACE

Suresnes
18
Paris
3
Argentan
1
Sougé
5
GERMAN - OCCUPIED
FRANCE
Les Ponts de Cé
1
Mezières
1
Poitiers
1
Dole
1
Garnat
1
Morez
1
SWITZERLAND
neutral
Gex
1
Nanteuil
4
Limoges
28
Eymoutiers
1
Cours
1
Lyon
9
Champier
1
Puy de Dôme
2
Voiron
1
Tourtoirac
3
Uzerche
3
Brantôme
9
Salignac
5
St. Etienne
2
Grenoble
1
Thenon
1
Brive
4
Hauteforte
4
Martignas
1
DORDOGNE
78
Bay
of
Biscay
Cognac
1
Mane
1
Villematier
4
Nice
5
Toulouse
6
Marseilles
1
Miremont
9
0 miles 60
0 kilometres 80
Mediterranean Sea
Pyrenees
SPAIN
neutral
GERMAN-OCCUPIED ITALY

© Martin Gilbert 1982

SOME BIRTHPLACES

© Martin Gilbert 1982

Map 248

JEWS, GREEKS AND ITALIANS DROWNED OFF POLEGANDROS, 6 JUNE 1944

SIPHNOS

HERAKLIA

AMORGOS

KILIMOS

POLINOS

IOS

ANTIMILOS

POLEGANDROS

SIKINOS

KARDIOTISSA

MILOS

960

SANTORINI

ANAPHI

THIRASSIA

PHTINI

PACHIA

MAKRA

CHRISTIANA
ASKANIA
ES'CHATI

A e g e a n

S e a

STANDIA

set sail 6 June

Canea
260 *Jews*
imprisoned
21 May

Rethymnon

deported
4 June

Heraklion
400 *Greek hostages*
300 *Italian prisoners-of-war*

C   R   E   T   E

0   miles   20

0   kilometres   30

© Martin Gilbert 1982

Jews had lived on Crete since Roman times. Often oppressed, in AD 440 they put their faith in a pseudo-Messiah, who offered to lead them 'dry shod' through the sea to the Promised Land. Hundreds were drowned.

On 21 May 1944 the Gestapo imprisoned all 260 Jews of Canea, and the five families of Rethymnon. On June 4 they were all deported to Heraklion, and two days later, put on board ship and sent across the Aegean Sea towards the island of Santorini.

Deported with the Jews were 400 Greek civilians, who had been seized as hostages, and 300 Italian prisoners-of-war, who for more than four years had been Germany's allies. All were taken 120 miles across the sea, where the ship was deliberately sunk, and all on board were drowned.

Only 7 Cretan Jews managed to survive the war, in hiding.

Despite the presence of Allied forces in southern Italy, and the Soviet advance into Eastern Galicia, the SS still sought out Jews to deport to Auschwitz. One of the areas of their search was the islands of the Ionian Sea, among them Zante, and Corfu, then only 50 miles from the Allied forces in south Italy.

Jews had lived on Corfu (*right*) since the thirteenth century. During the seige of the island by the Turks in 1716, the Jews had distinguished themselves in defence of the island. During the Italian occupation, from April 1941 to September 1943, there had been no serious hardship, nor did the German occupation on 27 September 1943 lead to any immediate persecution. But on 6 June 1944 all 1,800 Jews were seized by the Gestapo, and eight days later they were deported to what they were told would be 'resettlement' in Poland. The women went overland to Larissa, the men by sea. While at sea they were given nothing to eat or drink and several died. On June 20 all were sent northwards by train, reaching Auschwitz nine days later: 1,600 were sent at once to the gas chamber, and 200 to forced labour.

On Zante (*above*) both Archbishop Chrysostomos and Lukos Karrer, the mayor, refused to obey the Gestapo order that all 257 Jews on the island should be assembled at the quayside to board the boat from Corfu. 'If the deportation order is carried out', the Archbishop declared, 'I will join the Jews and share their fate.' All 195 able-bodied Jews were sent to safety in remote villages. Sixty old people and children were seized by the Gestapo and taken to the quayside to await the Corfu boat: but the boat was already so overcrowded that it did not stop.

Map 251

DISTANT DEPORTATIONS, JUNE 1944

North Sea

Baltic Sea

D-Day landings 6 June

HOLLAND **496** 3 June

Stutthof **20,000** women 29 June

Soviet forces

Auschwitz

Paris **1153** 30 June

13 June

Boryslaw **700** 22 June

Mauthausen

Oradour

0 ___ miles ___ 200

0 ___ kilometres ___ 300

Verona **485** Fossoli 26 June

HUNGARY **381,000** 15 May - 30 June

ITALY

Adriatic Sea

Florence **16** 4 June

Allied forces

Aegean Sea

Mediterranean Sea

Corfu **1,800** 14 June

Zante

© Martin Gilbert 1982

As Soviet forces drew nearer and nearer to Auschwitz, and Allied forces landed on the Normandy beaches on 6 June 1944, the deportations to Auschwitz continued. Trains reached Auschwitz throughout June *(above)* from Paris, Italy, Holland, the Eastern Galician town of Boryslaw and from Corfu, as well as from the massive continuing deportations from Hungary *(pages 196-201)*.

At the same time as these deportations into Auschwitz, the first evacuation of Jews away from Auschwitz had begun, when prisoners in the slave labour camps drawing their labour force from Birkenau were sent out by train, the men westwards to Mauthausen, the women northwards to Stutthof.

The concentration camp at Stutthof had

STUTTHOF AND ITS SATELLITE SLAVE LABOUR CAMPS

been set up in September 1939 (*page 34*). But it was not until August 1943 that any large number of Jews, several hundred survivors of the Bialystok ghetto revolt, were deported there (*page 164*).

It was in the area around Stutthof that the Germans had begun, in the spring of 1944, to set up more than 60 new labour camps, to replace those which had already been overrun by the Soviet forces. The map above shows the principal towns and camps to which prisoners were sent from Stutthof throughout the summer and autumn of 1944 (*pages 211*).

In the labour camps around Stutthof, conditions were barbaric: of 100 Jewish girls in the slave labour camp at Gerdauen, only three survived the war.

In Stutthof itself, tens of thousands of prisoners died of dysentery, typhus and starvation. Others were brutally clubbed to death while working in the nearby forests, or sadistically drowned in mud. Many were killed by means of phenol injections, and their bodies then burned in the crematorium, in specially designed 'high capacity' ovens.

Altogether more than 52,000 Jews passed through Stutthof, of whom at least 30,000 were women. Only about 3,000 survived the brutal treatment.

In France, four days after the Allied landings, the Germans killed more than 600 French villagers at Oradour-sur-Glane (*right*). The women and children were burned alive in the church, and the men were machine-gunned, as a reprisal against

SEVEN JEWS KILLED AT ORADOUR, 10 JUNE 1944

the killing in another village of an SS army commander by a resistance sniper. Seven of the 642 men, women and children killed at Oradour were Jews: refugees who had earlier been able to escape deportation to Auschwitz by hiding among the friendly villagers. Now they became the victims of another repeated feature of Nazi tyranny, reprisals against civilians. Among the seven were Joseph Kanzler, born in Budapest, and his two children, born in Strasbourg.

Map 254

DEPORTATIONS FROM CENTRAL HUNGARY, 15 MAY - 8 JULY 1944

Auschwitz

Dziedzice

GALICIA

Bielsko Biala

from Theresienstadt

2,503
15 May

2,500
16 May

2,500
18 May

Zywiec

G R E A T E R

G E R M A N Y

Zwardon

Zwardon

Zilina

MORAVIA

S L O V A K I A

Zvolen

Szecseny
250

Balassagyarmat
2,100

Losonc

Putnok
509

Mosonmagyarovar
350

Nagyoroszi

Ozd
500

Sajoszentpeter
500

Danube

AUSTRIA

Oroszvar
120

Ersekujvar
7,000

Vamosmikola
60

Petervasara
50

Eger
1,400

Miskolc
see map 242

Kisterenye
75

Saly
40

Harsany
50

Dunaszerdahely
8,000

Bercel
170

Paszto
380

Emod
60

4,000

Gyor

Acs
100

Tata
450

Gyongyos
1,600

Mezokovesd **750**

Kapuvar
300

Komarom
100

Kal
100

Fuzesabony
200

Tet
120

Gyomore
170

Budapest
and
region

Heves
350

Tiszafured
650

Beled
300

Jaszbereny
560

Jaszkiser
55

Csepreg
225

Papa and region
see map 258

H   U   N   G   A   R   Y

Tiszaroff
45

Szombathely
4,228

*see maps
257 and 259*

Korosladany
100

Balaton region
*see maps 256 and
262*

Danube

Izsak
25

Szarvas
100

Gyoma
48

Mezobereny
100

Sarkad
159

Kiskoros
580

Kiskunfelegyhaza
700

Szentes
400

2,000

Bekescsaba

Dunapataj
100

Kecel
30

Kiskunmajsa
126

Hodmezovasarhely
650

Gyula
450

Kalocsa
250

Kistelek
200

Totkomlos
100

Kiskunhalas
750

CROATIA

Janoshalma
200

Melykut
70

Baja
700

Mezokovacshaza
250

Nagybaracska
50

Bacsalmas
160

Mako
1,400

RUMANIA

B A C S K A
see page 185

B A N A T
see page 59

0   miles   40

0   kilometres   60

© Martin Gilbert 1982

Map 255

DEPORTATIONS FROM RUTHENIA AND NORTHERN TRANSYLVANIA, 15 MAY – 8 JULY 1944

Brody

VOLHYNIA

Auschwitz

Rzeszow

Lvov

Birkenau

Cracow

Tarnow

Przemysl

GENERAL GOVERNMENT

Soviet forces by 8 July 1944

Soviet forces advancing in May

Monowitz

Sanok

EASTERN GALICIA

Stanislawow

Stryj

Munkacs
25,000

Iza
3,000

Lubotin

Radvan

Presov

Ungvar
14,000

Kolomyja

Korosmezo

Kuty

SLOVAKIA

RUTHENIA

Bilke

Czernowitz

Huszt
10,000

BUKOVINA

Satoraljaujhely

Kassa
10,000

Beregszasz
10,000

Maramarossziget
12,000

Felsoviso
8,000

HUNGARY

Nagybanya

NORTHERN TRANSYLVANIA

Szekelyhid

Szalva

Beszterce
8,000

Des
10,000

Szilagysomlyo
7,000

Szaszregen
8,000

Nagyvarad
36,000

Kolozsvar

Marosvasarhely
6,000

22,000

miles 20

kilometres 30

RUMANIA

Sepsiszentgyorgy

© Martin Gilbert 1982

The deportation of Hungarian Jews to Auschwitz had begun on 15 May 1944 from eastern Hungary *(page 187)* and central Hungary *(opposite)*. Also starting on May 15, Jews were deported from two of the areas annexed in 1938 and 1940, Ruthenia and northern Transylvania *(above)*, where the number of victims exceeded 250,000 in just under eight weeks. The maps show some of these deaths and give an indication of the speed, scale and effectiveness of the Nazi plan; a plan put into operation more than four and a half years after the German invasion of Poland.

Each deportation train bore the deceptive inscription 'German worker-resettlers'. Up to 100 people were forced into each wagon. Like the earlier French, Dutch, Belgian and Greek deportees, they were allowed only a single bucket of water and a single waste bucket to each wagon. Hundreds died during the journey. Many committed suicide or were driven insane by confinement and fear. Others were killed or robbed whenever the train had to stop for traffic control.

The deportations were still in mid course on 'D-Day' when the forces of the Western allies landed on the Normandy beaches *(page 194)*. For more than two years the Nazi authorities, and even Hitler himself, had failed to persuade the Hungarian Government, or the Hungarian Regent, Admiral Horthy, to agree to these deportations. Now, in control of Hungary, the Germans hastened to destroy this last unmolested mass of Jewry before Soviet forces, steadily advancing towards Eastern Galicia, entered eastern Hungary.

THE HUNGARIAN DEPORTATIONS CONTINUE : THE LAKE BALATON REGION

Sarvar 600

Papa (and region) see map 258

Lovasbereny 50

Kapolnasnyek 80

Janoshaza 300

Varpalota 180

Szekesfehervar 1,750

Devecser 150

Csabrendek 50

Veszprem 800

Polgardi 50

Seregelyes 80

Nagyvazsony 30

Racalmas 25

Zalaszentgrot 100

Balatonfured 130

Balatonkiliti 50

Aba 50

Dunapentele 60

Tapolca 600

Kovagoors 40

Lake Balaton

Siofok 190

Enying 170

Keszthely see map 262

Balatonszemes 50

Balatonboglar 190

Iregszemcse 56

Simontornya 70

Dunafoldvar 300

Ozora 70

Cece 50

Pincehely 100

Kethely 45

Tamasi 200

Nagydorog 70

Danube

Nagykanizsa 1,800

Somogyszil 30

Gyonk 55

River

Nagybajom 90

0 miles 15
0 kilometres 20

© Martin Gilbert 1982

DEPORTATIONS FROM THE BUDAPEST REGION

0 miles 10
0 kilometres 20

Esztergom 400

Vac 1,400

Lorinci 200

Kallo 50

Szentendre 150

Aszod 200

Hatvan 450

Pomaz 20

see map 259

Tinnye 50

Zsambek 30

Godollo 260

Tura 90

Budapest

Isaszeg 60

Bicske 230

Pecel 90

Gyomro 130

Suburban Budapest 12,750

Nagykata 350

Martonvasar 70

River Danube

Tokol 59

Ocsa 140

Pilis 64

Ercsi 130

Bugyi 55

Dabas 50

Cegled 500

Adony 120

Domsod 90

Orkeny 78

Kunszentmiklos 121

Lajosmizse 30

Nagykoros 400

© Martin Gilbert 1982

The Hungarian deportations to Auschwitz continued throughout May and June: and were carried out systematically from region to region. Towards the end of June, and in the first week of July, the deportations were focused on the regions of Lake Balaton (*above*), Budapest (*left*), and the outer suburbs of Budapest (*opposite, below*). Jews from even the smallest of communities were seized (*opposite, above*), the Nazi aim being to deport every Hungarian Jew to Auschwitz. To this end, Adolf Eichmann personally supervised the deportations from an office in Budapest.

On reaching Auschwitz, only a few from each train, sometimes only a dozen men out of as many as 4,000 deportees, were kept alive for use as slave labourers; the vast majority was taken straight to the gas chambers, and murdered. The corpses were cremated.

The map opposite (*above*) shows the Jewish communities and families from the Papa region, who were deported to Auschwitz on 4 July 1944 and murdered there. In 1942 many of the young Jews of Papa had been sent to forced labour

THE JEWS OF THE PAPA REGION DEPORTED TO AUSCHWITZ, 4 JULY 1944

Marcalto **14**

Veszpremvarsany
Sonnenfeld family

Magyargencs **7**

Papateszer **5**

Kemeneshogyesz **11**

Papa **2,565**

Bakonykoppany **2**

Mezolak **5**

Vinar **2**

Adasztevel **1**

Ugod **12**

Kulsovat **4**

Mihalyhaza **1**

Daka **2**

Tapolcafo **5**

Bakonybel
Weisz family

Zirc **8**

Nemesszalok **60**

Dabrony **4**

Nagyalasony **7**

Csogle **18**

Kiscsosz **5**

Somlovecse **9**

Nagypirit **8**

Kispirit **3**

Iszkaz **6**

Somloszollos **16**

Kerta **6**

Doba **7**

Borszorcsok **1**

Kislod **8**

Kamond **5**

Somlovasarhely **15**

Ajka **35**

Apacatorna **10**

Tuskevar **32**

*Miklos Kohn
Gyula Scheiber
and his wife
Terez Scheiber
Mihaly Spierer
and his wife
Laszlo Spierer
Istvan Spierer*

Pusztamiske **10**

Padrag **2**

Halimba **7**

Ocs **3**

0 miles 8
0 kilometres 10

© Martin Gilbert 1982

on the Russian front (*page 184*). On 24 May 1944 the remaining 2,565 Jews of the town, and more than 200 Jews from nearby villages, had been confined to a ghetto. A few weeks later they were moved to a concentration camp set up in a factory in the town, in readiness for deportation.

As news of the deportations reached the West, together with the first accounts, by escapees, of the working of the gas chambers at Auschwitz, and of the gassing of Jews from the first trains from Hungary, protests poured in to Budapest: from the Allied leaders, from the King of neutral Sweden, from the President of the International Red Cross, and from the Vatican. These protests reached a climax in the first days of July, as the Papa Jews were about to be deported. Tragically, for them, the protests came too late. Even as the Hungarian Government was deciding to order a halt to the deportations, the 2,800 Jews of Papa were being made ready to be sent to Auschwitz; less than 300 survived. Among those who perished was their rabbi, J. Haberfeld.

DEPORTATIONS FROM THE BUDAPEST SUBURBS

0 miles 3
0 kilometres 5

Dunakeszi **200**

Ujpest **10,000**

Rakospalota **1,800**

Csomor **70**

Kistarcsa **75**

Pestujhely **400**

Rakosszentmihaly **660**

Rakosliget **176**

Budapest

municipal border 1944

Kobanya **4,000**

Rakoscsaba **400**

Rakoskeresztur **200**

Albertfalva **85**

Kispest **4,000**

Pestszentlorinc **500**

Pestszenterzsebet **3,000**

Torokbalint **80**

Csepel **700**

Soroksar **150**

Nagyteteny **140**

Map 260

DEPORTATION, MASS MURDER AND REVOLT, JULY 1944

Baltic Sea

Shauliai (Shavli) *ghetto 'liquidated'* 15 July

Kovno **8,000** *1 July*

Vilna **Ponary** **3,000** *2 July*

19-25 July

Stutthof

Jewish partisan units 8 July

GREATER GERMANY

Majdanek *liberated 23 July*

Radom *the last* **3,000** *slave labourers 26 July*

Lublin

Ostrowiec *David Kempinski*

Jewish partisan company led by *Yehiel Grynszpan*

Theresienstadt **4,000** *deported six months earlier, gassed at Auschwitz 12 July*

SILESIA

3 July Death march *6 July Death march*

Auschwitz

Soviet forces

Dachau

S L O V A K I A

Csorna **650** *5 July*

Sopron **1,286** *5 July*

Koszeg (Güns) **117** *4 July*

Szil **50** *5 July*

Papa **2,800** *4 July*

Mor **125**

Budapest

Dunaharaszti **100** *8 July*

Albertirsa **100**

Monor **200**

Paks **500**

Debrecen **13,000** *3-8 July*

Tolna **120** *6 July*

Bonyhad **800** *6 July*

Mohacs **500** *5 July*

Decs **40**

from Rhodes and Kos

© **Martin Gilbert 1982**

0 *miles* 80
0 *kilometres* 120

As Soviet forces approached Shauliai, Kovno, Vilna and Lublin during the first week of July, Jewish partisans were active behind the lines on all these fronts.

On July 2 the SS took the last 3,000 Jews of Vilna, labourers in a factory, and murdered them at Ponary (*above*). Thousands were also killed at Shauliai and Kovno, and thousands more evacuated to Stutthof and Dachau, as the Soviet forces drew near. At Ostrowiec, as the SS sent 2,000 slave labourers towards Auschwitz, some succeeded in breaking out and escaping.

On 4 July 1944 the Jews of Papa (*page 199*) were deported to Auschwitz (*above*). In all, during that first week of July, 50,000 more Hungarian Jews were sent to their deaths (*opposite, above*). Many of these deportees

lived in small communities to the south of Lake Balaton (*opposite, below*). Then, on July 8 the Hungarian Government bowed to the growing international pressure, and ordered the deportations to be stopped. The Germans gave way. More than 437,402 Hungarian Jews had been deported; 300,000 were still alive on July 8, most of them in Budapest, where the deportations had been about to begin, having already reached the suburbs (*page 199*).

Majdanek was entered by Soviet forces on July 23. The SS now accelerated the marches and evacuations away from Auschwitz (*above*), while from France and Belgium (*opposite, above*), as well as from Radom, the last few trains were still being sent into Auschwitz. Not only the final Hungarian

DISTANT DEPORTATIONS, JULY 1944

BELGIUM **563** *21 July*

Normandy landings

Paris **1,300** *29 July*

Toulouse **166** *30 July*

SWITZ.

SPAIN *neutral*

PORTUGAL

Bergen-Belsen
Buchenwald
Auschwitz

HUNGARY **50,000** *1-8 July*

Leningrad
Moscow
Kovno
Vilna
Soviet forces
Kiev
Stalingrad
Lvov
Odessa
Jassy

Rome

Yugoslav partisans
Adriatic Sea

Black Sea

TURKEY *neutral*

Kos **120**

Rhodes **1,700** *23 July*

SYRIA

PALESTINE

EGYPT

0 miles 400
0 kilometres 600

© Martin Gilbert 1982

deportees, but Jews from as far away as the islands of Kos and Rhodes were also still on their way to the gas chambers as more and more 'death marches' away from the camp were ordered, and hundreds of Jews were killed as men and women, weakened by hunger and ill-treatment, were marched westwards towards new labour camps.

In Yugoslavia, Jews fought among partisan units which were liberating larger and larger areas of the Balkans.

It was during these evacuations that Dachau, and soon also Bergen-Belsen, hitherto camps primarily for non-Jewish political prisoners, became camps into which tens of thousands of Jews were evacuated, mostly from the labour camp regions of the east, and in which, while not systematically murdered as in the eastern death camps, they perished in their hundreds from the brutality of the guards, and from starvation and disease.

MORE HUNGARIAN DEPORTATIONS, 1-8 JULY 1944

Vasvar **200**
Kormend **240**
Zalalovo **80**
Sumeg **250** *4 July*
Keszthely **825** *4 July*
Pacsa **50**
Hahot **30**
Lake Balaton
Karad **80**
Tab **400** *7 July*
Marcali **200** *7 July*
Nemesded **40**
Kaposvar **6,000** *2 July*
Dombovar **731**
Magocs **120** *5 July*
Csurgo **200**
Nagyatad **200**
Kadarkut **60**
Pecs **1,180** *6 July*

0 miles 20
0 kilometres 30

© Martin Gilbert 1982

JEWISH ORPHANS SEIZED ON 20-24 JULY 1944 AND DEPORTED TO AUSCHWITZ

River Seine

Drancy

Bobigny Station

Neuilly

Paris

to Auschwitz
300

Montreuil

500

Louveciennes

0   miles   5
0   kilometres   8

© Martin Gilbert 1982

BIRTHPLACES OF THIRTY-ONE OF THE CHILDREN DEPORTED ON 31 JULY 1944

BELGIUM

GERMANY

LUXEMBOURG

Longwy
Berthe Kerszbaum aged 12

Villerupt
Arnold Nadel aged 14
Leon Nadel aged 9

Thionville
Mireille Korman aged 12

Hayange
Jacqueline Korman aged 7
Hennette Korman aged 5

S A A R

F R A N C E

Metz

Alice Gliot aged 12
Louise Gliot aged 11
Adolf Gliot aged 10
Charles Gliot aged 7
Renée Grumberger aged 8
Jean Grumberger aged 7
Rolande Grumberger aged 6

Joseph Tabak aged 13
Jacques Tabak aged 7
Nathan Szklarz aged 12
Daniella Szklarz aged 6
Michelle Westreich aged 4

Forbach
Jacques Steinberg aged 9
Madeleine Steinberg aged 7

Sarreguemines
Leopold Ratz aged 12
Liliane Ratz aged 11

0   miles   15
0   kilometres   20

© Martin Gilbert 1982

David Holz aged 13
Joseph Holz aged 12
Jacques Holz aged 11
Marianne Holz aged 9
Paul Holz aged 6
Emmanuel Holz aged 4

Odette Krieger aged 13
Genette Krieger aged 9
Nina Krieger aged 7

Nancy

On 20 July 1944, while the Allies advanced towards Paris, the SS ordered the arrest of Jewish orphans in the Paris region. Within four days, 500 orphans had been seized, some 300 of whom were among a total of 1,300 Jews deported from Drancy to Auschwitz on 31 July 1944.

The map above, and the maps opposite, show the birthplaces and ages of 67 of these 1,300 deportees. On reaching Auschwitz, 800 of them were gassed, including all the children. Of the 500 adults selected for work in nearby labour camps, 350 survived the last ten months of the war.

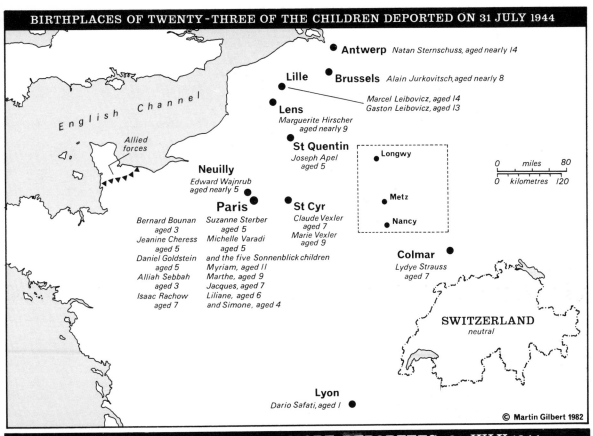

BIRTHPLACES OF TWENTY-THREE OF THE CHILDREN DEPORTED ON 31 JULY 1944

Antwerp — Natan Sternschuss, aged nearly 14
Brussels — Alain Jurkovitsch, aged nearly 8
Lille — Marcel Leibovicz, aged 14 / Gaston Leibovicz, aged 13
Lens — Marguerite Hirscher aged nearly 9
St Quentin — Joseph Apel aged 5
Longwy
Metz
Nancy
Neuilly — Edward Wajnrub aged nearly 5
St Cyr — Claude Vexler aged 7 / Marie Vexler aged 9
Colmar — Lydye Strauss aged 7

Paris:
Bernard Bounan aged 3
Jeanine Cheress aged 5
Daniel Goldstein aged 5
Alliah Sebbah aged 3
Isaac Rachow aged 7
Suzanne Sterber aged 5
Michelle Varadi aged 5
and the five Sonnenblick children
Myriam, aged 11
Marthe, aged 9
Jacques, aged 7
Liliane, aged 6
and Simone, aged 4

SWITZERLAND neutral

Lyon — Dario Safati, aged 1

English Channel / Allied forces

© Martin Gilbert 1982

BIRTHPLACES OF THIRTEEN MORE DEPORTEES, 31 JULY 1944

London — Milly Pomerance aged 50
Berlin
Frankfurt — Ruth Mentzel aged 12 and her mother Charlotte, aged 34
Paris / Drancy
Colmar
Lyon
Auschwitz
Soviet forces
Marseilles — Claude Korssia aged 5 and his youngest sister Elise, aged 3
Allied forces / Adriatic Sea
Black Sea
Behor Yeruchalmi aged 47
RHODES
Oran:
Gabrielle Korssia aged 14
Marcelle Korssia aged 7
Simone Korssia aged 9
and their mother Tama, aged 40
whose two youngest children had been born in Marseilles
Tlemcen — Mina Dahan aged 6
Jaffa — Eliezer Zlaskine aged 54
Cairo — Maurice Zeitoun aged 46
Mediterranean Sea

© Martin Gilbert 1982

THE ALLIED ADVANCE, 23 JUNE-25 AUGUST 1944

North Sea

Baltic Sea

Leningrad

Klooga

Riga

front line 7 August 1944

Vitebsk

Kovno

Vilna

Minsk

Grodno

Stutthof

Bialystok

front line 23 June 1944

Ravensbrück

Neuengamme

Warsaw

Kiev

Sachsenhausen

London

Bergen-Belsen

Berlin

Siedlce

Lublin

Majdanek

English Channel

front line 25 August 1944

Prague

Auschwitz

Lvov

Czernowitz

Odessa

Caen

Paris

Mauthausen

Kosice

Munkacs

Jassy

Dachau

Vienna

Bratislava

Black Sea

front line 14 August 1944

Budapest

Bay of Biscay

Lyons

Trieste

Bucharest

Bordeaux

Grenoble

Marseilles

Cannes

Adriatic Sea

Allied forces 25 August

| 0 | miles | 250 |
| 0 | kilometres | 400 |

© Martin Gilbert 1982

A LABOUR CAMP EVACUATION TO AUSCHWITZ, 22 JULY 1944

Lublin

Konopnica

Majdanek

`1,200`

left 22 July 1944

Niedrzwica Duza

Skarzysko-Kamienna

Wilkolaz

Ostrowiec Swietokrzyski

Annopol

Krasnik

Swiety Krzyz

Olbiecin

Kielce

Ozarow

Goscieradow

`180`

Wola Jachowa

Cmielow

Nowa Slupia

River Vistula

Auschwitz

arrived 1 August 1944

Cracow

`200`

gassed on arrival

| 0 | miles | 25 |
| 0 | kilometres | 40 |

© Martin Gilbert 1982

A 'DEATH MARCH' EVACUATION FROM WARSAW, 29 JULY 1944

Zychlin
arrived
1 August

River Vistula

Kampinos forest

Soviet forces

40
30 July

460
29 July

River Bzura

Lowicz
20   31 July

Warsaw
3,520
left
29 July 1944

600   not evacuated,
later took part in
the Warsaw uprising

© Martin Gilbert 1982

EVACUATED BY 'DEATH TRAIN' TO DACHAU, 4 AUGUST 1944

WARTHELAND

Berlin

Kutno

Zychlin
3,000
left
4 August 1944

Warsaw

SAXONY

River Elbe

SILESIA

River Oder

Soviet forces

GENERAL
GOVERNMENT

1,000

THURINGIA

River Vistula

Prague

BOHEMIA

MORAVIA

Auschwitz

BAVARIA

River Danube

SLOVAKIA

Dachau
2,000
arrived
9 August 1944

Munich

Vienna

© Martin Gilbert 1982

Between 23 June and 25 August 1944 both the Soviet and western Allied forces made considerable advances *(opposite, above)*. As Bialystok, Lublin and Lvov were liberated, the Germans accelerated the evacuation of Jews away from the advancing Soviet forces.

As Russian troops approached Lublin, 1,200 Jews, many of them prisoners-of-war who had been captured in September 1939, were marched away on foot, westwards to Kielce, where 180 were killed. The survivors were then sent by train to Auschwitz, where 200 were gassed on arrival.

A similar death march and death train evacuation, during which more than 2,000 Jews died, started from Warsaw a week later *(above)*. Those evacuated to Zychlin and then to Dachau were Jews who had been brought from Auschwitz to clear the rubble of the Warsaw ghetto. As this evacuation began, 50 of the slave labourers managed to escape into 'Aryan' Warsaw, and were to fight in the Warsaw uprising later that month *(page 206)*.

Map 271

DEPORTATIONS, DEATH MARCHES AND REVOLT, AUGUST 1944

© Martin Gilbert 1982

North Sea

Baltic Sea

from Estonia

Stutthof

Ravensbrück

0   miles   100

0   kilometres   200

Soviet forces

Warsaw
*uprising
1 August -
15 Sept*

Lodz
70,000
6-30 August

Ostrowiec
labour camp
2,000
3 August

Buchenwald

Gross Rosen

Drancy

Paris
51 *17 August*
*uprising
15-25 August*

Allied forces

Flossenburg

Auschwitz

Plaszow
evacuation begins

Mielec
slave labour camp
3,000
24 August

Banska Bystrica

Novaky
SLOVAKIA
*uprising
26 August*

Sered

Gusen

Mauthausen

Lyons
650
*uprising
26 August*   *11 August*

Verona
222
2 August

Györ

Lake Balaton

death march August - October

*several thousands
including the poet
Miklos Radnoti*

Castres
uprising

Allied forces

Marseilles

Mazamet
uprising

*Allied landing
15 August*

Pisa
7
1 August

Adriatic Sea

Allied forces

Novi Sad

Belgrade

6,000

Bor
August death march

As the Allied armies advanced, the killing of Jews continued (*above*), with deportations to Auschwitz from Paris, Lyons and Verona, as well as 70,000 sent to Auschwitz from Lodz, the last of the 'working' ghettos.

The evacuations away from Auschwitz were also gaining in intensity: hundreds died in deportation trains to Ravensbrück and Flossenbürg, Güsen and Mauthausen.

In Pisa the Nazis murdered the Catholic philanthropist Pardo-Roques and six Jews he had sheltered. Hundreds more Jews died when the slave labour camps in Estonia (*above*) were evacuated by sea.

During August 1944 Jewish units, and individual Jews, were active in partisan activity in France. In the Warsaw uprising about 1,000 Jews in hiding, and escaped or liberated Jewish slave labourers, took part, including a Jewish battle unit commanded by Shmuel Kenigswein. During the Slovak revolt, a Jewish battalion, as well as hundreds of individual Jews took part in the capture of three major towns.

Map 273

MASSACRE, DEPORTATION AND EVACUATION, SEPTEMBER 1944

North Sea

Baltic Sea

Narva
liberated 21 September

Klooga **3,000**
19-23 September

Lagedi **426**

Lake Pskov

Soviet forces

Riga
liberated 13 October

25 September

1,019 *3 September*
2,087 *4 September*

HOLLAND

Hamburg
Neuengamme

Westerbork

Stutthof

5,000
women evacuated

3,000
women evacuated

Lodz

Christianstadt

Kratzau

500
men evacuated

Brussels
liberated 3 September

Theresienstadt
2,499
28 September
1,500
29 September

Auschwitz

hundreds women evacuated

500 *evacuated*

Soviet forces

Nancy
liberated 15 September

Allied forces

Dachau

SWITZERLAND
neutral

Hungarian fascist forces

Csermo

Arad

liberated 22 September

Lugos

hundreds massacred 4 September

| 0 | miles | 200 |
| 0 | kilometres | 300 |

Adriatic Sea

© Martin Gilbert 1982

As Allied forces liberated city after city, the murder of Jews continued. During September 1944 four trains reached Auschwitz from Holland and Theresienstadt (*above*). Almost all the deportees, including all the old people and children, were gassed.

It was on one of these trains from Holland that Anne Frank, a Jewish girl whose parents had brought her to Holland as a refugee from Germany before the war, was most probably deported to Auschwitz. She later died at Bergen-Belsen.

Also during September 5,000 more women were evacuated out of Auschwitz to Stutthof, and 3,000 to Neuengamme. The photograph shows Himmler at Stutthof.

As Soviet forces approached Klooga, almost all the surviving slave labourers were slaughtered, among them 1,500 Jews from Vilna, 800 Soviet prisoners-of-war and 700 Estonian political prisoners. Only 85 inmates survived.

In the slave labour camp at Lagedi (*above*) all the Jewish prisoners, including women and babies, were killed only a few hours before the Soviet troops arrived. In northern Transylvania, as Hungarian fascist units seized control, hundreds more Jews were massacred.

Meanwhile, from the many slave labour camps of German-occupied Latvia (*opposite*), tens of thousands of Jews, many of them already deportees from Vilna and Dvinsk (*page 169*), were being evacuated by ship to the Stutthof concentration camp region, as Soviet forces cut off the Gulf of Riga.

Map 274

SLAVE LABOUR CAMP EVACUATIONS, 25 SEPTEMBER 1944

Map 275

DEPORTATION AND REVOLT, OCTOBER 1944

Death marches and death train evacuations took place from Auschwitz, and also from Budapest, throughout October 1944. At the same time, Jews from northern Italy and Theresienstadt continued to be sent to Auschwitz, as were more than 8,000 Jews fom Slovakia, deported as a German reprisal against the Slovak revolt *(page 206)*. Among those deported from Slovakia on October 28 was Tobias Jakobovits, author of a history of the Jews of Bohemia and a member of the staff of the Jewish Museum in Prague; he was sent to his death together with the rest of the museum staff.

In Auschwitz, recently arrived Polish, Hungarian and Greek Jews who were being forced to drag the bodies of those gassed from the gas chambers to the crematoria, having secretly managed to gather some explosives from four Jewish girls working in a nearby munitions factory, blew up one of the four crematoria on 7 October 1944. All those who took part in the revolt were subsequently killed, except for a single Jew, Isaac Venezia, from Salonica, who managed to get back into the main camp. In

the final evacuation of Auschwitz *(page 215)*, he was among those sent to Ebensee, where he died of starvation.

Throughout November 1944 every day saw further towns liberated or captured by the Allies. In the west the Americans were on German soil. In the east the Russians had entered East Prussia, and they had captured the two islands at the mouth of the Gulf of Riga *(page 209)*.

In Auschwitz 8,000 more Jews were gassed during November *(opposite)*, before Himmler ordered the gassing to cease. The last gassings took place on November 28. Thousands of Jews were now sent away from Auschwitz by train to concentration camps and labour camps inside Germany. Among those camps were Dachau and Bergen-Belsen, which, while not serving as extermination camps, were nevertheless the scenes of increasing hardship, hunger, disease and brutality. One group of prisoners from Auschwitz was sent to Lieberose, where they were put to work building a special 'city' at Ullersdorf, to serve as a future rest home for German officers.

Map 276

EVACUATIONS AND DEATH MARCHES, NOVEMBER 1944

North Sea

Baltic Sea

Soviet forces

EAST PRUSSIA

Neuengamme

Stutthof
12,000

Ravensbrück

Bergen-Belsen

Luckenwalde

Lieberose

Piotrkow
the last
400

Antwerp
*port opened
to the allies
26 November*

Allied forces

Buchenwald

Flossenburg

Saarebourg
*liberated
21 November*

Soviet forces

Auschwitz
8,000

Kremnicka
400

Vamosmikola
19 November

Mulhouse
*liberated
22 November*

Dachau

Strasshof

Sered
481
3 November

*Enzo Sereni
murdered
18 November*

Mauthausen

Vienna

SWITZERLAND
neutral

Budapest
50,000
*death march
2-8 November*
10,000
perished

Szolnok
*liberated
4 November*

*Havivah Reik
killed
20 November*

Allied forces

Nagykanizsa
*Hanna Szenes
captured
(murdered in
Budapest)*

*Enzo Sereni
captured*

Ligurian
Sea

Adriatic
Sea

Allied forces

Yugoslav partisans

0   miles   100
0   kilometres 150

© Martin Gilbert 1982

From Stutthof 12,000 Jews, including 4,000 women, were marched south-westward into Germany. Hundreds were killed, or died from exhaustion, on the march. From Piotrkow the last 400 slave labourers were sent to different camps. From Vamosmikola several thousand Jewish prisoners-of-war were sent on a death march across Germany to Luckenwalde. Hundreds died, or were shot, on the march.

On November 2 tens of thousands of Hungarian Jews were driven from Budapest, as Soviet forces approached the city. Whipped and shot by the SS, they were forced westwards towards Vienna: some 4,000 were saved by the intervention of Raoul Wallenberg, a Swedish diplomat, but more than 10,000 died during six days of terror.

Amid these catastrophies, Jewish parachutists, recruited by the British in Palestine and dropped behind the German lines, had tried to make contact with the various Jewish partisan groups. One of these parachutists, a woman called Havivah Reik, took part in the final phases of the Slovak uprising, but was killed at Kremnicka. Another, Enzo Sereni, who had been captured in the German lines in Italy, was taken to Dachau and murdered. A third, Hanna Szenes, captured near Nagykanizsa on the Hungarian-Yugoslav border, was taken to Budapest, tortured, and shot.

Map 277

A DEATH MARCH FROM LIEBEROSE, DECEMBER 1944

Sachsenhausen
900 arrive
Oranienburg

0 — miles — 15
0 — kilometres — 20

River Oder

Falkensee
Falkensee
Spandau

Berlin

Fürstenwalde

Wannsee
Potsdam
Waltersdorf
Wildau
Kablow **2,600** *die on the march*
Wusterhausen
Storkow
Scharmutzel See

Frankfurt-on-Oder

Schwielow See

Glienicke
Buchow
Lindenberg
Beeskow
Bahrensdorf
Friedland
Günthersdorf

Gross Schwiedloch See

Ullersdorf
3,500 *set off*

Luckenwalde

Lieberose

© Martin Gilbert 1982

In December 1944 the Jews who had been sent from Auschwitz to a camp at Lieberose (*page 211*) were evacuated again, forced to march on foot more than 100 miles to the concentration camp at Sachsenhausen (*above*). More than 3,500 set off. Several hundred, too sick to leave the camp infirmary, were shot, and the building set on fire. The march continued in snow and slush, from first light to darkness. Each night the marchers were ordered to make a left turn, march 20 paces, and lie down. At dawn those who could not rise, or could only stumble, were shot. By the time the march reached its destination less than 900 were still alive.

On 6 January 1945 several hundred Jewish women had been taken by train from the Slovak forced labour camp at Sered to Ravensbrück. As the Soviet forces again moved westward, the remaining labour camps on Polish soil were likewise hastily evacuated (*opposite, below*). At Skarzysko Kamienna, where 10,000 Jews had perished in two years, some 5,000 slave labourers were evacuated by train to new camps. A few were able to run away in the confusion, and to hide until the Soviet forces arrived.

Conditions were no better once the evacuees reached their new camps inside Germany. Brutality, savage beatings, sadistic tortures, hunger, senseless hard labour, and shooting at the whim of the guards, were common to all the remaining camps, where overcrowding reached incredible proportions as the evacuations intensified.

The Allied armies were now ready for their final assault on the German heartland (*opposite, above*). The first to advance, on 12 January 1945, were the Soviet forces. As they did so, the last 47 Jewish slave labourers at the former death camp at Chelmno, knowing that they were about to be shot by the SS as Soviet troops drew nearer, revolted, using a building to hold out in. The SS set fire to the building and then machine-gunned those who fled from it. Only one survived.

THE RED ARMY PREPARES TO ADVANCE, 12 JANUARY 1945

North Sea

Baltic Sea

Danzig • Stutthof

Ravensbrück • Stettin

Hamburg

Sachsenhausen

Bergen-Belsen • Berlin • Chelmno • Warsaw

The Hague

Lodz

Leipzig • Breslau • Skarzysko

Cologne • Gross Rosen • Czestochowa • Mielec

Brussels • Buchenwald • Auschwitz

Frankfurt • Prague • Plaszow

Zilina

Metz

Strasbourg • Dachau • Sered

Tuttlingen • Vienna

Belfort • Munich • Mauthausen • Budapest

Ebensee

SWITZERLAND
neutral

0 miles 150
0 kilometres 200

© Martin Gilbert 1982

Jasenovac

SLAVE LABOUR CAMP EVACUATIONS, AND REVOLT, 17 JANUARY 1945

Ravensbrück

Chelmno
revolt
the last **46** killed
1 escaped
17 January

Warsaw

Soviet forces

Berlin

River Oder

Lodz region
slave labour camps

Büchenwald

Skarzysko Kamienna
slave labour camp
10,000 ◄ killed
5,000 ◄ evacuated

Gross Rosen

Czestochowa

Mielec
slave labour camp

Prague

Plaszow
slave labour camp

0 miles 100
0 kilometres 150

© Martin Gilbert 1980

213

Map 280

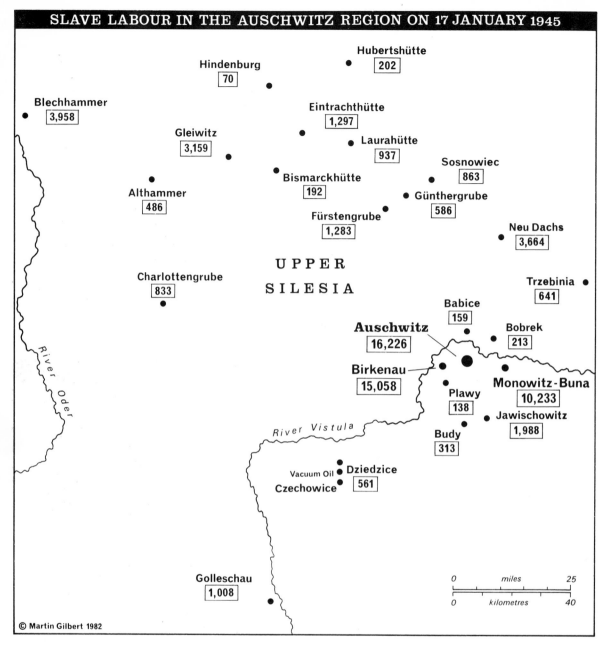

SLAVE LABOUR IN THE AUSCHWITZ REGION ON 17 JANUARY 1945

Hubertshütte
202

Hindenburg
70

Blechhammer
3,958

Eintrachthütte
1,297

Gleiwitz
3,159

Laurahütte
937

Sosnowiec
863

Bismarckhütte
192

Günthergrube
586

Althammer
486

Fürstengrube
1,283

Neu Dachs
3,664

UPPER
SILESIA

Charlottengrube
833

Trzebinia
641

Babice
159

Auschwitz
16,226

Bobrek
213

Birkenau
15,058

Monowitz-Buna
10,233

Plawy
138

Jawischowitz
1,988

Budy
313

River Vistula

River Oder

Vacuum Oil
Dziedzice
561

Czechowice

Golleschau
1,008

0   miles   25
0   kilometres   40

© Martin Gilbert 1982

On 16 January 1945, shortly after the last slave labourers had been evacuated from Czestochowa, Soviet troops entered the city (*opposite, below*). On January 17 the SS recorded (*above*) the number of slave labourers in the Auschwitz region: a total of more than 30,000 men and women. On the following day, January 18, orders were given for the immediate evacuation of all slave labour camps in Upper Silesia. The Jews were to go westward, at first on foot.

Hundreds died on these marches, or were shot as they walked. Many died because, too weak to rise after they had fallen down, they froze to death in the snow. The map opposite (*above*) gives the routes and numbers of only a few of these marches, and of the recorded deaths. Hundreds more died whose deaths were never recorded, or whose graves were never found. Several hundred escaped.

The lower map (*opposite*) shows the general direction of the train evacuations from 18 January 1945, and names 25 of the many dozens of camps to which the evacuees were sent. Many were forced to travel in open railway wagons, exposed to the full fury of winter, and hundreds died of starvation or exposure.

DEATH MARCH EVACUATIONS FROM THE AUSCHWITZ REGION, 18 JANUARY 1945

Blechhammer

to Gross Rosen

Gleiwitz

Neu Dachs **3,000**

600 in 18 days

50

Mikolow

Janinagrube **800**

Neu Berun

Zory

Sweirklany

Birkenau **1,500**

Monowitz **1,000**

Loslau

Rogozna **172**

Cwiklice

17 Auschwitz **2,500**

Wilchwy **5**

Studionka

3

43

Poreba **36**

159

Miedzna **71**

Jawischowitz **1,948**

Jastrzebia **32**

Mszana **26**

Bzie **4**

18

Dziedzice **200** *shot after evacuation*

Soviet front line on 18 January 1945

0 miles 8
0 kilometres 10

© Martin Gilbert 1982

THE RED ARMY ADVANCE AND THE AUSCHWITZ REGION EVACUATIONS

North Sea

Baltic Sea

Memel *liberated 27 January*

Neuengamme

Ravensbrück

Danzig

Stutthof

Hamburg

Bergen-Belsen

Salzwedel

Sachsenhausen

Gardelegen

Berlin

Warsaw

Dora

Cologne

Nordhausen

Buchenwald

Rehmsdorf

Ohrdruf

Fulda

Gross Rosen

Czestochowa **6,000** *evacuated*

Soviet forces on 23 January 1945

British and United States forces

French forces

Flossenbürg

Loslau Birkenau **4,200** *shot 20 January*

Auschwitz **98,000** *evacuated*

Soviet forces on 15 January 1945

Schömberg

Schörzingen
Spaichingen

Dachau

Gusen

Mauthausen

Tüttlingen

Munich

Vienna

SWITZERLAND *neutral*

Schlier

Gunskirchen

Ebensee

0 miles 100
0 kilometres 150

© Martin Gilbert 1982

Budapest *liberated 18 January*

Map 283

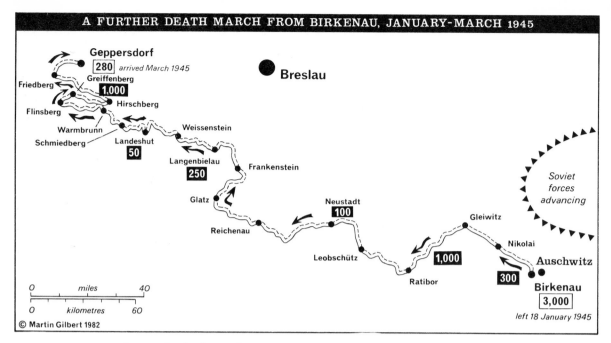

A FURTHER DEATH MARCH FROM BIRKENAU, JANUARY-MARCH 1945

Geppersdorf

280 arrived March 1945

Breslau

Greiffenberg

1,000

Friedberg

Hirschberg

Flinsberg

Weissenstein

Warmbrunn

Landeshut

Schmiedberg

50

Langenbielau

250

Frankenstein

Glatz

Neustadt

100

Reichenau

Soviet forces advancing

Gleiwitz

Leobschütz

1,000

Nikolai

Ratibor

300

Auschwitz

Birkenau

3,000

left 18 January 1945

0 miles 40

0 kilometres 60

© Martin Gilbert 1982

Among the death marches from Birkenau was one which lasted for more than six weeks. Of the 3,000 who set out on foot, only 280 survived. The map above shows their route, and the numbers who died, or were shot, along the way.

The map opposite shows the route both of this march from Birkenau to Geppersdorf, and of five other evacuations which began in the last ten days of January 1945. The shortest was from Königsberg to the Baltic fishing village of Palmnicken. Most of the 3,700 marchers were Jewish women who had been working in one of the branches of Stutthof camp, in Königsberg itself. They were told that they were to be evacuated by sea. On the way, 700 were shot, some at the whim of the guards, others because they stumbled and fell. Then, as the marchers neared the shore, ostensibly to board the boat, the SS opened fire on them with machine-guns. The women were weak and unarmed. But still the will to live was strong in them, and they tried desperately to escape the withering fire. Three thousand were massacred. But about 60 escaped.

From Danzig, and from Stutthof, 29,000 Jews, most of them women, were evacuated by boat and train to camps in Germany. But only 3,000 survived the journey. Three days earlier, from Lamsdorf camp near Breslau, thousands of Jewish prisoners-of-war (see pages 34-5) had been sent, on foot, westwards towards Thuringia. Their march, like that of the Jews to Geppersdorf, took

more than six weeks, and hundreds died or were killed during its course.

The fifth evacuation shown here had an equally tragic course, but a less terrible ending. Over 100 Hungarian Jews from Auschwitz had earlier been sent to work in a quarry in Golleschau. On 21 January 1945 they too were evacuated, this time by train, from Golleschau. Sealed in two cattle trucks, the Jews were shunted north, south, and west. No one on the route dared to open the trucks, which were labelled 'Property of the SS', and 20 of the Jews froze to death as the erratic journey continued. After six days the sealed wagons reached Zwittau, where they were detached from another train and left at the railway station. Learning of this, Oscar Schindler, a German Catholic who owned a number of factories, tried to get permission from the SS to shunt the wagons to his munitions factory at Brünnlitz. He was unsuccessful, but then decided to go personally to the railway station, where he found the bill of lading and wrote on the bottom: 'Final destination — Schindler Factory, Brünnlitz.' The wagons were sent on. When they reached his factory Schindler broke open the locks and released the Jews, giving them shelter, food and warmth, at the risk of his own life.

These were not the first Jews whom Schindler had saved. Earlier, he had brought to his factories prisoners from Plaszow, Gross Rosen and other camps, in theory to employ them as slave labour, but in fact to

Map 284

EVACUATION, MASSACRE AND RESCUE, 20-27 JANUARY 1945

SWEDEN
neutral

DENMARK

Baltic Sea

700
killed in
the march
to the shore

3,000
machined-gunned
at the shore

Palmnicken

Danzig
Stutthof

Königsberg

29,000
evacuated

26,000
*perish during
evacuation*

Ravensbrück

Stettin

Sachsenhausen

Berlin

Warsaw

Kittlitztreben

Breslau

Soviet forces

Buchenwald

THURINGIA

Geppersdorf

Lamsdorf
camp
*evacuated
22 January*

advancing 25 January 1945

Auschwitz

Fulda
*arrived
10 March*

Birkenau

648
*found dead at
liberation
27 January*

Prague

20

Zwittau

Golleschau
*evacuated
21 January*

Brünnlitz
*arrived
27 January*

85
saved

0   miles   100
0   kilometres   160

© Martin Gilbert 1980

protect them. One of these whom Schindler
had saved earlier was Moshe Bejski, a young
Polish Jew who was to become a Justice of
the Supreme Court in Israel 35 years later.
When Schindler died in October 1974, his
body was taken to Jerusalem; at his funeral
many of those whom he had saved walked in
final homage to his burial place on the
Mount of Olives.

On 27 January 1945, as Soviet troops
entered Auschwitz-Birkenau, they found 648
dead inmates: Jews, Poles and Gypsies.

A FORTY-TWO DAY DEATH MARCH, 26 JANUARY - 11 MARCH 1945

Soviet forces

Berlin

River Oder

Neusalz *slave labour camp*
1,000 *women left, 26 January 1945*

River Spree

Christianstadt
28 January

Muskau
1 February

18 February

S I L E S I A

River Neisse

Leipzig

River Elbe

Bautzen
28 February

Dresden

Breslau

Zinnwald
4 March

800
died or murdered on the march

Prague

Marienbad
7 March

Flossenbürg
200 *arrived on 11 March*

Weiden
10 March

| 0 | miles | 40 |
| 0 | kilometres | 60 |

© Martin Gilbert 1982

FROM DEATH MARCH TO DEATH TRAIN

Bergen-Belsen
arrived 24 March

Berlin

River Oder

Neusalz

Muskau

River Elbe

Bautzen

| 0 | miles | 60 |
| 0 | kilometres | 80 |

Weiden

Marienbad

Flossenbürg
left 19 March

Nuremberg

Prague

© Martin Gilbert 1982

One death march, lasting 42 days, consisted of 1,000 Jewish women who had been working as slave labourers at a camp at Neusalz. On 26 January 1945 they were ordered out of the camp and marched south westwards, accompanied by the beatings and shootings which had become a commonplace of death marchers. By the time the marchers reached Flossenbürg *(above)*, all but 200 had been killed. Eight days later the survivors were evacuated again, this time by train *(left)*, and several more had died by the time the train reached Bergen-Belsen.

On 18 February 1945, as the women deportees from Neusalz were crossing the River Spree, more than 500 Jews, hitherto protected because they were married to Christians, were seized throughout Germany and deported to Theresienstadt *(opposite)*. The photograph shows some of the hundreds of children who were sent to Theresienstadt.

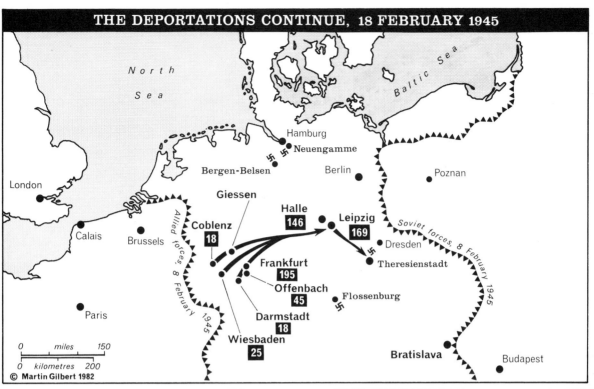

THE DEPORTATIONS CONTINUE, 18 FEBRUARY 1945

Map 288

EVACUATION AND REVOLT, MARCH-APRIL 1945

Rosen, 3,500 prisoners had been marched west and south, away from the advancing Russians. More than 500 died as they were forced through the rubble of Dresden to the concentration camp at Flossenbürg. A further 2,000 Jews from Gross Rosen were evacuated by train to Ebensee, one of the satellite camps of Mauthausen. In all, 49 died on the journey, and a further 182 during the disinfection procedure at the camp on the day of their arrival, 3 March 1945.

From the slave labour camp at Koszeg, where 3,000 Jews had died of hunger, disease, torture and execution in less than a year, the approach of the Russian army led to yet another death march, also to Ebensee, for the camp's 2,000 survivors (opposite). For several weeks they were marched through the hills and mountains of Austria. Anyone who could not get to his feet at the start of the daily march was shot.

Until the summer of 1944 Koszeg had a small Jewish community of 117 people. They had been among the very last Hungarian Jews to be deported to Auschwitz, on 4 July 1944 (page 200), two days before the deportations were brought to an end. Only 15 had survived. Among the dead was the rabbi of Koszeg, Isaac Linksz.

Later in 1944 Koszeg had seen the setting up of the slave labour camp which now, in March 1945, was itself being 'liquidated', in the Nazi terminology.

At Ravensbrück, north of Berlin, nine women who escaped were tracked down, and executed.

In the southernmost areas still under German control, less than 1,000 of Bosnia's 14,000 Jews were still alive, in the concentration camp at Jasenovac. There, on 22 April 1945, 600 prisoners, Jews and non-Jews, rose in revolt and attacked their guards. The guards had machine-guns and grenades. The prisoners had knives, sticks and bare hands. In all, 520 of the prisoners were killed: 80 escaped, of whom 20 were Jews.

The photograph is of a prisoner in Mauthausen who had decided to bring an end to his agony by running against the electrified wire. As more and more Jews and other prisoners were being brought into Mauthausen and its satellite camps the deaths there from brutality and starvation rose precipitately: more than 7,000 Jews died at Mauthausen in just over four months, 15,000 Gypsies, and more than 4,000 Soviet prisoners-of-war (pages 232-3).

In March and April 1945 Soviet forces drove deep into Germany. But the desire to kill Jews, and to make use of Jewish slave labour, still dominated Nazi policy. In Bratislava, as Soviet troops approached, the Nazis murdered all 497 members of a Jewish slave labour battalion (above).

From the concentration camp at Gross

Map 289

A DEATH MARCH ACROSS AUSTRIA, MARCH–APRIL 1945

Map 290

FIVE EVACUATIONS, 1-3 APRIL 1945

North Sea

Baltic Sea

Hamburg

Neuengamme

Stettin

Bergen-Belsen

Sachsenhausen
left early April

Berlin

Soviet forces

British forces 1 April 1945

River

Nordhausen
left 3 April

16 February–15 April

Oder

Artern
left early April

Kamenz

Dresden

Breslau
besieged

American forces 1 April 1945

Neustadt
arrived 22 April

Chemnitz

Teplitz

Leitmeritz

Theresienstadt

Sudeten mountains

Mainz

Prague

Heilbronn **42**

Crailsheim

Kochendorf
*left 1 April
Poles, Czechs,
French, Russians
and Jews*

Zobingen

Ulm

Linz

Amstetten
*left early
April*

Dachau

Wels

Melk

Hütten
47
*Lake
Constance*

Gmunden

Ebensee
arrived 18 April

Austrian Alps

Soviet forces

0	miles	100
0	kilometres	160

SWITZERLAND
neutral

© Martin Gilbert 1982

Map 291

From the first days of April it became clear that the Russian and western Allies would continue to advance until they met somewhere in the middle of Germany. But still Hitler hoped that the German army would be able to hold out in a mountainous area, either the Sudeten mountains or the Austrian Alps, and continue the war.

Two separate policies now drove the SS to prolong the agony of the death marches: the desire to prevent the Allies from liberating anyone who had been a witness of mass murder, and the wish to preserve for as long as possible a mass of slave labour for all the needs which confronted the disintegrating army: repairing roads and railway tracks, building up railway embankments, repairing bridges, excavating underground bunkers from which the battle could still be directed, preparing tank traps to check the Allied advance, and helping with the incredibly difficult work involved in preparing mountain fortresses deep underground.

Over and above these reasons, however, there remained the ever-present, all-pervading Nazi obsession that Jews were not human beings, that they must be made to suffer, and that it did not matter if they were to die, however cruel the circumstances. The death marches and death trains therefore continued, despite the increasing chaos on the roads and railways following the collapse of both the western and eastern fronts. The map on the left shows five such evacuations; the map on the right, three more, within less than a week.

With the rapid movement of armies, written records are scarce. The number of dead shown on these two maps represents only a fraction of the number of Jews who died from exhaustion, or brutality, in those four days.

Labour camps such as Ohrdruf had only been opened a few months earlier to enable a future army command centre to be built underground by tens of thousands of Jewish slave labourers who had been evacuated from the east. Now these same Jews were being evacuated again as American and British forces pressed in from the west. To go back east was impossible. Only north and south now lay open to traffic. And so thousands of Jews were taken by train to Bergen-Belsen, Dachau, Leitmeritz, Theresienstadt and Ebensee. In each of these camps conditions became so terrible, dominated by starvation and typhus, that hundreds died every day.

Map 292

AMERICAN TROOPS REACH OHRDRUF, 4 APRIL 1945

North Sea

Baltic Sea

Neuengamme

Ravensbrück

Bergen-Belsen

Gardelegen

Sachsenhausen

Berlin

Soviet forces

Mittelbau-Dora

Allied forces, 4 April 1945

River Oder

16 February to 15 April 1945

Buchenwald

Ohrdruf
*liberated
4 April 1945*

Gross Rosen

Theresienstadt

Allied forces, 4 April 1945

Flossenbürg

0   *miles*   60
0   *kilometres*   80

© Martin Gilbert 1982

On 4 April 1945 United States troops reached the village of Ohrdruf *(above),* where 4,000 camp inmates had died or been murdered in the previous three months, and where hundreds had been shot on the eve of the American arrival. Some of the victims were Jews, others Polish and Russian prisoners-of-war. All had been forced to build a vast underground radio and telephone centre, intended for the German army in the event of a retreat from Berlin.

The sight of the emaciated corpses created a wave of revulsion which spread back to Britain and the United States. General Eisenhower, who visited the camp, was so shocked that he sent photographs of the dead prisoners to Churchill, who at once arranged for several Members of Parliament to visit the camp.

On April 8 many Jewish inmates at Buchenwald, some of whom had only reached the camp from Auschwitz or Stutthof three months before, were marched out, leaving the non-Jewish prisoners to await the arrival of the Americans. The Jews were driven east, then south, to the concentration camp at Flossenbürg. Others, in camps at Aschersleben and Schönebeck, were driven south, then north again, then back south, first on foot and in trucks, then by train, to Leitmeritz. A third group was sent through the Sudeten mountains to Theresienstadt, 60 being murdered at the village of Buchau.

Map 293

FOUR FURTHER EVACUATIONS, 8-16 APRIL 1945

Magdeburg

Schönebeck
left 12 April

Barby

River Elbe

Soviet forces

Aschersleben
left 11 April

Zörbig

Bitterfeld

Torgau

Delitzsch

Leipzig

Colditz

Dresden

River Elbe

Freiberg

Buchenwald
left 8 April

Weimar

Eisenberg

Gera

Chemnitz

Jena

Weida

S A X O N Y

Leitmeritz

Theresienstadt

Plauen

Johanngeorgenstadt
left 16 April

S U D E T E N L A N D

Hof

Karlsbad

Podersam

Buchau
60

B A V A R I A

Eger

S U D E T E N L A N D

Marktredwitz

Bayreuth

Flossenbürg

Weiden

miles 0 — 30

kilometres 0 — 40

© Martin Gilbert 1982

Map 294

BRITISH TROOPS REACH BELSEN, 15 APRIL 1945

North Sea

Baltic Sea

British forces

Hamburg
Bremen
Lübeck
Neuengamme
Putlitz
Ravensbrück
Sachsenhausen

Stutthof
Soviet forces

Bergen-Belsen
liberated 15 April
Gardelegen
Berlin

front line 18 April

5,000 *deaths from weakness and exhaustion 15-25 April after liberation*

Nordhausen
Mittlebau-Dora
Torgau

Soviet forces
15 April

0 miles 100
0 kilometres 150

Ohrdruf
Buchenwald
Dresden

American forces

liberated 11 April

Theresienstadt

Prague

Nuremberg
liberated 16 April
Flossenburg

Moravska Ostrava

French forces
Stuttgart

Brno

Schömberg
Schörzingen
Spaichingen
Tuttlingen

Dachau
Munich

Mauthausen
Günskirchen
Ebensee

Vienna
liberated by Soviet forces 13 April

SWITZERLAND

© Martin Gilbert 1982

On 15 April 1945, eleven days after American troops had discovered the mass graves of Ohrdruf, British troops entered Belsen *(above)*. Here the British found evidence of mass murder on an even vaster scale. Of 10,000 unburied bodies, most were victims of starvation. Even after liberation 500 inmates died each day from typhus and starvation; deaths which continued for more than a week after liberation.

Photographs, films and articles about Belsen circulated widely by the end of April, making so great an impact that the word 'Belsen' was to become synonymous with 'inhumanity'. For these were not reports of discoveries by other armies in the distant corners of the Reich, but of horrors as seen by men from London and Manchester, from the Midlands and the North of England, familiar enough with the horrors of war by April 1945, but shocked as they never

thought they could be by the sights that confronted them. 'There had been no food nor water for five days preceding the British entry', a British army review reported. 'Evidence of cannibalism was found. The inmates had lost all self respect, were degraded morally to the level of beasts. Their clothes were in rags, teeming with lice, and both inside and outside the huts was an almost continuous carpet of dead bodies, human excreta, rags and filth.'

Soldiers and nurses set to work to save those who could be saved. But even the arrival of food was too much for hundreds of the inmates, who died as a result of the 'richness' of the British army rations: dried milk-powder, oatmeal, sugar, salt and tinned meat.

On the same day that British troops entered Belsen, American troops entered yet another camp at Nordhausen, where

Map 295

DEATH MARCHES FROM RAVENSBRUCK AND SACHSENHAUSEN, 19-25 APRIL 1945

Kölpinsee

Waren

Plauersee

Neubrandenburg

Soviet forces advancing

Plau

Malchow

Neu Strelitz

Müritzsee

Fürstensee

Putlitz

Ravensbrück

17,000 *women*

Stolpsee

Wittstock

Pritzwalk

Zechlin

thousands

Dossow

thousands

Fretzdorf

Rheinsburg

hundreds

Rossow

Rogelin

Katerbow

Alt Ruppin

Lindow

hundreds

Walsleben

Neu Ruppin

Grieben

Löwenburg

Herzberg

Dretzsee

Beetz

Sommerfeld

hundreds

Kremmen

Sachsenhausen

40,000 *men*

Oranienburg

0 miles 15

0 kilometres 20

© Martin Gilbert 1982

hundreds of slave labourers were found, 'in conditions', as the United Stated Signal Corps recorded, 'almost unrecognizable as human. All were little more than skeletons: the dead lay beside the sick and dying in the same beds: filth and human excrement covered the floors. No attempt had been made to alleviate the disease and gangrene that had spread unchecked among the prisoners.'

At yet another camp, Gardelegen, the American troops found, in a huge open pit, the still burning logs on which the bodies of the dead had been cremated.

As the western Allies now had all the evidence they needed of Nazi atrocities, there could be no purpose in further evacuations. Nevertheless, on 15 April 1945, as the western and Soviet armies drew together, 17,000 women and 40,000 men were marched westwards from Ravensbrück

and Sachsenhausen (*above*). A Red Cross official who was present, by chance, as the marchers set off from Ravensbrück wrote in his report: 'As I approached them, I could see that they had sunken cheeks, distended bellies and swollen ankles. Their complexion was sallow. All of a sudden, a whole column of those starving wretches appeared. In each row a sick woman was supported or dragged along by her fellow-detainees. A young SS woman supervisor with a police dog on a leash led the column, followed by two girls who incessantly hurled abuse at the poor women.' Many hundreds died of exhaustion in the effort of the march. Hundreds more were shot by the wayside. The march was quite purposeless, except in the pain and death it caused. For the American and Russian troops had almost come together at Torgau in the centre of the Reich, and were to meet there on April 25.

Map 296

FRENCH FORCES REACH FOUR MASS MURDER SITES, 25 APRIL 1945

In southern Germany it was the turn of French troops to stumble across the evidence of mass murder, and of recent killings. Even amid the beautiful spring fragrance of the Swabian Alps and the upper Danube, it was the stench of death which assailed them.

At four villages mass graves were found of Jews who had earlier been deported from camps and ghettos in the east. With typical Gestapo thoroughness, the names, ages and birthplaces of the victims had all been recorded. The map opposite (above) shows some of these birthplaces. The 39-year-old Peisach Rudnitzki had been born in distant Swieciany, where, in September 1941, nearly 4,000 Jews had been murdered, but where several hundred had managed to escape (page 77), including his own nephew, Yitzhak Rudnitzki, who survived the war as a partisan with the Red Army, and was later to become (as Yitzhak Arad) chairman of Yad Vashem, the holocaust memorial and archive in Jerusalem.

The Second World War was almost over. Yet no corner of the dwindling Reich was free from killing: on 25 April 1945, the day on which French forces reached Tüttlingen, six Jews were taken by the Gestapo at Cuneo, and shot (opposite, above).

Elsewhere, it was a day of historic importance: the meeting at Torgau of Russian and United States forces. Germany had been cut in half. A day later, the Germans evacuated the last survivors of Stutthof by sea to Lübeck (opposite, below). Hundreds died during the voyage. Four days later, while the evacuation ships were still at sea, Soviet troops entered Ravensbrück. In that one camp alone 92,000 Jews and non-Jews, most of them women and children, had been murdered in just over two years. But as the Soviet troops overtook the 'death marchers', several thousand were still alive.

That same day, 30 April 1945, Adolf Hitler committed suicide in Berlin.

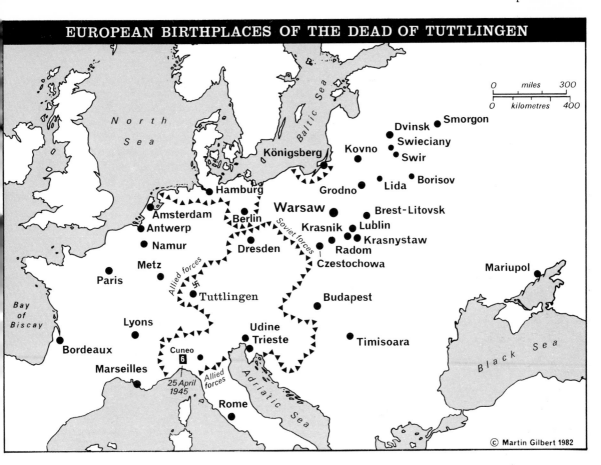

EUROPEAN BIRTHPLACES OF THE DEAD OF TUTTLINGEN

North Sea

Baltic Sea

Smorgon
Dvinsk
Swieciany
Kovno
Königsberg
Swir
Borisov
Grodno
Lida
Hamburg
Warsaw
Brest-Litovsk
Amsterdam
Berlin
Krasnik
Lublin
Antwerp
Krasnystaw
Dresden
Radom
Namur
Czestochowa
Metz
Soviet forces
Mariupol
Paris
Allied forces
Tuttlingen
Budapest
Bay of Biscay
Lyons
Udine
Trieste
Timisoara
Bordeaux
Cuneo
6
Black Sea
Marseilles
25 April 1945
Allied forces
Adriatic Sea
Rome

© Martin Gilbert 1982

THE STUTTHOF SEA EVACUATION, 26 APRIL 1945

DENMARK

SWEDEN
neutral

Copenhagen
Malmo

Baltic Sea

North Sea

SCHLESWIG-HOLSTEIN

Eckernförde
Neustadt

Soviet forces

Stutthof
evacuated 26 April 1945

MECKLENBURG

Lübeck
arrived 3 May 1945

Hamburg
Bremen

Ravensbrück
liberated 30 April

Stettin

British forces

Soviet forces

American forces

Berlin

© Martin Gilbert 1982

Map 299

THREE EVACUATIONS, APRIL - MAY 1945

Hamburg

Lübeck

Neuengamme
left early April

Ravensbrück
150 *released*
5 *killed by Allied bombing*

Stettin

Soviet forces

Berlin
*occupied
2 May*

American and Soviet
forces meet
25 April

Torgau

Nordhausen

Leipzig

Buchenwald

United States forces

Dresden

Rehmsdorf
2,775
*left
20 April*

Theresienstadt
575
survived

1,200

Marienbad
1,000 *27 April*

Pilsen

Nuremberg

0   miles   60

0   kilometres   80

Dachau
*liberated
29 April*

Munich

Mauthausen

Günskirchen

Schlier

Salzburg
*captured
4 May*

Ebensee
arrived 1 May 1945

Innsbruck
*captured
3 May*

© Martin Gilbert 1982

Shortly before American troops had liberated Nordhausen on April 15, one last train of concentration camp inmates had been dispatched southwards from Neuengamme, on the long and difficult journey across the war zones, to Ebensee.

At the very moment when the German army itself was made up of those formerly unfit to serve, many of the guards on the deportation trains and in the concentration camps themselves remained the highly trained criminal élite of the totalitarian state. They also remained killers to the end: on 27 April 1945, during a death march in which 2,775 Jewish slave labourers were sent eastward from Rehmsdorf, a satellite camp of Buchenwald, 1,000 marchers were killed by machine-gun fire and grenades at Marienbad station. A further 1,200 were killed as the march continued eastward to Theresienstadt, where 500 were killed on arrival. Only 75 of the marchers survived.

On April 28 the Red Cross arranged with the SS for the transport of 150 Jewesses from Ravensbrück to Sweden, the first of 3,500 Jewish and 3,500 non-Jewish women to be transferred to safety in the last ten days of the war (*page 236*). On their way through Germany, five of the women were killed during an Allied air-raid.

On April 29 American forces entered Dachau. The photographs opposite are amoung thousands that were taken that day, and in the following week. The top photograph shows the camp as seen from one of the guard towers. Hundreds of bodies still lie in the perimeter ditch and in the open space between the huts and the ditch. The lower photograph, taken by an American serviceman, shows the scene that confronted the Allied troops. Some of the photographs taken after the liberation of Dachau are so terrible that they have never been reproduced, nor have I felt able to reproduce them here.

After the war Dachau was used as a prison for Nazi war criminals, and at a series of war crimes trials in the town of Dachau, 260 SS functionaries were sentenced to death. The principal war criminals were tried at Nuremberg in 1945 and 1946.

In the last year of the war more than 40,000 prisoners had died in Dachau, of whom 80 per cent were Jews. At Buchenwald, which American forces had liberated two weeks earlier, on April 1, 56,549 had died of starvation, disease, or from the deliberate sadism of the guards.

JEWS MURDERED IN MAUTHAUSEN, JANUARY - MAY 1945

NORWAY 1
DENMARK 2
LATVIA 5
HOLLAND
ENGLAND 1
56
GERMANY 187
POLAND 3,777
SOVIET UNION 25
70
BELGIUM LUXEMBOURG 4
CZECHOSLOVAKIA 135
Mauthausen
HUNGARY 3,214
RUMANIA 16
FRANCE 248
YUGOSLAVIA 13
ITALY 67
BULGARIA 1
STATELESS 37
TURKEY 1
GREECE 169

Baltic Sea
Adriatic Sea
Black Sea
Aegean Sea
Mediterranean Sea

0 miles 300
0 kilometres 400

© Martin Gilbert 1982

FIFTEEN THOUSAND GYPSIES MURDERED IN MAUTHAUSEN, JANUARY - MAY 1945

North Sea
HOLLAND 3
POLAND 175
SOVIET UNION 14,876
LUXEMBOURG 14
CZECHOSLOVAKIA 7
Mauthausen
Bay of Biscay
FRANCE 28
HUNGARY 1
RUMANIA 6
CROATIA 2
SPAIN 1
ITALY 5
YUGOSLAVIA
Adriatic Sea
Black Sea
GREECE 3
Aegean Sea
Mediterranean Sea

0 miles 200
0 kilometres 300

© Martin Gilbert 1982

The last concentration camp to be liberated by the Americans was Mauthausen, together with its satellite camps at Gunskirchen and Ebensee *(pages 234-5)*. In just over four months, more than 30,000 people had been murdered at Mauthausen, or had died from starvation and disease. Jews and Gypsies *(left)*, formed the largest groups of those killed. But other groups had also been singled out by the Nazis for cruel deaths: homosexuals, Jehovah's Witnesses, Soviet prisoners-of-war, and tens of thousands of Spanish republicans. These Spaniards had been interned in France in September 1939, deported by the Germans to Mauthausen in 1940, and systematically worked to death in the stone quarry there, or shot at random, until only 3,000 remained alive by January 1945. Of these, 2,163 were killed in the last months *(opposite, below)*. The commandant of Mauthausen, Franz Ziereis, once boasted that he gave his son 50 Jews 'for target practice' as a birthday present.

All inmates at Mauthausen — Jews, Gypsies, homosexuals, religious prisoners, Russians and Spaniards — were subjected to the same vicious cruelties. Among those held in the camp was a British naval officer, Lieutenant Commander Pat O'Leary, GC, DSO. Leary's biographer, Vincent Brome, has recorded in *The Way Back,* published in London in 1968, how Leary 'became familiar with the gas lorries and the sight of prisoners loaded into them who died on the way to nowhere. He saw men kicked, strangled and beaten to death.'

On one occasion, Leary witnessed what happened when another prisoner, who had managed to escape, was recaptured; an SS guard, Leary recalled, 'launched a tremendous blow to the man's jaw. The prisoner's hand went up to ward off a second blow and the guard kicked him savagely in the stomach. As the man doubled up another sledgehammer blow hit his jaw. He fell down. "Up! Up!" The SS man kicked him to attention again. Then alternately he slogged his jaw and kicked his stomach, eight, nine, ten, eleven times, until one tremendous kick in the pit of the stomach brought blood gushing from the man's mouth; he screamed and fell down. The guard continued kicking him in the face, head, groin and legs. The twitching form at last lay quite inert and the pavement was quickly thick with blood.'

Such beatings were commonplace at Mauthausen: hundreds of prisoners being murdered each month by similar savagery.

A FINAL DEATH MARCH, 1-5 MAY 1945

River Danube

Linz

Leonding

Gusen *concentration camp*

Traundorf

Ebelsberg

Pichling

Pichling See

concentration camp

Mauthausen

Traun

Ansfelden

Asten

Kristein

River Danube

Pucking

St.Florian

Enns

Ennsdorf

Wels

Haid

Kremsdorf

River Traun

River Enns

St.Valentin

concentration camp

Gunskirchen

Thalheim

Schleissheim

Weisskirchen

concentration camp

Steyr

0 miles 5

0 kilometres 8

© Martin Gilbert 1982

THE DEATH OF GEZA HAVAS, 5 MAY 1945

0 miles 40

0 kilometres 60

deported to Germany 1944

Brno

evacuated to Mauthausen April 1945

with other Hungarian Jews, interned in various forced labour camps, 1941–1944

Linz

Mauthausen

Bratislava

Vienna

Günskirchen

died a few hours before the arrival of the Allied forces, 5 May 1945

River Danube

A U S T R I A

Neusiedler Sea

Budapest

worked as a journalist from 1936, aged 21. Edited a collection of essays on socialism

borders of 1937

Graz

Lake Balaton

H U N G A R Y

© Martin Gilbert 1982

Nagykanizsa

born 1905

Map 307

On 1 May 1945, as the American army approached Mauthausen, the last death marches of the war began, from Mauthausen itself, Gusen and St. Valentin, to Günskirchen (*opposite, above*). Hundreds of marchers fell to the ground as they marched, dying in the mud from sheer exhaustion.

Among those who reached Günskirchen alive was the Hungarian writer and journalist, Geza Havas. But on May 5, only a few hours before the Americans arrived, he died (*opposite, below*).

Starvation, disease and brutality continued to take their toll to the end. From one transport of 4,000 Hungarian Jews, brought earlier to Mauthausen from Auschwitz, and then marched to Günskirchen and Ebensee, only 300 were alive on the day of liberation. Of 1,000 Polish civilian workers, non-Jews, brought to Ebensee from Warsaw in September 1944, only 100 survived. At Ebensee, as the American armies approached, all 30,000 prisoners were ordered into a tunnel packed with explosives. As the historian of Mauthausen, Evelyn Le Chêne, has written: 'The prisoners, to a man, blankly refused. The SS guards were paralysed with indecision. The hordes of humans swayed and murmured. For the first time since their arrest, the prisoners who were not already dying saw the possibility that they might just survive the war. Understandably, they neither wished to be blown up in the tunnel, nor mown down by SS machine-guns for refusing. But they knew that in these last days, many of the SS had left and been replaced by Volksdeutsche. A quick consultation with some of his command made it clear to the Commandant that they too were reluctant either to force the men into the tunnel, or to shoot them down. With the war all but over, they were thinking of the future, and the punishment they would receive for the slaughter of so many human beings was something they still wished — even with their already stained hands — to avoid. And so the prisoners won the day.'

When American troops reached Mauthausen, they found nearly 10,000 bodies in a huge communal grave. Of the 110,000 survivors, of whom 28,000 were Jews, more than 3,000 died after liberation (*right*). Some died because they were too weak or sick to be nursed back to health, others because they left the camp before they were strong enough to begin normal life again.

235

Map 308

WOMEN SURVIVORS OF THE CAMPS DYING IN SWEDEN, MAY - NOVEMBER 1945

0 miles 250
0 kilometres 400

Stockholm

SWEDEN
Karlstad
Norrköping

Göteborg

Halmstad

Kalmar

Helsingborg

Malmo

North Sea

Baltic Sea

Vilna
Henia Azulanscha aged 20

Hamburg

Ravensbrück
7,000
evacuated 28 April

Warsaw
Rozika Rosenbaum aged 30

Lodz Rachela Galster aged 40

Amsterdam

Dresden
Helena Hausmann aged 20

Sosnowiec
Zofia Alterwein aged 29

Czestochowa Bronislawa Dorfman aged 16

Cracow Cesia Kleiner aged 18

Lena Veffer aged 21
Anna Watterman aged 24
Eugelina Lissauer aged 14
Rosette Bas aged 20
Fre van Leer aged 28

Prague
Anne Goldschmidt aged 46
Gerda Fischelova aged 23

Uzhgorod Dina Rothstein aged 22

Novoselitsa Helen Abrahamovitsch aged 22

Lucenec
Sara Ehrenfeld aged 23

Beregszasz
Rozalia Katz aged 20

Györ
Hedwig Gestettner aged 25

Budapest
Ilona Delikat aged 34
Erzsebet Kohn aged 33
Judit Sandor aged 17

Cluj (Kolozsvar)
Sarolta Samu aged 41
Ewa Aron aged 17

ITALY
Regina Cepparo aged 43

Belgrade
Sara Krystik age unknown

Adriatic Sea

Black Sea

© Martin Gilbert 1982

On 8 May 1945 the Allies accepted the unconditional surrender of Germany. More than eleven million civilians had been murdered in cold blood since the German invasion of Poland more than five years before. Among those eleven million were six million Jews (*page 244*).

Czechs, Frenchmen, Greeks, Italians, Poles, Russians and Serbs had been among the millions of non-Jewish civilians killed in reprisal actions, and in mass executions. But only the Jews had been systematically searched out for death from every region, city, town, village and hamlet of German-dominated Europe. The Nazi aim was to ensure that not one single Jew survived, and 'Jew' was defined as anyone with Jewish parents, a single Jewish parent, or even a single Jewish grandparent.

Despite the Nazi intention, and as a result of the sudden collapse of the German armies, between 250,000 and 300,000 Jews survived the concentration camps and death marches. But the coming of the Allied victory could

not save tens of thousands of these 'survivors', who, as at Dachau, Belsen and Ebensee, were too weak and too sick to live more than a few days, weeks or months, despite all the care and attention lavished upon them, by their liberators. Also, as the historian Evelyn Le Chêne has written: 'Many died from sheer joy. They had lived on hope, on fear and on their nerves for so long that the sudden relaxation of tension, when it came, was too much for them.'

The map above gives the names, ages and birthplaces of 26 out of 3,500 Jewish women who, released from Ravensbrück after Red Cross intervention on April 28 1945 (*page 230*) and sent from there to Sweden, died in the Swedish towns shown here, between May and November 1945. The oldest was 46, the youngest, 14. These women all died after liberation, as had more than 5,000 prisoners at Belsen (*page 226*) and 3,000 at Mauthausen (*page 235*). Others, amid the confusions and hardships of the immediate post-war world, slowly regained their strength.

Map 309

THREE YOUNG SURVIVORS REACH ULM

Among the survivors who reached western Germany after the German surrender in 1945 were several hundred children who were taken to a children's home at Ulm (above). There, each child was photographed, and such details as they could recall were set down. Three of those children are shown on the left.

Of Idel Levitan (top), born in Lithuania, the son of Micha and Mira Levitan, those who questioned him noted: 'He was with his parents in the Ghetto in Kovno. His parents gave him to Christians. Parents were killed. An aunt took him from the Christians, to Lodz, from where he came with a Kibbutz to Ulm, to the Children's Home.'

Of Renja From (middle), born in Eastern Galicia, the interviewer noted: 'She thinks that at the outbreak of the war her mother gave her to Poles. She knew then that she is Jewish, but the Christians with whom she was living forbad her to speak about it. She learned that her mother was murdered by the Germans and thrown into a ditch. She does not remember her father. An acquaintance of her family took her to Germany, to the Children's Home at Ulm.'

Of Zlata Tauber, born in 1941, the person who interviewed her wrote: 'She does not remember her parents, she only knows that she has been in Russia. One brother is in Poland, but he does not want to be Jew because of the persecutions they had to go through. She therefore renounced on him.'

SOME BIRTHPLACES OF DACHAU SURVIVORS

Baltic Sea

Borders of 1937

Gdynia

Bialystok

Mlawa

River Vistula

Gostynin

Warsaw

Klodawa

Kutno

Lodz

Mszczonow

Kalisz

Sieradz • Pabianice

Radom

Lublin

Belchatow

Piotrkow

Wielun

Szydlowiec

P O L A N D

Kielce

Sandomierz

Czestochowa

Zawierce

Bedzin

Olkusz

Radomysl

Sosnowiec

Auschwitz

Tarnow

Cracow

Bielsko

Nowy Targ

C Z E C H O S L O V A K I A

Kosice

Satoraljaujhely

Miskolc

Komarom

Eger

Esztergom

Hatvan

Vac

Jaszbereny

Sopron

Györ

Tatabanya

Budapest

Papa

Monor

Debrecen

Szombathely

H U N G A R Y

Lake Balaton

River Danube

Bekescaba

Nagykanizsa

Szeged

Kaposvar

Baja

Mako

Pecs

© Martin Gilbert 1982

MORE DACHAU SURVIVORS

Baltic Sea

Riga

North Sea

Vilna

Oszmiana

Kovno

Amsterdam

Berlin

Warsaw

Rotterdam

Lodz

Przemysl

Kiev

Beregszasz

Dachau

Vienna

Cluj

Budapest

Rome

Salonica

Corfu

Rhodes

Mediterranean Sea

© Martin Gilbert 1982

The map on the left and the map above show the birthplaces of most of the Jews who had been liberated by the Americans in Dachau. Gradually restored to physical health, many were still distressed. 'It seems to us', Dr Zalman Grinberg told his fellow survivors at the end of 1945, 'that for the time being mankind does not understand what we have gone through and what we have experienced. We fear we will not be understood in future. We unlearned to laugh, we cannot cry any more, we do not understand our freedom yet, all this because we are still with our dead comrades... We belong in the mass-graves of those shot in Kharkov, Lublin and Kovno. We belong to the millions gassed and burned in Auschwitz and Birkenau. We belong to those tens of thousands tormented by milliards of lice, living in mud on a starvation diet, with coldness and despair as companions. We are not alive. We are dead!'

The photograph, taken after the liberation of Buchenwald, shows some of the survivors of death marches and evacuation trains (*maps 261, 271, 276, 279, 282, and 284*).

The majority of those who survived the Holocaust sought a new life beyond Europe. The map opposite gives the approximate number who went to the principal havens.

Map 312

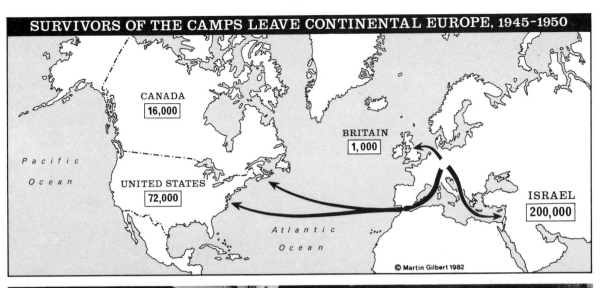

SURVIVORS OF THE CAMPS LEAVE CONTINENTAL EUROPE, 1945-1950

CANADA
16,000

BRITAIN
1,000

Pacific
Ocean

UNITED STATES
72,000

ISRAEL
200,000

Atlantic
Ocean

© Martin Gilbert 1982

Map 313

ONE MAN'S JOURNEY, 17 JANUARY - 24 OCTOBER 1945

Baltic Sea

Kovno
Vilna
17 January
Minsk
18 January
Baranowicze
19 January
Brest-Litovsk
21 January
Kowel
22 January
Przemysl
9 February
Rzeszow
26 February
Lvov
23 January and 31 January
Sanok
2 March
Stanislawow
27 January
Ungvar
5 March
Beregszasz
6 March
Satu Mare
8 March
Oradea Mare
9 March
Szombathely
11 July
Graz
12 July
Budapest
7 July
Cluj
10 March and 2 June
Milan
15 August
Tarvisio
17 July
Arad
5 July
Alba Julia
3 July
Padua
24 August
Mestre
22 July
Bucharest
11 March to 30 June
Bologna
13 September

miles 150
kilometres 250

Adriatic Sea

© Martin Gilbert 1982

Bari
15 September

to **Palestine**, 24 October

Between 1944 and 1948 some 200,000 survivors left Europe for Palestine, then a British Mandate. Incredibly, the killing of Jews had continued in Poland for more than two years after Germany's surrender (*opposite*). It was this Polish anti-semitic violence that gave a strong impetus to the 'Bricha', or flight of the Jews to Palestine. Thus, after the killing of two young Jews in Biala Podlaska, all 30 survivors left. In Lublin, Leon Felhendler, one of the leaders of the Sobibor revolt (*page 173*), was likewise killed; also killed in Lublin, on 19 March

1946, was Chaim Hirschmann, one of only two survivors of Belzec death camp.

The flight to Palestine gained its culminating force with a pogrom in Kielce in which 41 Jews were killed. But the 'Bricha' itself had begun with each region's liberation Thus, shortly after the liberation of Vilna, Dov Levin, a young Jew from Kovno who had fought with the Soviet partisans, embarked on a typical, but nevertheless remarkable journey (*above*). The war ended while Levin was in Bucharest. But he continued his journey to Palestine.

Map 314

POST-WAR KILLINGS AND THE FLIGHT OF THE SURVIVORS, 1944-1948

North Sea

SWEDEN

Baltic Sea

BALTIC STATES

Hamburg

Stettin

Kovno
Vilna

Boleslawiec

Berlin

GERMANY

Sokoly **7**
Bialystok

POLAND **1,000** *Jews murdered between liberation and mid-1947*

100,000 *fled from Poland*

Warsaw

Biala Podlaska **2**
Parczew **4**
Turek **1**
Nachod
BOHEMIA
Kielce **41**

Lublin **2**
Piaski **6**
Mordy **7**
Polaniec **5**

VOLHYNIA

Ulm
Munich
Feldafing
AUSTRIA
Salzburg
Villach

SLOVAKIA
Snina **16**

Bratislava

Skarzysko-Kamienna **5**
Diosgyor **1**

UKRAINE

BESSARABIA

FRANCE

Port de Bouc
Marseilles
Le Ciotat

Spezia

Sisak

Budapest

HUNGARY
Kunmadaras **3**

BUKOVINA

RUMANIA

Bucharest

Ancona

Adriatic Sea

ITALY

YUGOSLAVIA

Bari

GREECE

Burgas

BULGARIA

Black Sea

Athens

TURKEY

Mediterranean Sea

CYPRUS
British

PALESTINE
British Mandate

0   *miles*   300
0   *kilometres*   500

© Martin Gilbert 1982

Map 315

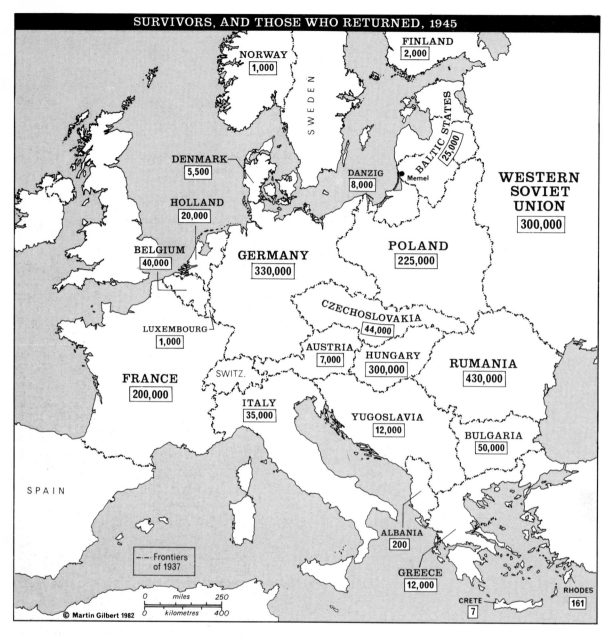

SURVIVORS, AND THOSE WHO RETURNED, 1945

NORWAY
1,000

FINLAND
2,000

SWEDEN

DENMARK
5,500

DANZIG
8,000

Memel

BALTIC STATES
25,000

WESTERN
SOVIET
UNION
300,000

HOLLAND
20,000

BELGIUM
40,000

GERMANY
330,000

POLAND
225,000

LUXEMBOURG
1,000

CZECHOSLOVAKIA
44,000

AUSTRIA
7,000

HUNGARY
300,000

RUMANIA
430,000

FRANCE
200,000

SWITZ.

ITALY
35,000

YUGOSLAVIA
12,000

BULGARIA
50,000

SPAIN

ALBANIA
200

GREECE
12,000

RHODES
161

CRETE
7

—·—· Frontiers
of 1937

0   miles   250
0   kilometres   400

© Martin Gilbert 1982

In addition to the 300,000 survivors of the concentration camps, over a million and a half European Jews survived Hitler's efforts to destroy them. Some were fortunate, as in Germany, to escape from Europe before the outbreak of war or, as in Hungary, that liberation came before the plans for their destruction could be completed. Others, as in Rumania, were saved when their Government, hitherto anti-Jewish, changed its policy in anticipation of an Allied victory. The Jews of Bulgaria were saved by the courage of the Bulgarian people *(page 153)*. The majority of the Polish Jews shown here survived because they found refuge in 1939 and 1940 in Soviet Central Asia. More than 20,000 French, Belgian and Dutch Jews had found refuge in Switzerland, Spain and Portugal. Denmark's Jews had been smuggled to safety in Sweden *(pages 166-7)*.

Some Jews everywhere, but particularly in France, Belgium, Holland and Italy, survived because the Germans took longer to deport them than time finally allowed: the Allied landings on continental Europe coming while deportations were still in progress. Other Jews all over Europe escaped deportation altogether because they were sheltered by individual non-Jews who risked their own lives to save Jews.

In all, as the map opposite shows, more than 1,600,000 of the Jews who were alive in Europe in September 1939, were still alive in May 1945. The photograph shows one such survivor, in Dachau on the day of the camp's liberation, 29 April 1945.

Map 316

JEWS MURDERED BETWEEN 1 SEPTEMBER 1939 AND 8 MAY 1945: AN ESTIMATE

FINLAND
11

NORWAY
728

ESTONIA
1,000

LATVIA
80,000

MEMEL
8,000

LITHUANIA
135,000

furthest German advance 1942

DENMARK
77

North Sea

Baltic Sea

HOLLAND
106,000

BELGIUM
24,387

WHITE RUSSIA

WESTERN RUSSIA

FREE CITY OF DANZIG
1,000

GERMANY
160,000

POLAND
3,000,000

SOVIET UNION
1,000,000

VOLHYNIA

PODOLIA

UKRAINE

LUXEMBOURG
700

CZECHOSLOVAKIA
217,000

GALICIA

RUTHENIA
60,000

BUKOVINA
124,632

BESSARABIA
200,000

CRIMEA

AUSTRIA
65,000

HUNGARY
200,000

NORTHERN TRANSYLVANIA
105,000

FRANCE
83,000

RUMANIA
40,000

Black Sea

ITALY

Adriatic Sea

YUGOSLAVIA
60,000

8,000

7,122
4,221

MACE-DONIA

THRACE

Aegean Sea

ALBANIA
200

KOS
120

GREECE
65,000

RHODES
1,700

CRETE
260

Mediterranean Sea

miles
0   300

kilometres
0   400

Frontiers (Northern Transylvania, in 1940)
of 1937

LIBYA
562

© Martin Gilbert 1982

By the most exact estimates of recent research, the number of Jews killed in Europe between September 1939 and May 1945 was nearly six million. This estimate is a minimum; the deaths shown opposite total just over 5,750,000, and are based on such country-by-country and region-by-region records as survive. These records are listed in the bibliography which follows.

Such a total, however, can never be complete. Thousands of infants and babies were murdered, by the Nazi killings squads in the autumn of 1941, for example, before their birth could be recorded for any 'statistical' purpose. Thousands more individuals, especially in the remoter villages of Poland, were 'added' to the deportation trains which left larger localities, without any numerical register being made of their existence or fate. For several hundred Jewish communities throughout Europe, the most that the historical research of more than 35 years has been able to record is some phrase such as: 'the fate of this community is unknown'. Yet that community, perhaps of 100, or even 1,000 Jews, had existed in 1939, and had been destroyed by 1945.

Throughout Europe, the traveller to this day comes across monuments and gravestones to the victims. Stones mark the mass graves of individuals of whom nothing will ever be known: not their names, their ages, their birthplaces, nor indeed their total number. The photograph shows one such 'war grave', to 11 'unknown' Jews, killed in Austria in the early months of 1945.

Bibliography

I have restricted this bibliography to those works which I have personally consulted in assembling the facts for this Atlas, and have indicated against particular titles those specific maps for which the title was of service. I have also indicated those sources which provided comprehensive material on deportations and other facts incorporated on the maps. To avoid any danger of exaggeration, whenever two sources conflict in the precise number of those murdered in any instance, I have chosen the lower figure. For example, in the case of the Nazi killing squad massacre at Rowne in November 1941, page 81, where contemporary German sources indicate a death toll of at least 18,000, while one recent Jewish source has had reason to estimate that the figure could be as high as 22,000, I have retained the lower figure.

Unpublished sources
The unpublished sources which contained material for individual maps included the following eye-witness testimonies in the archives of Yad Vashem, Jerusalem:
the deportations from Germany to Poland in 1938 (map 19), testimony of Theodor Hatalgy 03/3206;
the Hajerat-M'Guil labour camp in the Sahara (map 59), testimony of Avraham Alfassi, 03/963;
the Jassy death train (map 73), testimony of Binyamin Rabinovitz, 03/897;
the deportation from Norway to Auschwitz (map 164), testimony of Dr L. Eitinger, a German refugee doctor, 01/255;
the deportation from Corfu to Auschwitz (map 250), testimony of Eliahu Uschman, 03/3041;
the deportation from Rhodes to Auschwitz (map 261), testimony of Hanna Zironi, 03/3171;
the deportation of Jews from Albania to Bergen-Belsen (map 230), testimony of Yisrael Teitelbaum, 03/3252;
the Warsaw to Zychlin death march (map 269), testimony of Henech Abramovitch, M I/E, 1605/1489;
the 42-day death march from Neusalz (map 285), testimony of Alisa Besser, 03/3394;
the Stutthof death camp and death marches (map 298), testimony of Pninna Sela, 03/638;
the Palmnicken massacre (map 284), testimony of Celina Moskowitz, 03/1108;
the rescue of Jews by Oskar Schindler (map 284), 01/164;
the post-war murder of Jews in Poland (map 314), at Sokoly near Bialystok, testimony of Icchak Szajder, and at Skarzysko-Kamienna, M 11/B, 244 and M1/PZ;10/632.
For a general guide to all European localities, deportations, slave labour camps, resistance, escape to the partisans, and death marches of the period, I consulted Yehuda Bauer (editor), *Guide to Unpublished Materials of the Holocaust Period,*

volume 3, Jerusalem 1975; volume 4, Jerusalem 1977 and volume 5, Jerusalem 1979.
For the death march from Mauthausen to Gunskirchen (map 305), I found important material on a single-sheet map, 'Weg des Todesmarsches Mauthausen-Gunskirchen', in the Yad Vashem archives, O 15/23-1-4.
For many of the other death marches between June 1944 and May 1945 (maps 290, 291, 292 and 299), I drew on material in 'Vol. 2, Death Marches (Marches de la Mort), Routes and Distances', issued on 28 May 1946 by the Intelligence Section of the UNRRA Central Tracing Bureau.
For the location of mass murder sites, revolts and slave labour camps in eastern Poland, now western White Russia (including maps 88, 98 and 216), I was fortunate to be able to consult 'The Jewish Underground in the Ghettos of Western Byelorussia during the Holocaust', a doctoral thesis submitted by Dr Shalom Cholawski to the Senate of the Hebrew University of Jerusalem in December 1977.
The fate of the Jews of Bessarabia (map 78) is described in 'The Rumanian Jewry between 23.8.1944 and 31.12.1947', a doctoral thesis submitted by Dr Jean Ancel to the Senate of the Hebrew University of Jerusalem in September 1979.
For further details of the slave labour camps in the Sahara (map 59), I consulted the letter and documents submitted by Dr E. Schaefer to the Wiener Library, London, 16 April 1958.
Other unpublished materials from which I have drawn material include:
'Treatment of Jews in Upper Silesia', 6 May 1938, a report by R. F. O'N Bashford, the British Vice-Consul in Breslau, copy in Foreign Office papers 371/21635 (map 8);
'Concentration, Work and Punishment Camps in the British Zone, I Germany, II Austria', Foreign Office papers 371/57528 (map 278): lists camps known to have existed between 1939 and 1945 in the British Zones of Germany and Austria, with notes on location, type of camp, and conditions inside the camps;
'Jews in Nazi Europe, February 1933 to November 1941', memorandum submitted to the Inter-American Jewish Conference, Balitmore, Maryland, 23 November 1941, by the Institute of Jewish Affairs (including maps 43, 44 and 52): includes a list of 27 towns and villages from which Jews were expelled in German-occupied Poland, 19 localities to which the Jews of Cracow were expelled, and 21 cities and towns in which ghettos had been established, with the number of Jews in each;
'List of Persons Imprisoned in Terezin/Theresienstadt', Czechoslovak Relief Action, London, March 1945 (alphabetical list of names, ages and last domicile);
'Tableaux Recapitulatif des Israelites et Tziganes deportés du camp de rassemblement de Malines vers les camps d'Extermination de Haute

Silesie', Brussels 28 November 1977 (lists 25 deportations from Belgium to Auschwitz, with dates and details, and 4 deportations elsewhere: also 11 attempts at escape, with dates);

'Overzicht van de uit Nederland Gedeporteerde Joden', Rijksinstituut voor Oorlogsdocumentatie (Netherlands State Institute for War Documentation), Amsterdam n.d. (lists 68 deportations from Holland to Auschwitz, 19 to Sobibor, 7 to Theresienstadt and 8 to Bergen-Belsen, with dates and numbers of those deported).

'German Extermination Camps — Auschwitz and Birkenau', issued by the Executive Office of the President, War Refugee Board, Washington D.C., 26 November 1944 (includes the report of four escapees from Birkenau, Rudolf Vrba and Alfred Wetzler, 33 pages, and Czeslaw Mordowicz and Arnost Rosin, 6 pages).

The Palestine High Commissioner's comment at the time of the 'Struma' disaster (map 103) is in his telegram No. 257, Most Secret, in the Colonial Office papers, London, reference 733/446/76021.

I based the map on page 240 (map 313) on Dov Levin's diary of his journey from Vilna to Palestine, and on his letter to me of 3 July 1980.

I obtained further information used in this Atlas in conversation in Jerusalem on 23 December 1980 with:

Shmuel Krakowski, recollections of the evacuation of Dziedzice (map 281), and of the Rehmsdorf to Theresienstadt evacuation (map 299).

Judge Moshe Bejski, recollections of the Schindler Jews (map 284).

Hadassa Modlinger, recollections of the evacuation from Ravensbrück to Sweden (map 299).

I received further spoken testimony from:
Hugo Gryn, the Ruthenian deportations (map 255) and the Lieberose death march (map 277), in conversation in London, 11 January 1979, and from
Leon Pommers, the escape of Jews across the Trans-Siberian railway, (map 69) in conversation in Jerusalem, 14 May 1979.

I am also grateful to Alexander Pechersky, the leader of the revolt at Sobibor (map 222), for his letter of recollections, sent from Rostov-on-Don, on 16 December 1980.

I have based two maps (maps 310 and 311), on 'Sharit Ha-Platah', 5 volumes, Dachau 26 June 1945 (names, birthplaces and dates of birth of survivors in the former concentration camps). Volume 1, revised Munich 1946, covers Dachau; volume 2, Buchenwald and others; volume 3, Bergen-Belsen, Salzwedel, Gardelegen and Theresienstadt; volume 4, Linz, Buchenwald (children aged 16-17), Dachau, Braunschweig, Mannheim, Mauthausen, Innsbruck, Celle, Regensburg; volume 5, Feldafing, Dachau, Allauch and others.

The map on page 224 (map 292) was based in part on 'Atrocities and other conditions in Concentration Camps in Germany', Report of the Committee Request by Gen. Dwight D. Eisenhower through the Chief of Staff, Gen. George C. Marshall, to the Congress of the United States, 79th Congress, 1st Session, Document No. 40, Washington 15 May 1945.

Published documents
Two principal published sources from the point of view of German policy and practice are the *Trial of the Major War Criminals before the International Military Tribunal: Official Text,* 42 volumes, Nuremberg 1947-1949 and the *Trial of War Criminals Before the Nuremberg Military Tribunals under Control Council Law No. 10,* 15 volumes, Washington D.C., 1949-1953.

There is also a comprehensive guide to more than 3,000 of the documents submitted at the Nuremberg Trials in Jacob Robinson and Henry Sachs (editors), *The Holocaust, The Nuremberg Evidence, Part One: Documents,* Jerusalem 1976. I have plotted details on the maps from many of these documents, reference L, NG, NO, NOKW, PS, RF and D, and in particular from the documents dated:

26 October 1938, expulsion of Polish Jews from Germany, reference NG 2014 (map 19);

8 November 1938, report of explusion of Polish Jews from Germany, NG 2010 (map 19);

27 February 1940, statistics of Warthegau expulsions, NO 5348 (map 43);

29 February 1940, further statistics of Warthegau expulsions, NO 5402 (map 43);

28 March 1940, Stettin and Schneidemühl deportations to Lublin region, NG 2490 (map 37);

31 October 1940, report of 6,504 German Jews deported to the Pyrenees, NG 4934 (map 49);

3 July 1941, only 2,000 Jews left in Siauliai, NO 4537 (map 73);

7 July 1941, 400 Jews killed in Riga, NO 2935 (map 73);

13 July 1941, 500 Jews being shot every day in Vilna, NO 2937 (map 73);

27 August 1941, murder of 11,000 Hungarian Jews at Kamenets Podolsk, PS 197 (map 74);

27 August 1941, 4,000 Jews killed in Jassy, NG 4962 (map 74);

3 September 1941, 300 Jews shot at Ananayev, NOKW 1702 (map 86);

19 September 1941, *Einsatzkommando A,* reports 46,692 Jews killed in Lithuania in less than three months, NO 3149 (map 87);

19 September 1941, 1,303 Jews killed at Berdichev, NO 3149 (map 86);

2 October 1941, report of 33,771 Jews killed at Babi Yar on 29 and 30 September 1941, NO 3137 (map 86);

11 October 1941, 449 shot in Belgrade area in three days, NOKW 497 (map 86);

13 October 1941, death of Dutch Jews in Mauthausen NG 2710 (map 90);

15 October 1941, *Einsatzgruppe A,* reports having killed 125,000 Jews and 5,000 non-Jews, L 180;

24 October 1941, deportation of 50,000 Reich

Jews to Riga and Minsk, PS 3921 (map 92);

26 October 1941, Jews shot in Odessa, NO 3403 (map 86);

29 October 1941, 8,000 Jews shot at Mariupol, NOKW 1529 (map 86);

1 November 1941, 7,000 Jews murdered at Borisov, NOKW 3146 (map 94);

3 November 1941, *Einsatzgruppe C,* reports on killing of 75,000 Jews, NO 3157;

14 November 1941, *Einsatzgruppe B,* reports on killing of 45,000 Jews, NO 2825;

19 November 1941, 10,000 Jews killed in Dnepropetrovsk, NO 2832 (map 94);

25 November 1941, 1,200 Buchenwald inmates deported to Bernberg, NO 907 (map 94);

30 November 1941, 14 Jews killed at Armyansk, NOKW 1532 (map 94);

8 December 1941, report of 15,000 Jews killed in Rovno (Rowne) a month earlier, NO 2827 (map 94);

12 December 1941 'shooting on the spot' a solution in Serbia, NG 3354 (map 96);

12 December 1941, *Einsatzgruppe D,* reports killing 55,000 Jews, NO 2828;

14 December 1941, killing of 76 Jews at Karasubazar, NOKW 2029 (map 96);

end 1941–early 1942, the 'Jaeger report' on *Einsatzgruppe A* killings in Lithuania and Latvia, totalling 137,346 deaths, listed under men, women and children, between July 4 and 25 November 1941, PS 2273;

1 January 1942, killings at Simferopol on previous day, NOKW 2231;

14 January 1942, Estonia 'cleared of Jews' and 26,900 Jews killed in Riga, NO 3279 (map 98);

17 January 1942, 22 Jewish partisans shot at Evpatoria, NOKW 1524 (map 102);

20 January 1942, minutes of Wannsee Conference, NG 2586 G(7) (maps 99 and 100);

28 February 1942, 36 Jews executed at Feodosiya, NOKW 1862 (map 102);

8 April 1942, murder of 91,678 Jews in the Crimea, NO 3338 and NO 3359 (map 102);

1 May 1942, 22 Jews executed at Feodosiya, NOKW 1717 (map 102);

1 May 1942, Warthegau extermination 'in progress', NO 246 (map 117);

30 May 1942, Dr Clauberg proposes medical experiments at Auschwitz, NO 211 (map 122);

9 June 1942, despatch of a gas van from Belgrade to Riga, PS 501 (map 127);

30 June 1942, report of 52,000 Slovak Jews already deported, NG 4553 (map 126);

9 July 1942, deportations from Belgium, NG 002 (map 134);

6 August 1942, Dr Clauberg requests second sterilization unit for Auschwitz, NO 210 (map 122);

11 August 1942, Hungarian protests against anti-Jewish measures, NG 1856 (map 238);

20 August 1942, Italian refusal to deport Croat Jews, NG 2368 (map 89);

27 August 1942, 95,000 Jews executed in Baranowicze district, and 6,000 escape to partisans, NG 1315 (map 224);

3 September 1942, 27,069 French Jews already deported, RF 1227;

11 September 1942, reports of 17,000 Dutch Jews already deported, NG 2631;

18 September 1942, Jews to receive no meat, meat products or eggs in Greater Germany, NG 1651;

24 September 1942, further Italian refusal to deport Croat Jews, NG 3165;

25 September 1942, Rumanian Jews deported from France, NG 1971 (map 155);

3 October 1942, Jewish resistance groups in Germany reported to the Ministry of Justice in Berlin, NG 683;

20 November 1942, third Italian refusal to deport Croat Jews, NG 2345;

6 December 1942, forced labour in Tunisia, NG 2099 and NG 3150 (map 188);

18 February 1943, report of 86,632 Jews murdered in Minsk, NO 3339 (map 193);

4 March 1943, planned deportation of Croat Jews, NG 2348 (map 205);

16 May 1943, the Stroop report on the destruction of the Warsaw ghetto, PS 1061 (map 204);

7 June 1943, Dr Clauberg reports sterilization rate at Auschwitz of 1,000 women a day, by a single physician with assistants, NO 212 (map 206);

7 June 1943, pro-Jewish demonstrations in Sofia, NG 2357 (map 197);

21 June 1943, Jewish skeleton collection plans for Strasbourg, NO 091 (map 208);

30 June 1943, total of 434,329 Jews deported from Galicia by 27 June 1943, L 018 (map 206);

5 July 1943, six Jews shot earlier at Heraklion, NOKW 2907 (map 208);

15 July 1943, order to deport all 800 Jews still alive in Croat concentration camps, NG 2413 (map 208);

4 October 1943, Danish resistance to deportation of Jews, NG 3920 (map 213);

17 October 1943, Jews arrested in Rome, NO 315 (map 221);

2 November 1943, 73 Jews and 30 Jewesses from Auschwitz to Natzweiler, for a collection of Jewish skeletons, NO 086 (map 208);

6 April 1944, arrest of Jewish children in children's homes, and deportation to Drancy, RF 1235;

14 April 1944, report of deportation of Greek Jews on 23–25 March 1944, NOKW 2520 (map 232);

23 April 1944, deportation of Hungarian Jews to start on 15 May 1944, NG 2233 (map 240);

28 April 1944, Corfu deportation plans, NOKW 1985 (map 250);

4 May 1944, progress of ghettoization and deportation plans for Ruthenia (200,000 ghettoized) and Transylvania (110,000 to be ghettoized), NG 2262 (map 240);

8 June 1944, statistics of Hungarian deportations, NG 5620 (map 241);

16 June 1944, renewal of Slovak deportations, NG 2261 (map 251);

3 July 1944, deportations from Rhodes, NOKW 1795 and NOKW 1802 (map 261);

10 September 1944, Jewish forced labourers, 6,000 in all, at Bor, NOKW 981 (map 273);

15 October 1944, order for destruction of Jewish skeleton collection at Strasbourg, NO 807 (map 208);

27 October 1944, deportation of total of 437,402 Jews from Hungary reported, NG 5573 (map 260);

22 January 1945, Stutthof death march orders, NO 3796 (map 284);

25 January 1945, Stutthof death march schedule, NO 3792 (map 284);

23 May 1945, testimony of Franz Ziereis, Commandant at Mauthausen, NO 1973 (map 300);

18 March 1946, affidavit by Baron van Lamsweerde on the Rehmsdorf to Theresienstadt death march, D924 (map 299);

6 June 1947, affidavit by Paul Blobel on Unit 1005 to obliterate traces of mass graves, NO 3829 (map 217);

23 October 1947, eye-witness account of gas vans used in Riga, NO 5511 (map 127).

Single sheet maps

Among the historical atlases and maps consulted were several single-sheet maps on specific themes, including:

Jean Ancel, *Transnistria Inclusiv Provinciile Afectate De Deportari Masive,* Jerusalem, n.d. (the Transnistrian camps and death marches) maps 78 and 80;

Dokumentačná Akcia, *Deportácia Židov zo Slovenska,* Bratislava, June 1948 (deportation routes and numbers from Slovak towns and villages) maps 126 and 128;

Herbert Froboess, *Deutschland 1945,* Munich n.d. (location of concentration camps and sub-camps in Greater Germany, including the Natzweiler and Mauthausen sub-camps) map 278;

Dr Gollert, *Die Territoriale Verteilung der Juden in Warschau nach Polizeikommissariaten, Volkszahlung vom 24 Februar 1940* (gives percentage of Jews throughout Warsaw, before the expulsions into the ghetto) map 55;

C. Jablonski, *Podzialy Administracyjne Wojewodztwa Lodzkeigo i Obszarow Przyleglych 1939-1945r.,* Lodz 1972 (wartime administrative boundaries of the Lodz region) map 42;

Edward Kossoy, *Judenvernichtung im Donauraum,* Munich, n.d. (deportation routes with dates and numbers, from Austria, Slovakia, Bukovina, Ruthenia, Transylvania, Banat, Bacska and Serbia, with inset of concentration, labour and internment camps in Italy);

Edward Kossoy, *Polen,* Munich, n.d. (concentration camps and labour camps throughout Poland, with insets on France, Transnistria, North Africa, Upper Silesia, and Warsaw region);

Edward Kossoy, *Polen und Balticum am Ende des sweiten Weltkrieges,* Munich, n.d. (death camps,

concentration camps, slave labour camps, deportation routes with dates and number, from the General Government, the Baltic States, Upper Silesia, Danzig-West Prussia, East Prussia and the Warthegau);

League of Nations, *Territory of Saar Basin,* scale 1:100,000, 3 May 1919 (map provided as annex 2 to the Treaty of Versailles), London 1919, map 7;

Militärgeographischen Institut in Wien, single sheet maps of western Russia (borders of 1914), reprinted Vienna 1940, scale 1:200,000;

Mitteleuropa in der ersten Hälfte des Jahres 1945 n.d. (concentration camps and their satellite camps, with front lines on 1 April, 14 April and 6 May 1945, and the dates on the liberation of the camps maps 290 to 294 and map 307;

Lieutenant Popescu, *Transnistria,* 1.43, maps 78 and 80.

Zidovske Pracovne Tabory A Strediska Na Slovensku, Bratislava, 5 July 1943 (locates Jewish labour camps in Slovakia) map 216.

Atlases

Several Atlases provided historical as well as geographical information not obtainable elsewhere, among them:

O. A. Beloglazova (editor) *Atlas S.S.S.R.,* Moscow 1954;

Wladyslaw Czaplinski and Tadeusz Ladogorski, *Atlas Historyczny Polski,* Warsaw 1968;

Deutscher Generalatlas, 1:200,000, Stuttgart 1967-1968;

George Goodall (editor), *Philips' International Atlas,* 5th edition, Liverpool 1945 (includes the boundaries of German-occupied Poland, plates 53-54, of German-occupied Czechoslovakia, plates 59-60, and of Hungarian-occupied Transylvania, plates 63-64);

Dimitri Kosev and others, *Atlas po Bulgarska Istoria,* Sofia 1963;

Janusz Lopatto (editor), *Samochodowy Atlas Polski 1:500,000,* Warsaw 1979 (road Atlas of Poland, 34 map spreads, town plans and gazetteer);

Dr Oswald Muris, *Hansa Weltatlas,* Leipzig 1943 (includes the European frontiers of September 1943, and the internal administrative divisions of Greater Germany);

T. Dodson Stamps and Vincent J. Esposito, *A Military History of World War II: Atlas,* West Point 1953 (168 campaign maps, including 7 maps on the Polish campaign, 5 maps on the Balkan campaign, 22 maps on the war in eastern Europe, 26 maps on the war in western Europe, 15 maps on the war in North Africa and 16 maps on the operations in Italy).

Books and articles

There are now nearly five hundred 'memorial' books on the destroyed Jewish communities of Europe; including more than 400 for Poland, 20 for Rumania, 13 for Russia, 5 for Lithuania, 4 for Czechoslovakia, 4 for Germany, 1 for Yugoslavia (Sombor), 1 for Greece (Salonica) and 1 for

Latvia. I have tried to make the fullest possible use of these books, some of which are listed in the bibliography, and to which there is, up to 1973, a comprehensive guide in David Bass, 'Bibliographical List of Memorial Books Published in the years 1943-1972', in *Yad Vashem Studies,* ix, Jerusalem 1973, pages 273-321.

The Bulletin of the Jewish Historical Institute in Warsaw, founded in 1951, contains many important articles on the fate of Polish Jewry. Of particular value are the tables of deportations from towns, villages and hamlets throughout Poland, prepared by Tatiana Berenstein (Berensztyn), Danuta Dabrowska, Adam Rutkowski and Szymon Datner, and which I have listed in the bibliography of published works.

For the basic historical facts of more than a thousand separate communities overtaken by the Holocaust, as well as for the country-by-country entries, and a specific Holocaust section, each with its own bibliography, I have used Cecil Roth (editor in chief), *Encyclopaedia Judaica,* Jerusalem 1972, 16 volumes. The individual community entries in these sixteen volumes are being substantially supplemented by the Yad Vashem project, *Pinkas Hakehillot Encyclopaedia of Jewish Communities,* of which the following six volumes have already been published and which provide detailed information on the life and destruction of several hundred of the communities plotted in this Atlas:

Rumania, volume 1, Jerusalem 1969;

Germany-Bavaria, Jerusalem 1972 (including maps 108 and 109);

Hungary, Jerusalem 1976;

Poland: the Communities of Lodz and its Region, Jerusalem 1976;

Poland: Eastern Galicia, Jerusalem 1980;

Rumania, volume 2, Jerusalem 1980.

Other published works which proved indispensable in the preparation of this Atlas were:

Activité des Organisations Juives en France sous L'Occupation, Paris 1947.

S. Adler-Rudel, 'The Evian Conference on the Refugee Question', in *Leo Baeck Institute Year Book* xiii, 1968, pages 235-73.

Reuben Ainsztein, *Jewish Resistance in Nazi-Occupied Eastern Europe,* London 1974.

Henry Allainmet, *Auschwitz en France: La Vérité sur le seul camp d'Extermination en France, Le Struthof,* Paris 1974 (about Natzweiler).

American Jewish Committee, *The Jews in Nazi Germany: A Handbook of Facts Regarding the Present Situation,* New York 1935 (documents on anti-Jewish measures and the text of laws affecting the Jews).

Jacob Apenszlak (editor), *The Black Book of Polish Jewry,* New York 1943.

Jacob Apenszlak and Moshe Polakiewicz, *Armed Resistance of the Jews in Poland,* New York 1944.

Yitzhak Arad, *Ghetto in Flames: the Struggle and*

Destruction of the Jews in Vilna in the Holocaust, Jerusalem 1980 (lists all murder 'actions' in Vilna between 1941 and 1944).

Yitzhak Arad, *The Partisan,* New York 1979 (the story of Swieciany, Vilna, and Jewish partisan activity).

Schlomo Aronson, *Beginnings of the Gestapo System: the Bavarian model in 1933,* New Brunswick, New Jersey 1969.

Z. Asaria, *Zur Geschichte der Juden in Osnabrueck,* Osnabrück 1969.

K. J. Ball-Kaduri, 'Berlin is "Purged" of Jews: The Jews in Berlin in 1943', in *Yad Vashem Studies,* v, Jerusalem 1963, pages 271-316 (includes lists of 11 deportations from Berlin to Auschwitz between 12 January and 12 March 1943, and 8 to Theresienstadt between 12 January and 17 March 1943).

Yehuda Bauer *Flight and Rescue: Brichah,* New York 1970 (map 314).

Yehuda Bauer, 'Rescue Operations Through Vilna', in *Yad Vashem Studies,* ix, Jerusalem 1973, pages 215-223 (map 69).

Arieh L. Bauminger, *Roll of Honour,* 2nd edition, Tel Aviv 1971 (non-Jews who saved Jews).

Norman H. Baynes (editor) *Hitler's Speeches,* 2 volumes, London 1941.

Wladyslaw Bednarz, *Das Vernichtungslager zu Chelmno am Ner,* Warsaw 1946.

Tatiana Berenstein, 'Eksterminacja Zydow w Galicji 1941-1943' *Biuletyn Zydowskiego Instytutu Historycznego,* number 61, Warsaw, 1967 (12 statistical tables of the ghettoization, deportation and destruction in 139 Jewish communities in Eastern Galicia between 1941 and 1943).

Tatiana Berenstein, 'Martyrologia, opór i zaglada ludnosci zydowskiej', in *Biuletyn Zydowskiego Instytutu Historycznego,* number 21, pages 56-83, Warsaw 1957 (10 statistical tables listing the size, deportation and destruction of Jewish communities in the Lublin district between 1939 and 1944).

Adolf Berman, 'The Fate of Jewish Children in the Warsaw Ghetto', in Yisrael Gutman and Livia Rothkirchen (editors), *The Catastrophe of European Jewry,* Jerusalem 1976, pages 400-421.

Blackbook of Localities whose Jewish Population was Exterminated by the Nazis, Yad Vashem, Martyrs' and Heroes' Remembrance Authority, Jerusalem 1965 (lists the number of Jews town by town and village by village, according to the pre-war census returns, in Poland, Germany, Yugoslavia, Austria, Hungary, Rumania, Greece, Czechoslovakia, Holland, Norway, Luxembourg, Estonia, Latvia, Lithuania and the Soviet Union).

Nachman Blumenthal (editor), *Yizkor Baranow: A Memorial to the Jewish Community of Baranow,* Jerusalem 1964.

Joseph Borkin, *The Crime and Punishment of I. G. Farben,* New York 1978 (slave labour at Auschwitz-Monowitz, based on the published Nuremberg War Crimes Trials records).

Randolph L. Braham, *The Destruction of*

Hungarian Jewry: A Documentary Account, 2 volumes, New York 1963 (documents on German deportation policy, with facsimiles).

Randolph L. Braham, *The Politics of Genocide: the Holocaust in Hungary,* 2 volumes, New York 1981.

Randolph L. Braham, *Hungarian-Jewish Studies,* 3 volumes, New York 1966, 1969, 1973.

Randolph L. Braham, 'The Kamenets Podolsk and Delvidek Massacres: Prelude to the Holocaust in Hungary', in *Yad Vashem Studies,* ix, Jerusalem 1973, pages 133-156.

B. Brilling (editor), *Westfalia Judaica.*

Zvie A. Brown and Dov Levin, *The Story of an Underground: the resistance of the Jews of Kovno (Lithuania) in the Second World War,* Jerusalem 1962.

T. Brustin-Berenstein, 'Deportacje i Zaglada Skupisk Zydowskich w Dystrykcie Warszawskim' in *Biuletyn Zydowskiego Instytutu Historycznego,* number 3, Warsaw 1952 (11 statistical tables of the ghettoization, deportation and destruction of Jews in Warsaw, and of Jewish communities throughout the Warsaw region).

Tadeusz Bystrycki (general editor) *Skorowidz Miejscowci Rzeczpospolitej Polskiej,* 4 volumes, Warsaw and Przemysl, 1934 (lists the location of all towns, villages and hamlets in inter-war Poland).

Frederick B. Chary, *The Bulgarian Jews and the Final Solution, 1940-1944,* Pittsburgh 1972 (map 197).

Marta Cohen (editor and translator), *Hanna Senesh: Her Life and Diary,* London 1971 (map 276).

Congrès Juif Mondial, Section de Roumanie, Commission d'Etudes, *Le Massacre des Juifs de Jassy,* Bucharest 1946 (photographs and documents of the town and train massacres, June-July 1941) (map 73).

Danuta Czech, 'Deportation und Vernichtung der griechischen Juden', in *Hefte von Auschwitz,* II, 1970 (lists 19 train deportations to Auschwitz from Salonica between 20 March and 18 August 1943 and two from Athens and Corfu on 11 April and 30 June 1944).

Danuta Czech, 'Kalendarium der Ereignisse im Konzentrationslager Auschwitz-Birkenau', in *Hefte von Auschwitz,* numbers 2-9, Oswiecim, 1959-64 (records all deportation trains reaching Auschwitz between March 1942 and November 1944, with dates, and the fate of those on them).

D. Dabrowska, 'Zaglada Skupisk Zydowskich w "Kraju Warty" w okresie Okupacji Hitlerowskiej' in *Biuletyn Zydowskiego Instytutu Historycznego,* number 13, Warsaw 1955 (16 statistical tables of the ghettoization, deportation and destruction in the city of Lodz and other towns and villages of the Warthegau).

Szymon Datner, 'Eksterminacja Zydow w Okregu Bialostockim', in *Biuletyn Zydowskiego Instytutu Historycznego,* number 60, Warsaw 1966 (8 statistical tables of the ghettoization, deportation and destruction in Bialystok and the Bialystok region), see in particular map 168.

Szymon Datner, *Las Sprawiedliwych* (the forest of the righteous), Warsaw 1968 (the story of non-Jewish Poles who helped Jews in Poland).

Szymon Datner, *Walka i zaglada bialostockiego ghetta,* Lodz 1946 (the Bialystok ghetto revolt) (map 210).

Szymon Datner, *55 Dni (i.ix-15. x 1939) Wehrmachtu w Polsce,* Warsaw 1967 (map 29).

A. de Cocatrix, *The Number of Victims of the National Socialist Persecution,* International Tracing Service, Arolsen, 12 April 1977.

Louis de Jong, 'The Netherlands and Auschwitz' in *Yad Vashem Studies,* vii, Jerusalem 1968, pages 39-55.

Lucjan Dobroszycki, 'Restoring Jewish Life in Post-War Poland', in *Soviet Jewish Affairs,* volume 3, number 2, London 1973 (details of Jews killed by Poles after liberation) (map 316).

Giuliana Donati, *Deportazione Degli Ebrei Dall' Italia,* Milan, March 1975 (lists 14 deportations from Italy to Auschwitz, and 7 other deportations, between 16 September 1943 and 14 December 1944, with the fate of the deportees).

Giuliana Donati, *Ebrei in Italia: Deportazione, Resistenza,* Florence 1975.

S. M. Dubnow, *History of the Jews in Russia and Poland from the earliest times until the present day,* 3 volumes, Jewish Publication Society of America reprint, Philadelphia 1946 (map 3).

Krzysztof Dunin-Wasowicz, 'Zydowscy wiezniowie KL Stutthof', *Biuletyn Zydowskiego Instytutu Historycznego,* number 63, Warsaw 1967 (lists 26 deportations of Jews into Stutthof between 29 June 1944 and 14 October 1944; and 14 deportations of Jewish men, women and children out of Stutthof between 21 July 1944 and 12 December 1944).

Dr Max Freiherr du Prel, *Das General-Gouvernement,* Würzburg 1942 (preface dated Vienna, 10 March 1942: a 404-page German survey of the General Government, with maps and photographs).

Georges Dunand, *Ne perdez pas leur trace!,* Neuchatel 1951 (the fate of the Jews of Bratislava, by an eye-witness between September and December 1944).

Ralph Durand, *Guernsey under German Rule,* London 1946.

Stanislaw Duszak, *Majdanek,* Lublin 1980.

Helmut Eschwege, 'Resistance of German Jews against the Nazi Regime', *Leo Baeck Institute Year Book* xv, 1970, pages 143-180.

Liliana Picciotto Fargion, *L'occupazione tedesca e gli ebrei di Roma: documenti e fatti,* Milan 1979.

Benjamin B. Ferencz, *Less Than Slaves: Jewish Forced Labor and the Quest for Compensation,* Cambridge Massachusetts, 1979.

M. R. D. Foot, *S.O.E. in France: An Account of the British Special Operations in France 1940-1944,* London 1966.

Josef Fraenkel (editor), *The Jews of Austria, Essays on their Life, History and Destruction,* London 1967.

Philip Friedman, *Roads to Extinction: Essays on the Holocaust,* New York and Philadelphia 1980 (includes essays on the destruction of the Jews of

Lvov, the Gypsies, and Jewish resistance).

Główna Komisja Badania Zbrodni Hitlerowskich w Polsce, *Obozy hitlerowskie na ziemiach polskich 1939-1945: Informator encyklopedyczny,* Warsaw 1979 (lists 5,877 labour camps, ghettos, concentration camps and other mass murder and atrocity sites with a comprehensive bibliography for each of these localities).

Dr Branko Gostl (and others), editors, Federation of Jewish Communities in Yugoslavia *Spomenica 1919-1969,* Belgrade 1969.

Günter Grass (and others), *Danzig 1939: Treasures of a Destroyed Community,* New York 1980.

Yisrael Gutman, 'The Genesis of Resistance in the Warsaw Ghetto', in *Yad Vashem Studies,* ix, Jerusalem 1973, pages 29-70.

Yisrael Gutman, *The Jews of Warsaw 1939-1943 Ghetto-Underground-Uprising,* Jerusalem 1977 (in Hebrew) (lists the monthly deaths from starvation in Warsaw in 1941 and 1942).

Yisrael Gutman and Efraim Zuroff (editors), *Rescue Attemps During the Holocaust,* Jerusalem 1977 (proceedings of the second Yad Vashem International Historical Conference, Jerusalem, 8-11 April 1974).

Gideon Hausner, *Justice in Jerusalem,* New York 1966 (the Eichmann Trial, narrative and extracts from evidence).

Heinz Heger, *The Men with the Pink Triangle,* London 1980 (memoirs of a homosexual at Sachsenhausen and Flossenbürg, with an historical introduction by David Fernbach).

Celia S. Heller, *On the Edge of Destruction: Jews of Poland Between the Two World Wars,* New York 1977 (map 12).

I. Heller and Z. Vajda, *The Synagogues in Hungary,* New York 1968.

Raul Hilberg, *The Destruction of the European Jews,* Chicago 1961 (New Viewpoints edition, New York 1973).

Raul Hilberg (editor), *Documents of Destruction, Germany and Jewry 1933-1945,* London 1972.

Sir John Hope-Simpson, *The Refugee Problem: Report of a Survey,* London 1939.

International Committee of the Red Cross, *Documents relating to the work of the International Committee of the Red Cross for the benefit of civilian detainees in German Concentration Camps between 1939 and 1945,* Geneva 1965 (contains an eye-witness account of the evacuations from Ravensbrück and Sachsenhausen in April 1945) (map 295).

Jewish Black Book Committe, *The Black Book: the Nazi Crime Against the Jewish People,* New York, 1946 (a Soviet source for German war crimes against Jews and others).

Albert Kalme, *Total Terror: An Exposé of Genocide in the Baltics,* New York 1951.

Abraham I. Katsh (editor and translator), *The Warsaw Diary of Chaim A. Kaplan,* New York 1965.

Robert Katz, *Death in Rome,* London 1967 (the Ardeatine caves massacre of 24 March 1944) (map 233).

Yitzhak Katznelson, *Vittel Diary (22.5.43-16.9.43),* Kibbutz Lohamei Haghettaot, Israel 1972 (map 231).

Donald Kenrick and Gratton Puxon, *The Destiny of Europe's Gypsies,* London 1972 (map 182).

Joseph Kermish, 'The Warsaw Ghetto Uprising in the Light of a hitherto Unpublished Official German Report', in *Yad Vashem Studies,* ix, Jerusalem 1973, pages 7-27.

Serge Klarsfeld, *Additif au Mémorial de la Déportation des Juifs de France,* Paris 1981.

Serge Klarsfeld, *Le Mémorial de la Déportation des Juifs de France,* Paris 1978 (lists dates of each deportation from France, executions in France, and the names of all deportees and others killed) (see in particular maps 51, 113, 114, 136, 148 to 150, 155, 159, 169 to 172, 243 to 147, 153 and 263 to 266).

David Knout, *Contribution à l'histoire de la Résistance Juive en France 1940-1944,* Paris 1947.

Edward Kossoy, *Handbuch zum Entschädigungsverfahren,* Munich 1958 (details of camp numbers and regional origin of deportees at Auschwitz, Dachau and elsewhere; a note of Jewish names in all European languages, and the date of all Jewish holy days during the war; also Displaced Persons camps, reparations, and emigrant ships to Palestine).

Yehezkiel Korn, *Jewish Agricultural Settlement in the Crimea, 1922-1947,* Jerusalem 1973 (in Hebrew) (map 102).

Shmuel Krakowski, 'The Fate of Jewish Prisoners of War in the September 1939 Campaign' in *Yad Vashem Studies,* volume xii, Jerusalem 1977 (maps 32 and 35).

Shmuel Krakowski, *Jewish Armed Resistance in Poland 1942-1944,* Jerusalem 1977 (in Hebrew).

David Kranzler, *Japanese, Nazis and Jews: the Jewish Refugee Community of Shanghai, 1938-1945,* New York 1976 (map 16).

Kriegstagebuch des Oberkommandos der Wehrmacht, 4 volumes, Frankfurt-am-Main, 1965 (dates on which the German army captured, and then lost, towns and territory: volume 1, 1 August 1940 to 31 December 1941; volume 2, 1942; volume 3, 1943; volume 4, 1944-45, edited respectively by Hans-Adolf Jacobsen, Andreas Hillgruber, Walther Hubatsch and Percy Ernest Schramm).

Gedalia Lachman, 'The Destruction of Skala', in Max Mermelstein-Weidenfeld (chairman, editorial committee), *Skala,* Tel Aviv 1978.

Isaac Landman (editor), *The Universal Jewish Encyclopaedia,* 10 volumes, New York 1939 (contains details of anti-Jewish violence through eastern Europe during the 1930s) (maps 10 to 12).

Jehuda-Gyula Lang, *A Pápai Zsidóság Emlékkönyve,* Tel Aviv 1973 (lists the villages and names the deportees from Papa and the Papa region) (map 258).

I. M. Lask (editor), *The Kalish Book,* Tel Aviv 1968 (maps 44 and 54).

Evelyn Le Chêne, *Mauthausen: The History of a Death Camp,* London 1971 (maps 300 to 304).

Eugene Levai, *Black Book on the Martyrdom of Hungarian Jewry,* Zurich 1948.

Liberated Jews Arrived in Sweden in 1945, 2 volumes, Malmö 1946 (includes list of Jewish refugees dying in Sweden in 1945, part 1 Czechoslovakians, part 2 Dutchmen, part 3 Hungarians, part 4 Italians, part 5 Poles, part 6 Rumanians, part 7 Stateless formerly Germans, and part 8 Yugoslavs) (map 308).

Liste Alphabetique des Personnes, en majorité Israelites, Deportées Par Les Convois Partis du Camp de Rassemblement de Malines entre le 4 Aout 1942 et le 31 Juillet 1944, 3 volumes, Brussels, 1 July 1954.

Dora Litani, 'The Destruction of the Jews of Odessa in the Light of Rumanian Documents', *Yad Vashem Studies,* vi, Jerusalem 1967, pages 135–154.

Czeslaw Madajczyk (editor), *Zamojszczyzna-Sonderlaboratorium SS,* 2 volumes, Warsaw 1979 (documents on the expulsion and massacre of Poles in the Zamosc province) (map 179).

Ber Mark, *Uprising in the Warsaw Ghetto,* New York 1975 (map 204).

Albert Menasche, *Birkenau (Auschwitz II), Memoirs of an eye-witness, how 72,000 Greek Jews Perished,* New York, 1947.

Sybil Milton (translator and editor), *The Stroop Report: The Jewish Quarter of Warsaw Is No More!* facsimile edition, New York 1979 (map 204).

S. Moldawer, *The Road to Lublin,* New York 1940 (map 37).

Michael Molho, *In Memoriam: Hommage aux Victimes Juives des Nazis en Grèce,* Salonica 1973 (lists numbers of Greek Jews murdered, community by community) (maps 196 and 232).

Werner Nachman and Heinrich Freund, *Sie Sind Nicht Vergessen,* Mannheim, n.d. (the deportation of Jews from the Saar, Baden and the Palantinate to Gurs, in October 1940) (maps 49 and 50).

Donald L. Niewyk, *The Jews in Weimar Germany,* Baton Rouge, Louisiana 1980.

Albert Nirenstein, *A Tower from the Enemy: Contributions to a History of Jewish Resistance in Poland,* New York 1959.

Miram Novitch, *Le Passage des Barbares: Contribution à l'Histoire de la Déportation et de la Résistance des Juifs Grècs,* Nice, n.d.

Miriam Novitch (editor), *Sobibor: Martyrdom and Revolt, Documents and Testimonies,* New York 1980 (map 222).

Miklos Nyiszli, *Auschwitz: A Doctor's Eye-witness Account,* New York 1960.

Opinia, Warsaw, 25 July 1946, page 7 (lists those killed in the Kielce pogrom).

Wila Orbach, 'The Destruction of the Jews in the Nazi-Occupied Territories of the USSR', in *Soviet Jewish Affairs,* volume 6, no. 2, 1976 (lists localities with Jewish death tolls).

Nissan Oren, 'The Bulgarian Exception: a Reassessment of the Salvation of the Jewish Community', in *Yad Vashem Studies,* vii, Jerusalem 1968, pages 83–106 (map 197).

Papers Concerning the Treatment of German Nationals in Germany, Command Paper 6120 of 1939, Germany No. 2 of 1939, London 1939 (treatment of German Jews in German concentration camps, 1933–1939).

Edmond Paris, *Genocide in Satellite Croatia: A Record of Racial and Religious Persecution,* Chicago 1961.

Robert O. Paxton, *Vichy France: Old guard and New Order, 1940-1944,* London 1972.

Stanislaw Piotrowski, *Hans Frank's Diary,* Warsaw 1961.

Republic of Poland, Ministry of Foreign Affairs *The German Occupation of Poland, Extract of Note addressed to the Governments of the Allied and Neutral Powers on May 3, 1941,* London 1941.

Polish Ministry of Information, *The German New Order In Poland,* London 1942.

Walter Poller, *Medical Block, Buchenwald: the Personal Testimony of Inmate 996, Block 36,* London 1961.

Bernard Postal and Samuel H. Abramson, *The Traveler's Guide to Jewish Landmarks of Europe,* New York 1971.

Werner Präg and Wolfgang Jacobmeyer (editors), *Das Diensttagebuch des deutschen Generalgouverneurs in Polen, 1939-1945,* Stuttgart 1975 (contains Hans Frank's speeches to his officials on ridding the General Government of Jews).

Miklós Radnóti, *The Witness* (selected poems, translated from the Hungarian by Thomas Orszag-Land), London 1977 (map 271).

Leyzer Ran (editor), *Jerusalem of Lithuania Illustrated and Documented,* 3 volumes, New York 1974 (the story of the Jews of Vilna through photographs).

Jacques Ravine, *La Résistance Organisée des Juifs en France 1940-1944,* Paris 1973.

Gerald Reitlinger, *The Final Solution: The Attempt to Exterminate the Jews of Europe 1939-1945,* London 1953.

Eugen Rosenfeldt, *Tuttlingen,* Tuttlingen 1947 (maps 296 and 297).

Herbert Rosenkranz, *Verfolgung und Selbstbehauptung Die Juden in Österreich 1938-1945,* Vienna 1978 (details of all emigration and deportations from Austria).

Ryszard Rosin (editor), *Zbrodnie Hitlerowskie w Lodzi i Województwie Lódzkim,* Lodz 1942 (Nazi crimes in Lodz and the Lodz region).

Henryk Ross, *The Last Journey of the Jews of Lodz Litzmannstadt,* Tel Aviv 1950.

Livia Rothkirchen, *The Destruction of Slovak Jewry: A Documentary History,* Jerusalem 1961.

Royal Institute of International Affairs, *Chronology of the Second World War,* London 1947.

Yitskhok Rudashevski, *The Diary of the Vilna Ghetto, June 1941-April 1943,* Tel Aviv 1973 (map 202).

A. Rutkowski, 'Zaglada Zydow w dystrykcie radomskim', *Biuletyn Zydowskiego Instytutu Historycznego,* number 15, Warsaw 1955 (13 statistical tables of the ghettoization, deportation and destruction in the Radom district, including the cities of Radom and Kielce, between 1939 and 1945).

Ernst Schäfer (editor), *Ravensbrück,* Berlin 1960

Rabbi Israel Schepansky, *Holocaust Calendar of Polish Jewry,* New York, July 1974 (in Hebrew).

Gertrude Schneider, *Journey Into Terror: Story of the Riga Ghetto,* New York 1979.

A. J. Sherman, *Island Refuge: Britain and Refugees from the Third Reich 1933-1939,* London 1973 (map 15).

Dušan Sindik (editor), *Secanja Jevreja na Logor Jasenovac,* Belgrade 1972 (memoirs of Jews in the Jasenovac camp).

Derrick Sington, *Belsen Uncovered,* London 1946 (map 294).

Tadeusz Skutnik, *Stutthof: Informator historyczny,* Gdansk 1979

George H. Stein, *The Waffen S.S., Hitler's Elite Guard at War 1939-1945,* London 1966

Zosa Szajkowski, *Analytical Franco-Jewish Gazetteer 1939-1945,* New York 1966.

Zosa Szajkowski, *Jews, Wars and Communism,* 2 volumes, New York 1972 and 1974.

Zvi Szner (editor) *Extermination and Resistance: Historical Records and Source Material,* volume 1, Kibbutz Lohamei Haghettaot, Israel 1958.

Arieh Tartakower and Kurt R. Grossman, *The Jewish Refugee,* New York 1944 (maps 15 and 16).

Totenbuch Theresienstadt, Vienna 1971, volume 1, 'Deportierte Aus Osterreich' (lists 50 deportations into Theresienstadt between 21 June 1942 and 15 April 1945, and 66 deportations out of Theresienstadt, with numbers and destinations between 9 January 1942 and 28 October 1944).

Michael Tregenza, 'Belzec Death Camp', in *The Wiener Library Bulletin,* 1977, volume xxx, pages 8-25.

Germaine Tillion, *Ravensbrück,* Garden City, New York, 1975.

Max Ungar (printer), *Mauthausen 8.8.1939-5.5.1945,* Vienna n.d.

Dr A. Ungerer (editor), *Verzeichnis von Ghettos, Zwangsarbeitslagern, und Konzentrationslagern,* Munich 1953 (lists date of establishment of ghettos in Poland and also expulsions, labour camps and concentration camps).

Zorach Warhaftig, *Uprooted: Jewish Refugees and Displaced Persons After Liberation,* New York, November 1946 (maps 312 and 315).

Leon Weliczker Wells, *The Janowska Road,* New York 1963 (maps 222 and 223).

Janusz Wieczorek (editor), *Scenes of Fighting and Martyrdom Guide: War Years in Poland, 1939-1945,* Warsaw 1968 (town-by-town and locality-by-locality notes of monuments to Nazi atrocities in Poland, post-1945 boundaries).

Mary H. Williams (editor), *Chronology 1941-1945,* United States Army in World War II, Special Studies, Washington 1960.

Leni Yahil, *The Rescue of Danish Jewry,* Philadelphia 1969 (map 213).

The Yellow Spot, the outlawing of half a million human beings, London 1936 (documents on anti-Jewish measures in Germany between 1933 and 1935, introduction by the Bishop of Durham dated 12 February 1936) (map 6).

Yitzhak Zuckerman, 'The Jewish Fighting Organization — Z.O.B. — its Establishment and Activites', written in Warsaw in March 1944, published in Yisrael Gutman and Livia Rothkirchen (editors), *The Catastrophe of European Jewry,* Jerusalem 1976, pages 518-548 (map 131).

Index of Places
(with map numbers)

Melnik, 23
Melun, 169
Melykut, 254
Memel, 4, 5, 6, 11, 18, 24, 25, 33,
    42, 272, 274, 282, 315, 316
Memelland, 25
Memmingen, 116
Menzel Bou Zelfa, 188
Meppel, 129
Merano, 1, 219, 221
Merchweiler, 7
Mergentheim, 51
Meridja, 59
Merignac, 133, 169
Mersch, 134
Mertzwiller, 237
Merzig, 7
Mestre, 313
Metkovic, 218
Metz, 170, 190, 264, 278, 297
Mexico, 16
Mexico City, 172
Meyreuil, 200
Mezieres, 246
Mezobereny, 254
Mezocsat, 242
Mezokovacshaza, 254
Mezokovesd, 254
Mezolak, 258
Miadziol, 224
Michalovce, 128
Michalowo, 168, 211
Michelstadt, 21
Michow, 121, 123
Mickun Bridge, 209
Middlefart, 213
Miedzna, 281
Miedzyrzec Podlaski, 28, 48, 140,
    160, 166, 173, 180, 208,
    215, 219
Miedzyrzec Volynsk, 72, 88, 119,
    154
Mielec, 29, 48, 101, 107, 215, 271,
    278, 279
Mielnica, 72, 143, 161
Mierzwin, 12
Mihalyhaza, 258
Mihova, 79
Mikolajow, 143
Mikolow, 281
Mikulince, 76, 139
Milan, 1, 221, 223, 225, 313
Milea, 79
Milejczyce, 168, 211
Miliana, 174
Milos Island, 248
Mineralnye Vody, 146
Minsk, 3, 71, 73, 92, 94, 100,
    106, 111, 113, 131, 193,
    198, 208, 215, 219, 222,
    224, 267, 313
Minsk Mazowiecki, 12, 29, 132,
    140, 180, 183, 207

Miory, 128
Mir, 94, 137, 224
Miremont, 246
Mirgorod, 70
Miskolc, 240, 241, 242, 254, 310
Missour, 59
Mistelbach, 13
Mittelbau-Dora, *see* Dora
Mizocz, 72, 162
Mlada Boleslav, 93
Mladenovac, 68
Mlawa, 48, 104, 173, 310
Mlyniec, 40
Mlynow, 72, 165
Mnichov, 17
Mnisek, 23
Modena, 221
Modliborzyce, 57, 160
Modling, 13
Modrica, 84
Mogador, 159, 245
Mogilev (Podolia), 78, 80, 94, 233
Mogilev (White Russia), 3, 58, 71,
    86, 96
Mohacs, 260
Moisakula, 82
Moknine, 188
Mokotow, 55, 204
Mokrin, 63
Molczadz, 128, 131, 244
Moldavia, 155
Moldova River, 79
Moldova Sulita, 79
Moldovita, 79
Molsheim, 237
Mommenheim, 237
Monasterzyska, 165
Monastir (Macedonia), 177
Monastir (Tunisia), 188
Monastyrshchina, 94
Monor, 260, 310
Monostor, 239
Monostor-Kapolnok, 240
Monowitz, 122, 255, 280, 281
Montauban, 198
Monte Carlo, 2
Montevideo, 172
Montreuil, 262
Moosburg, 32
Mor, 260
Moravia, 18, 22, 24, 26, 31, 93,
    219, 220
Moravska Ostrava, 26, 37, 93,
    164, 207, 220, 221, 294
Mordy, 140, 314
More, 46
Morez, 246
Morocco, 59, 99, 159
Mosbach, 50, 198
Mosciska, 173, 203
Moscow, 69, 71, 73, 96, 97, 98,
    100, 106, 147, 167, 202,
    208, 217, 219, 228, 244

Mosonmagyarovar, 254
Mosorin, 239
Mostaganem, 159, 174
Mostar, 85, 218
Mosty, 168
Mosty Wielkie, 76
Mozyr, 101
Mratin, 23
Mrzyglod, 27
M'Sila, 174
Mszana, 281
Mszczonow, 56, 149, 310
Muhlheim, 51
Mulhouse, 2, 186, 190, 276
Munich, 1, 2, 4, 6, 9, 18, 20, 22,
    47, 49, 89, 92, 192, 198,
    247, 270, 278, 282, 294,
    299, 307, 314
Munkacs (Mukacevo), 1, 18, 170,
    238, 240, 241, 255, 267,
    275
Munster, 20, 96
Murafa, 78, 80
Murawica, 165
Murska Sobota, 65
Muskau, 285, 286
Mustvee, 82
Muttersholz, 237
Myczkow (near Baligrod), 27
Myczkow (near Lesko), 27
Myena, 70
Myslenice, 12
Myslowice, 195

N

Nabeul, 188
Nachod, 314
Nadalj, 239
Nadworna, 94
Nagyalasony, 258
Nagyatad, 262
Nagybajom, 256
Nagybanya, 240, 255
Nagybaracska, 254
Nagydorog, 256
Nagyecsed, 242
Nagyhalasz, 242
Nagykallo, 240, 241, 242
Nagykanizsa, 256, 276, 306, 310
Nagykata, 257
Nagykoros, 257
Nagyoroszy, 254
Nagypirit, 258
Nagyszollos, 240
Nagyteteny, 259
Nagyvarad (Oradea Mare), 4,
    155, 240, 255, 313
Nagyvazsony, 256
Nakskov, 213
Nalbach, 7
Naleczow, 123
Namestovo, 128

Slutsk, 88, 167, 224
Smederovo, 68, 98
Smerek, 27
Smolensk, 71, 113, 126
Smolnik, 27
Smorgonie (Smorgon), 202, 297
Smyela, 3
Smyrna (Izmir), 113, 170, 244
Sniadowo, 168, 211
Sniatyn, 86, 115, 145
Snina, 314
Sobibor, 106, 115, 119, 120, 121, 124, 125, 128, 131, 137, 160, 165, 166, 180, 182, 192, 198, 201, 202, 205, 206, 207, 208, 210, 217, 219, 222
Sobienie Jeziory, 160
Sochaczew, 43, 56
Sofia, 10, 11, 62, 150, 170, 176, 194, 195, 197
Sojki, 152
Sokal, 34, 73, 115, 151, 165, 205, 244
Sokola, 211
Sokolka, 168, 183
Sokolow (near Rzeszow), 131
Sokolow Podlaski, 132, 153
Sokoly, 168, 211, 314
Sokul, 72
Solec, 55
Soliman, 188
Solina, 27
Solska Forest, 125
Soly, 202
Sombor, 239
Somloszollos, 258
Somlovasarhely, 258
Somlovecse, 258
Sommerfeld, 295
Somogyszil, 256
Sompolno, 104
Sonnenstein, 53
Sonta, 239
Sopockinie, 168, 211
Sopron, 260, 310
Soroca, 77, 78
Soroksar, 259
Sor Trondelag, 46
Sosnitsa, 70
Sosnowiec, 28, 29, 61, 114, 122, 128, 137, 191, 207, 210, 215, 223, 225, 280, 306, 310
Sotern, 7
Souflion, 194, 195
Souge, 246
Souk Ahras, 174
Souk el-Arba, 188
Sousse, 159, 188
South Africa, 16, 158
South China Sea, 158
South Holland (province), 129

Soviet Union (USSR), 4, 10, 11, 14, 33, 34, 35, 36, 37, 41, 42, 44, 45, 47, 60, 69, 71, 73, 74, 82, 97, 98, 99, 103, 120, 158, 175, 300, 301, 304, 315, 316
Sowin, 152
Spaichingen, 282, 294, 296
Spain, 15, 100, 301, 304
Spandau, 277
Speyer, 50
Split (Spalato), 89, 219, 229, 233
Spomysl, 23
Spree River, 285
Srbobran, 239
Srebrenica, 84
Srednie, 27
Srem, 63, 66
Sremska Mitrovica, 66
Sremski Karlovci, 66
Stablack, 32
Stalingrad, 71, 97, 146, 147, 167, 175, 176
Stalowa Wola, 180
Standia Island, 248
Stanestii, 79
Stanimaka, 197
Stanisic, 239
Stanislawow (Eastern Galicia), 28, 33, 76, 86, 111, 120, 131, 139, 144, 183, 193, 255, 313
Stanislawow (near Warsaw), 157
Stanitz, 8
Stankowa, 27
Stanleyville, 158
Starachowice, 163
Stara Gradiska, 84, 85
Stara Pazova, 66
Stara Role, 17
Stara Zagora, 197
Stare Kanjiza, 239
Stargard, 32
Stari Becej, 239
Starodub, 3, 70, 71, 86
Starogard, 40
Stary Sacz, 141
Stary Sambor, 139
Staszow, 173
Stawiszyn, 38
Stawy, 12
Stawiany, 12
Stawiski, 74, 168, 211
Stefanesti, 155
Steinach, 108
Stepan, 72, 142
Stepkow, 152
Sterdyn, 12, 153
Stettin, 2, 20, 37, 49, 164, 278, 284, 288, 290, 298, 299, 307, 314
Steyr, 91, 305
Steznica, 27

Stip, 194
Stockerau, 13
Stockholm, 11, 214, 308
Stoczek, 12, 153
Stok, 12
Stolin, 147
Stolp, 252
Stolpce, 74, 119, 224
Stolpsee, 295
Stopnica, 149, 166
Storkow, 277
Storojinet, 79, 80
Straja, 79
Stralsund, 37, 213
Strancice, 23
Strasbourg, 208, 237, 244, 247, 253, 278
Strasshof, 276
Straz, 17
Stribro, 17
Struth, 237
Stryj, 73, 76, 94, 143, 165, 173, 193, 205, 255, 309
Strzelno, 40
Strzyzow, 29, 131, 149
Studionka, 281
Stulpicani, 79
Stuttgart, 19, 294
Stutthof, 30, 47, 210, 216, 225, 234, 243, 251, 252, 260, 267, 271, 272, 273, 274, 276, 278, 282, 284, 294, 298
Styria, 289
Subotica, 62, 239
Suceava, 10, 79
Sucevita, 79
Suchawa, 105
Suchedniow, 173
Suchowola, 168, 211
Sudetenland, 17, 18, 19, 20, 22, 24, 93, 293
Sudeten Mountains, 290
Sudzha, 70
Sulejow, 163
Sulina, 155, 244
Sulita, 3
Sulmierzyce, 138
Sumeg, 262
Sumen, 197
Sumy, 70
Sunda, 272
Sunja, 64
Suprasl, 168, 211
Surabaja, 158
Suraz, 12
Suresnes, 57, 58, 246
Susleni, 77
Suwalki, 12, 33, 42, 191
Svenborg, 213
Svinare, 23
Swabian Alps, 296
Sweden, 11, 15, 33, 45, 46, 47,

Index of Individuals

(with page numbers)

OTHER BOOKS BY MARTIN GILBERT

The Churchill biography
Volume III, 'The Challenge of War', 1914–1916
Volume III, Documents, Parts I and II
Volume IV, 'The Stricken World', 1917–1922
Volume IV, Documents, Parts I, II and III
Volume V, 'The Prophet of Truth', 1922–1939
The Exchequer Years, Documents, 1922–1929
The Wilderness Years, Documents, 1929–1935
The Coming of War, Documents, 1936–1939
Volume VI, 'Finest Hour', 1939–1941
At the Admiralty, Documents, 1939–1940
Volume VII, 'Road to Victory', 1941–1945
Volume VIII, 'Never Despair', 1945–1965

Historical works
The Appeasers (with Richard Gott)
The European Powers, 1900–1945
The Roots of Appeasement
Britain and Germany Between the Wars (documents)
Plough My Own Furrow: the Life of Lord Allen of Hurtwood (documents)
Servant of India: Diaries of the Viceroy's Private Secretary (documents)
Sir Horace Rumbold: Portrait of a Diplomat
Churchill: a Photographic Portrait
Churchill's Political Philosophy
Auschwitz and the Allies
Exile and Return: the Struggle for Jewish Statehood
The Jews of Hope: the Plight of Soviet Jewry Today
Shcharansky: Hero of our Time
Jerusalem: Rebirth of a City, 1838–1898
Final Journey: the Fate of the Jews in Nazi Europe
The Holocaust: the Jewish Tragedy
The Second World War
Churchill, A Life

Atlases
Dent Atlas of American History
Dent Atlas of the Arab–Israeli Conflict
Dent Atlas of British History
Dent Atlas of the First World War
Dent Atlas of Jewish History
Dent Atlas of Recent History (*in preparation*)
Dent Atlas of Russian History
The Jews of Arab Lands: Their History in Maps
The Jews of Russia: Their History in Maps
Jerusalem: Illustrated History Atlas
Children's Illustrated Bible Atlas